HERE COMES THE CIRCUS

HERE COMES THE CIRCUS

BY PETER VERNEY

PADDINGTON PRESS LTD
NEW YORK & LONDON

Library of Congress Cataloging in Publication Data

Verney, Peter, 1930–
Here Comes the Circus

Includes index.
1. Circus. I. Title.
GV1817.V47 791.3 77-13987
ISBN 0-448-23115-8

Printed in England by Cox & Wyman Ltd., Fakenham, Norfolk

Designed by Colin Lewis
Endpapers: A cartoon of "Charivari" by Dame Laura Knight.
Courtesy of Sotheby Parke Bernet & Co.

IN THE UNITED STATES
PADDINGTON PRESS
Distributed by
GROSSET & DUNLAP

IN THE UNITED KINGDOM
PADDINGTON PRESS

IN CANADA
Distributed by
RANDOM HOUSE OF CANADA LTD.

IN SOUTHERN AFRICA
Distributed by
ERNEST STANTON (PUBLISHERS) (PTY) LTD.

TABLE OF CONTENTS

BEGINNINGS

It is half-past four on a hot summer's afternoon in London in the year 1770. A steady stream of people is crossing Westminster Bridge over the River Thames, and from time to time grand carriages make their way through the throng. Whatever it is drawing the crowd it would seem to be an attraction for the rich and for the common folk alike.

They appear to be making their way toward a new wooden-walled, wooden-roofed building with a high paling fence which proclaims itself to be Astley's Riding School where, if the handbills are to be believed, there is to be displayed an "Activity on Horseback by Mr. Astley, Sergeant-Major in His Majesty's Royal Regiment of Light Dragoons," and which, amazingly, will include nearly "Twenty Different Attitudes" performed on "One, Two or Three Horses Every Evening." The doors are to be "Open at Four. He will Mount at Five. Seats One Shilling; Standing Places Sixpence." They are going to the circus.

There had been examples of what we can call individual circus acts, or turns, over the ages and in many different countries – acts of skill, balance, strength and agility or with performing animals; but it is now accepted that Philip Astley is father of the modern circus. It was he who first brought together juggler and ropewalker, clown and "curiosity," spectacle and pageantry, horsemanship and animal mastery in his efforts to satisfy the human demand for the circus.

The origins of these circus acts may be found in every civilization; recorded for posterity on pottery or papyri, illustrated in books or illuminated manuscripts. It is now generally known that in the stadium of Olympia in ancient Greece professional acrobats tumbled and performed other skills alongside runners, wrestlers and the other athletes involved in the traditional Olympic sports. Audiences at the Circus Maximus and the other amphitheaters in Rome and

GUILDHALL LIBRARY, CITY OF LONDON

TIGHT ROPE
ASTLEY'S
RIDING SCHOOL
SIEUR JONES

elsewhere in the huge Roman Empire, enjoyed trick riding and other circus skills amid the vast and grisly spectacles for which that period is better known. As time passed, these acts were carried on by small troupes of performing artistes – the gleemen and *banquistes* – jugglers, mimics, cord dancers and puppet masters who traveled Europe in the Middle Ages. These wandering bands would give performances in the towns as they passed and soon became an accepted feature of the fairs in France and England, the *Jahrmarkten* of Germany and the street fairs of the Low Countries. Their skills were passed from generation to generation, and many of these troupers were the lineal ancestors of some of the great circus families of the last 150 years. One can begin to sense the international freemasonry of the circus, the amity which transcends frontiers, the feeling of being members of a huge and distinguished family of performers and artistes.

The acts of these old troupers live on in many of the circus turns we see today, and they have a delightfully old-fashioned ring about them – the *Saut de Singe* (the Monkey Jump), the *Saut du Lion* (the Lion Jump), the *Danse du Corde* (the Cord Dance). These acts are as old as time, but still thrill audiences everywhere.

The fairs persisted, with their traveling medicine men – known as mountebanks – their jugglers, ropewalkers and tumblers, but showmen across Europe were beginning to see an exciting prospect before them and starting to sense that people liked watching such performers and were prepared to pay money to do so. In 1755 a Frenchman called Defraine founded the Hetz Theater in Vienna, an open-air arena where animal combats took place on the lines of the bestial spectacles which so delighted the blood-hungry populace of ancient Rome. Judging that the audience wanted more than gore and death, the shrewd Defraine introduced what he called *chevauchées* - demonstrations and acts of riding skill often accompanied by music and fanfares. Elsewhere, in Vaux Hall in London and also in Paris, performances of trick riding gained popularity.

The small village of Islington, on the outskirts of London, became the home of such trick riding. Here in 1766 it was announced that a "Mr. Price will exhibit Horsemanship, This and Every Afternoon, if the Weather Permits, in the Field adjoining the Three Hats, Islington" where "Gentlemen and Ladies may be accommodated with Coffee and Tea, Hot Loaves and Sullybubs." In nearby Mile End around this time a Mr. Sampson, "Lately Discharged from Lord Ancrum's Light Dragoons," would stand in the saddle on one leg, dismount at full gallop and jump on again, ride two horses at once and, most remarkable of all, would ride at a gallop with his head on the saddle and his feet in the air. Another performing at this time was called Johnson; known as the Irish Tartar, he would ride three horses at the same

Thomas Johnson; The Irish Tartar.

time – standing on two with a third between – a feat now called Roman Riding.

Others copied and extended these feats. One Jacob Bates had a four-horse act and displayed this and other astonishing riding skills on a triumphant tour of Europe where, as he proudly related, he performed before no less than nine crowned heads including the emperor of Germany and Catherine the Great of Russia. He was one of the first to bring his riding prowess across the Atlantic and in 1773 was performing in New York. Another, Daniel Wildman, introduced a novelty which has never been repeated – trick riding with a swarm of bees around his head. The highlight of the act came when he fired his pistol, the signal for half the bees to march across a table and the other half to return to their hive. This would seem to be the only recorded incident involving trained bees! It was around this time that Philip Astley came onto the stage.

Born in 1742, Astley was the son of a cabinetmaker in the small town of Newcastle-under-Lyme in the Midlands of England. But like many sons he had no taste for his father's trade. Whenever a stagecoach pulled into the local hostelry, the young Astley would rush off to help handle the horses. His schooling suffered and Astley passed through life with little or no education. At the age of seventeen, enticed by stories of the great fair at Coventry which took place every November, Philip Astley fled his father's house. At the fair he fell

VICTORIA AND ALBERT MUSEUM

into the snare of a recruiting sergeant and so young Astley – by now a strapping lad with the shoulders of a prizefighter, the makings of the stentorian voice for which he later became quite famous, and a magical touch with horses – joined Colonel Elliott's 15th Light Dragoons.

OPPOSITE:
Philip Astley.

Two years after enlisting, Astley embarked for Germany with his regiment to serve the king of Prussia. He was a corporal by then, and had already made his mark when placed in charge of the regiment's remounts. When he returned a few years later, Sergeant Philip Astley was a hero, the toast of England, having distinguished himself by capturing the enemy flag at the Battle of Emsdorf and performing other acts of bravery.

A promising career lay before him in the army, but the young man was restless. He had long harbored a desire to run a riding school for the nobility, and prompted by the financial success of the Irish Tartar whom he had seen perform, Astley bought his discharge.

He started work breaking horses and soon afterward married an equally accomplished equestrienne. For £5 they bought a small horse with "eyes bright, lively, resolute and himpudent," as Astley put it, "that will look at an object with a kind of disdain." He named the horse Billy and taught him all the tricks then current in the horse world. In 1768, in a field in Lambeth called Halfpenny Hatch, Astley and his wife ringed off a small arena. There with Astley's own charger and Billy, who he now took to calling the Little Military Learned Horse, they performed before a standing audience. In the center of the arena stood an old dovecot, which they converted into a bandstand where a small drummer boy played. At the end of each performance Astley, hat in hand, would go round seeking halfpennies.

Soon Astley made a startling discovery. He found that it was much easier to stand on the back of a moving horse if it was going round in a circle and that, in order to have the horse at the best angle for balancing, the circle should be forty-two feet across – the circus ring had been invented.

Astley's experiment was an immediate success. His fame spread and soon the field at Lambeth was attracting not only the common people, but the nobility as well. The next year he bought some land near Westminster Bridge, built a ring with a shed attached and charged an entrance fee. He called the place Astley's Riding School. Outside, immaculate in his full dress uniform and astride his great charger, Astley beckoned one and all to "This 'ere Riding School." Inside, he thrilled the house by his remarkable feats on horseback. He would stand on two horses and put them both over obstacles; he would stand on one leg with his other foot in his mouth and jump the horse over a fence while doing so; there seemed no end to the accomplishments of this remarkable horseman.

Over the years Astley added other turns: trampoline performers, wire-walkers, slack-rope features and clowns as well as freaks – both animal and human. The circus as we know it had been born. By 1770 all the seats were covered; by 1778 the whole building was roofed; in 1794 it was burned down but quickly built up again. In all, Astley's was burned down three times and its owner was the first proprietor to experience the terrible hazard of a circus fire.

So Astley prospered. By now another star performer had been added: his son John, who proved to be an even more outstanding equestrian than his father. At the age of ten – although he was billed as being only five – his acts had all London agog at his skill, particularly at his "most amazing equilibrium" as he played on a violin while standing on a galloping horse. This feat prompted one correspondent to write, "The violin concerto performed by young Astley on horseback has disconcerted several brethren of the firing. They say it is introducing a bad custom, as moving Orchestras would greatly impede the execution of the semi-demi quavers."

In 1775, three years before Astley's Riding School became a fully enclosed theater, the versatile showman had made another move, this time to Paris, at the invitation of the French ambassador to London – and so it came about that Philip Astley founded not only the English circus but also that of France. The visit was hugely popular and in 1785 he was invited back, by the royal command of Queen Marie Antoinette. Immediately, though, he ran into trouble, for a stage monopoly decreed that Astley would only be permitted to perform acts on horseback, denying him the right to show the tumblers, jugglers and other turns which were now an accepted part of his troupe. Undismayed, the resourceful Astley circulated a handbill announcing that all his acts would indeed be performed on the backs of horses, and all of Paris came to see how he had outwitted the magistrates.

Great as Astley's own success was, it was nothing to that of his son. Paris adored young John. Pronounced a prodigy of nature, his minuets, his agility and comic dances all performed on horseback astounded everyone who saw him by their grace and precision. The queen dubbed him her English Rose and doubtless both father and son were suitably gratified when each was presented with a gold medallion as a mark of Marie Antoinette's favor. But Philip Astley was less impressed by her consort; in his booming voice he was heard to proclaim, "That there King, he can't be father of the Dolphin. Why he's omnipotent!"

An early performer with Astley in Paris was a certain Antoine Franconi, a Venetian who had been forced to leave Italy after killing a local landowner in a duel. For a while he wandered with nothing to do and nowhere to go, but finding himself in Lyons he offered to work as a tamer of wild beasts,

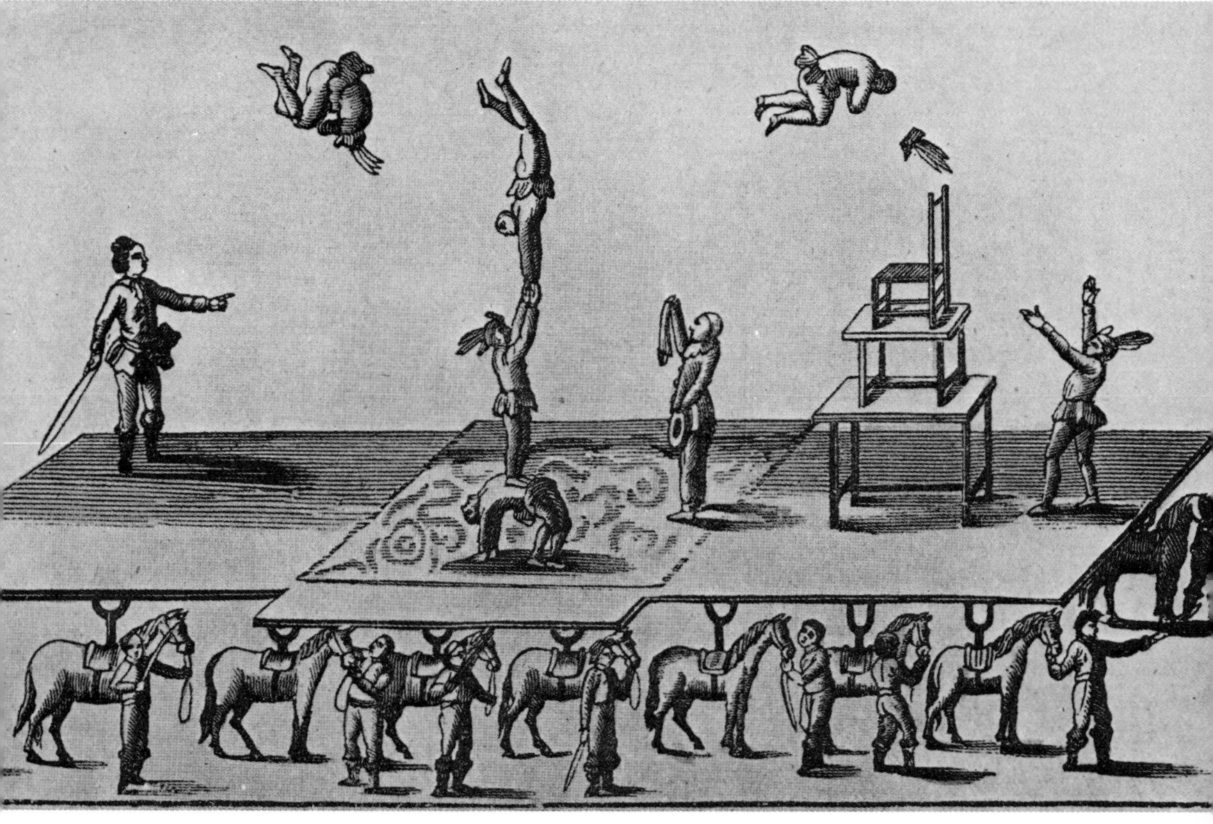

Philip Astley in Paris. Banned by the authorities from producing any act not done on horseback, this was how he overcame the problem.

although he had never entered a lion cage in his life. Evidently the resident lion sensed this, for on his first attempt at taming he was mauled. Despite this, Franconi was soon put in charge of the menagerie. Tiring of that, he then went to Spain where he saw his first bullfight. Immediately taken by the spectacle he decided to introduce a *Combat de Taureaux* at Rouen in France. The year 1785 saw him in Paris, this time in a bird act with Astley. When the latter was forced to leave Paris at the onset of the French Revolution, L'Amphitheatre Astley became L'Amphitheatre Franconi: so started the Franconi circus connection and a circus dynasty which was to span the circus world in France for the rest of the century.

Before he had left London for Paris, Astley was already being assailed by rivals. When he made his involuntary return it was to find that his circus was being aped by several others, particularly a certain Charles Hughes, who had been one of Astley's early clowns, or Mr. Merrymen, as they were known. A disagreeable-looking, swarthy man but with a peculiar charm and a handsome face and figure, he was reputed to be strong enough to carry an ox. In 1782 Hughes opened the Royal Circus at Blackfriars, a mile or so downstream of Astley's own amphitheater, and it became an immediate success, despite Astley's scathing references to the newcomers as "These 'ere pretenders to horsemanship."

Rivalry between the two was intense. To compete with

the famous Billy, Hughes introduced his Horse of Knowledge. He also brought over the celebrated equestrienne Sobieska Clementina, who performed unrivaled acts of skill, grace and courage. His imitation hunt in which no less than twelve couples of hounds, two foxes and a stag took part, was the rage of London for months. Snared in a law which the magistrates said forbade anything beyond simple drama, both circuses were closed down, albeit temporarily. Exasperated by this, Astley turned to writing and produced a widely acclaimed book called *L'Art Equestrien*; Hughes decided to take his troupe on a tour which went as far afield as Sardinia, Spain and even Morocco.

Soon they were both back, but once again ran foul of the law. Hughes this time accepted a commission from a Russian nobleman to collect blood stallions and brood mares and bring them to St. Petersburg to improve Russian stock. As his performing stud was idle, Hughes decided to take it with him as well and on their arrival a command performance before Empress Catherine was soon arranged. Captivated by all she saw – not least the impressive Hughes who, if rumor is to be believed, soon became one of her many favorites – she built two circuses for him. For a year he remained in Russia teaching the equestrian arts and from time to time performing himself. Then he wearied of the country and, leaving his troupe to satisfy imperial needs, he returned to England.

It was not Hughes, though, who was to make the greatest mark in the spread of the circus but one of his star pupils, John Bill Ricketts, who made his way westward after the closure of the Royal Circus.

Apart from Jacob Bates, there had been other equestrians to cross the Atlantic and bring the art to America. In 1771 a man by the name of John Sharp performed at Salem in Massachusetts. One by the name of Poole set up a kind of circus in Philadelphia in 1787, while an Irishman called John Brenon was both an equestrian and a slack-wire artiste. But Ricketts is commonly accepted as setting up the first true circus on American soil, for he constructed an imposing building on the corner of 6th and Chestnut Streets in Philadelphia and in 1792 gave his first performance in public. He himself was the star attraction, his turns astonished all who saw them. While standing up on the back of his horse, and with apparently effortless ease, he would leap over a ribbon held no less than twelve feet from the ground. Another favorite act was to jump over ten horses placed side by side, and his pyramid with two other riders at full gallop was the talk of the town. He was no mean juggler, either, and the highlight of his act was to juggle with two oranges and a fork, which ended up with the oranges impaled on the fork – the whole performance done at a gallop.

Ricketts went from strength to strength. From Phila-

HISTORICAL SOCIETY OF PENNSYLVANIA

"Mr Ricketts, the Equestrian Hero" – an early picture of John Bill Ricketts, father of the American circus.

CIRCUS WORLD MUSEUM, BARABOO, WISCONSIN

Ricketts's Circus on the corner of 6th and Chestnut Street, Philadelphia.

CIRCUS.

~~Saturday and ...~~ Wednesday the 24h of April, Will be performed, a Great Variety of NEW

Equeſtrian Exerciſes,

At the CIRCUS, in Market, the Corner of 12th Streets.-------The Doors Will be opened at FOUR, and the Performance begin at FIVE O'CLOCK preciſely.

Mr. Ricketts Leaps over a Riband, ſuſpended 12 Feet high, and at the ſame time thro' a CANE held in both hands and

alights on the other SIDE, with his FEET on the SADDLE, the HORSE being in full Speed.

PART I.---------Maſter RICKETTS, hangs by one Leg, ſweeps both his Hands and the Plume of his Cap on he Ground.----Likewiſe mounts his Horſe in full ſpeed, with one Foot on the Saddle in a pleaſing Attitude.

PART II.-----Mr. RICKETTS, rides a ſingle Horſe, turning round like the fly of a Jack, vaulting from the Horſe to the Ground and from thence to the Horſe.----Likewiſe from the near Side to the off Side, and from thence to the near Side.

HE Stands with his Feet on the Saddle, and puts Himſelf in Various Graceful Attitudes, the Horſe in full Gallop.

PART III.-----------Mr. RICKETTS, Will ride a ſingle HORSE, ſtanding erect, and

☞ Throws up a BOTTLE and MARBLE, playing with the ſame in the Air, then receives the Marble into the Mouth of the Bottle, the Horſe being in full gallop.

HE throws up an ORANGE and receives it on the Point of a SWORD, at the ſame time ſtanding on the Saddle without the Aſſiſtance of the Bridle Reins, turns about and Throws a Somerſet.

PART IV.-----HE will Ride Two Horſes ſtanding erect, at the ſame time throwing up Two Oranges, and a Fork, playing with them in the air, and receives the orange on the point of the Fork.

HE will put a GLASS of WINE in a HOOP, turning it round rapidly, the Glaſs remaining at the ſame Time in its place, takes the ſame and drinks to the company the horſe being in full Gallop, and all without the Aſſiſtance of the Reins.

PART V.-----------He Rides a SINGLE HORSE, in FULL GALLOP,

Standing on his Head on the SADDLE, at the ſame time.

PART VI.--------HE Will Perform a HORNPIPE on a ſingle HORSE, with and without the Bridle. Likewiſe Leaps from his horſe to the Ground, and with the ſame ſpring leaps from the Ground with one Foot on the ſaddle in the Attitude of Mercury, the horſe in full Gallop.

PART VII-------HE rides a Single Horſe, ſprings from the Seat erect without touching the Saddle with his Hands. Then Forms the Attitude of MERCURY without the Aſſiſtance of the Reins.

HE leaps from the Horſe to the Ground and with the ſame Spring re-mounts with his Face towards the Horſes Tail. And throws a Somerſet Backwards.

The Whole to conclude [by Particular Deſire] with Mr. RICKETTS carrying his young Pupil on his Shoulders,

In the ATTITUDE of MERCURY,

Standing on Two Horſes, in Full Gallop.

TICKETS Sold at the Circus, and at Mr. Bradford's, BOX One Dollar, Pit Half Dollar.

☞ The PRESIDENT and his LADY will honor the CIRCUS with their Company this Evening.

delphia he moved to New York City and then to Boston, ousting as he went the foreign – principally French and Italian – troupes of artistes who had begun to find their way across the Atlantic to the new nation. His equestrian turns were now supplemented by rope dancing performed by the "Celebrated Spinacuta," as the bills proclaimed, as well as comic singers, pantomimes and Monsieur Amboise's Fire Works. His stage displays won him endless praise and when George Washington retired from political life, it was Ricketts's amphitheater which was chosen as the scene for the farewell dinner. Here Ricketts produced an illuminated display which showed Washington, the "Founder of America," taking leave of the nation and the audience wept with emotion. But it was Ricketts's love for the spectacular which was to prove his undoing: once, while the troupe was depicting Don Juan on his journey to Hades to atone for his manifold misdeeds, the whole set was caught in an all-too-realistic Hell Fire and Ricketts's theater was burned to a cinder. Deeply discouraged by this turn of events, Ricketts sailed for Europe only to be lost at sea.

The circus was gathering momentum in Europe and America. By the turn of the century the first tenting circuses had taken to the roads of Europe; but at this stage they were little more than groups of fairground performers banding together to create a better show. Nevertheless, these were the precursors of the mighty rolling shows of a later age, and the blood of some of those old showmen flows in many a circus artiste today.

The permanent circuses too were gaining popularity. Astley's "Royal Amphi-Theatre of Arts," as he grandiloquently called his rebuilt riding school, now possessed a proper circus ring, a stage and seats on three sides with three full tiers. Here were performed his equestrian acts – still the centerpieces for circuses everywhere, as they would be for much of the century – and other turns, the tumblers, jugglers and rope artists which he had brought in from the fairgrounds.

Astley had now vastly extended his repertoire. His own Twenty Different Attitudes had been succeeded by The different Cuts and Guards Made Use of by Elliott's, the Prussian and Hessian Hussars, and by such acts as the famous monkey General Jackoo which he brought back from Paris, a Learned Pig and others. Particularly fine was *La Force d'Hercule*, or the Egyptian Pyramid, billed as an "Amusing Performance of Men Piled on Men" – the forerunner of the more modern Brother Act. And there were more "transcendent performers" besides Astley, father, mother and son, for they had been joined by a Mr. Taylor, a Signor Markutchy and a Miss Vangable who, "mounted on Droll Horses" would convulse the audience with her comic sketches. There was also James Lawrence, the Great Devil, who somersaulted over twelve horses in his *Grand Sault du*

Trampoline – another forerunner of a famous circus act. His presence prompted one wit to point out that no less than two thousand persons walked nightly to the devil – at Astley's. In addition there was a clown who galloped upside down with his head on "a common pint pot" and another lady who stood on more pint pots mounting "Pot by pot higher still, to the terror of all who see her," on the back of a galloping horse. Astley was always ready to seize on any topical event as a source of stage drama, so on the fall of the Bastille, he hurried to France to collect original souvenirs including a number of wax effigies from a Doctor Curtius whose niece became the renowned Madame Tussaud. These he added to his other "curiosities," or "monstrosities," as others preferred to call them, such as the woman whose golden hair swept to the ground, or the Newcastle Musical Child a bare three-year-old who played several "favourite airs on the piano," a veritable "Infant Orpheus."

Astley was a born showman, perhaps the first man who really deserved the title. He had the showman's gift of turning apparent adversity to his profit. On one occasion he imported some Automaton Figures which played the German flute in a manner "beyond conception." To such a degree were they beyond conception that Astley was arraigned before a court for being in league with the devil. A huge procession of his animals and performers led him on his way to court and the case collapsed amid a welter of publicity when he admitted to having borrowed the idea of his musical figures from a well-known London clock.

Publicity came naturally to him and one of his earliest efforts at bringing the riding school to public notice was when he sponsored a balloon ascent, a few months after the celebrated Montgolfier flight in Paris. This was the first ascent by hot-air balloon in England and, as it happened, within hours of another flight in Edinburgh. On another occasion he swam down the Thames on his back with a flag in each hand advertising his new Floating Bath – a form of bathing machine, another invention of Astley's fertile mind. Nor was the old soldier slow to realize, like Barnum and others in their time, that although ordinary people provide the mass of their audience, the way to gain publicity was by appealing to the well-to-do. So invariably his bills and press notices were addressed to "The Nobility, Gentry and others."

That his efforts were appreciated is clear from the following written by an enthusiastic reporter:

> Astley is in possession of the best Tumblers in the world, his Dancing Dogs have their peculiar laughable performances; the English Bull Dogs not to be equalled; General Jackoo is the first Rope-Dancer in the world; the whole Train of Horsemanship, and the Exercises of the celebrated Clown, are feats so uncommon, that the

> audience seem to vie with each other who shall applaud most; the Strong Man is really astonishing; and Mr. Darley, in the Prussian Dragoon, seems to be quite at home. The pantomime has a splendid variety of good machinery; the Musical Child a great phenomenon and the Fireworks do the artist the highest credit. [Astley always called them Philosophical Fire Works, for reasons best known to himself.] On the whole, there never was an entertainment so generally followed and admired.

OVERLEAF:
L'Ecole de Mars, *A cotillion on horseback.*

Astley was also the first to feature a dialogue between clown and ringmaster, himself. Another turn which was to have a great influence on the circus and prove a favorite with audiences for decades was entitled The Taylor Riding to Brentford. This was an adaptation of the age-old story of John Gilpin. In its first form it was a tale of awkwardness, of how a tailor – always the butt for stupidity and ineptness at anything apart from the needle – with a regiment rode to town to collect cloth for the uniforms. As the tailor was no horseman, the predicaments he got into may best be imagined but all culminated with the tailor running away with his horse in hot pursuit. That was the "Tailor," as it was affectionately known across the western world, in its purest form; but over the years and in different countries the story developed and the title varied. Billie Buttons or The Tailor Humorously Riding to New York, were two examples from America, the first performed as long ago as 1773 by Jacob Bates in New York. In France it was called *Le Tailleur Alsacien* or *Le Tailleur Gascon* or *Rognolet et Passe-Carreau.* In Germany it was *Der Reisand Schneider mit dem bosen Pferd* (the Traveling Tailor and the Bad Horse).

Having seen fires "of a most menacing and dreadful nature" destroy two of his London theaters and his third comfortably into its second decade of prosperity, Philip Astley died in Paris. By then the French circus was well launched, for in 1807 the Franconi, Antoine and other members of his vast family, opened the Cirque Olympique. Built in imitation of Astley's former amphitheater, here for nine years they produced their circuses and drama until the theater was taken over by the state. But finding Astley's old building now vacant, Franconi reopened there, and remained in residence until in 1826, after a performance of The Burning of Salins, this theater burned down too. And so the third and final Cirque Olympique was born in the Boulevard du Temple – more usually referred to as Le Boulevard du Crime, birthplace of some of the greatest French entertainment – and here it stayed until 1862 when it was demolished with other famous theaters along this notorious street to make way for the new Paris.

Already the interchange of performers between countries and between circuses, which is so characteristic of the

Sold by all the
Music Sellers
in Town & Country
The New Music to the popular Cotillion
Perform'd with unbounded applause at the
The Melody adapted to the

de Mars
Dance, executed by Several Celebrated Horses
VILION Newcastle Street, Strand
ps By Mr. Astley Sen.
Price 2 Shill.
Enter'd at
Stationers Hall 1807

VICTORIA AND ALBERT MUSEUM

The Royal Circus in London. A typical act of horsemanship.

circus, was becoming a conspicuous feature. Dancing dogs on one of Astley's bills had come from "France and Italy and other Genteel Parts of the Globe"; other foreign performers were frequent visitors to the London circuses. As Europeans went to America, so Americans came to Europe. One of the first of these was Stickney who performed in the 1830s in England and delighted audiences with his trick riding; he is believed to be the first man to do a double somersault on a bareback. Another to show his skills was Levi J. North a decade or two later. An accomplished horseman known as The Apollo on Horseback, he challenged the Englishman Price to a somersaulting contest over twelve hourly sessions. In the first hour North completed no less than thirty-three somersaults to Price's twenty; and he finally came out an easy winner with a total of 414 to his opponent's 357. Whatever else they may have been, the early circus performers were a pretty tough breed.

The earliest known circus to move complete across the Atlantic was that of Thomas Taplin Cooke. His father had worked the fairs in Scotland as long ago as the 1720s, and Thomas Taplin was himself a renowned ropewalker, rider and strongman – his most famous feat was to support ten men on a board across his chest while he braced himself with his legs and feet. In 1816 he took his circus on a triumphant trip to Lisbon, and lost most of his horses in a storm in the Bay of Biscay on the way back. On his return he so impressed King William IV and his queen that thereafter he was permitted to call his circus Cooke's Royal Circus. In 1836, though, he decided to try his luck across the Atlantic. So, chartering a 3,000-ton ship, the *Royal Stuart*, he and his company of 120 which included no less than 40 members of the Cooke family, 42 horses, and 14 ponies set sail for America.

The circus arrived safely in New York City – although by now there were 41 Cookes on board as a girl, appropriately christened Oceana, had been born on the way (she became a noted tightrope walker, the rage of Paris in her time). Thomas Taplin Cooke then set to work building a permanent amphitheater for 2,000 people in the Bowery and here he played before packed houses for six months until fire destroyed the circus. He moved to Philadelphia, then to Baltimore where fire struck once again destroying all his horses. But the old showman refused to be defeated. Public subscription and his own hard work and good humor enabled him to keep going. With a small troupe he moved to Boston and finally returned to Scotland. He left behind a daughter who later married a William H. Cole, a contortionist, and produced a son William Washington Cole, who became famous in American circus annals as "Chilly Billy" Cole. Another of Thomas Taplin's relations was Thomas Edwin Cooke who remained in the circus world all his life, until his untimely death at the age of ninety-six which was hastened, so they said, by his activities on a bicycle which he had just learned to ride.

The Cookes are one of the oldest circus families in the business. A while ago, a famous circus writer, W. S. Meadmore, discovered that the Cookes had intermarried with, among others, such celebrated circus families as Chadwick, Ginnett, Wirth, Woolford, Austin, Clarke – of the Clarkonians, a famous aerial act – Crockett, Pinder, Sanger, and Yelding. To take the lineage further, the Sangers married into the Pinder, Coleman, Austin, Hoffman, Freeman, and Ginnett families: the Kayes with the Bakers, the Bakers with the Paulos, the Paulos with the Fossetts, the Fossetts with the Yeldings, the Yeldings with the Barretts. In 1897, there were over two hundred lineal descendants of Thomas Taplin Cooke, and most of those were involved in the circus in one way or another. The tentacles of circus genealogy wind round each other – for the circus was, and still is, a close-knit community.

The tide of population in the United States was on the move westward. Entertainment was scarce, and levity of any kind was frowned on by the powerful church communities and thundered at from the pulpit. The people already living inland craved diversion and particularly the diversion of the circus, which they had heard about from travelers or read about in their papers, or even seen themselves on infrequent excursions to the city. This was the breeding ground of the legendary mud shows and the start of a revolution in circus history.

These shows were made up of a few horse-drawn wagons – the horses, having pulled the circus into town or hamlet, often had to double as performers – and a troupe of three or four artistes who did everything from announcing the show to taking part in every act. Up and down the eastern seaboard, and as far inland as they could get, these little mud shows traveled every spring and summer. Gradually their technique improved, their acts and their publicity became more sophisticated, their performances slicker and more professional. Their audiences demanded more and more and they got it. There were deeds of daring and skill by transcendent performers of all kinds, eye-catching spectacles "never before seen in this country" – so the papers announced. Already the extravagant claims which everyone loves, and no one believes, were becoming part of the way of life of the circus: "Elegant Frolics," "Lofty Vaulting," "Miss Payne will perform for the first time here the much applauded feat of the MERMAID" – who could possibly resist such mouth-watering delights?

The rolling shows had come to stay, but their technique was rough. It needed the genius of one or two individuals to exploit the great opportunity presented by a vibrant, emergent country and a people craving excitement and entertainment.

So it came about that one evening four gentlemen from North Salem, New York – in an area to become known as the "Cradle of the American Circus," because so many shows and showmen originated from there or thereabouts – started discussing the possibilities that a well-organized show presented. Their talk centered on the fact that a few years previously the greatest crowd draw ever seen had been Old Bet, an elephant. Old Bet had been acquired from a sea captain for $1,000 by one Hackaliah Bailey and she had been shown around New England attracting admiring and wondering crowds wherever she went. There was no doubt that people would pay good money to see a "ponderous pachyderm," as she was billed, and other peculiar animals. Bailey had been succeeded in the ownership of Old Bet by another showman from their own area, "Uncle Nate" Howes of Brewster's Station, and Howes had continued to show the beast with conspicuous success all over New England.

People wanted entertainment, the four from North Salem mused, there was no doubt about that. People also wanted to see strange beasts and would pay to do so. So the four men pooled their resources and acquired a show which they called the Zoological Institute, a traveling menagerie which began to tour the country. Not until the late 1830s, however, were menagerie and circus combined and allowed to roll together. Thus the four bold owners formed the first circus syndicate in the United States. They became known as the Flatfoots, a nickname derived, according to that great circus authority Earl Chapin May, from the time another circus threatened what they considered their exclusive territory. The four were said to have exclaimed, "We put our foot down flat, and shall play New York."

The syndicate conceived by John J. June, Lewis B. Titus, Sutton Angevine and Jerry Crane grew apace and when the Flatfoots finally passed from the circus scene in 1880 they had incorporated the circuses of such great American names as Lewis B. Lent, John J. Nathans, Dick Sands, and several others.

The year 1836 must go down in circus annals in letters of gold. For it was then that two individuals, each to make an indelible mark on circus and showman history, first appeared on the scene. Each year the Zoological Institute returned north for the winter and it was after one of their early rolling seasons that they elected to come to a small town called Ridgebury in Connecticut. Here dwelt Aron Turner, a shoemaker, who now became fascinated by the circus, as did his two sons, and together they decided to form a circus and go trouping. They needed help, and called in a neighbor, George F. Bailey, a nephew of Old Bet's Hackaliah Bailey who had retired to become landlord of a tavern in North Salem. George F. later married Aron Turner's daughter and became one of the great early circus managers of the American circus. The other who joined was a young man called Phineas Taylor Barnum, the greatest opportunist the entertainment world has known, the King of Showmen.

By then Barnum was twenty-six and had tried his hand at many things: storekeeper, promoter of curiosities – his Joice Heth, a withered negress supposedly 161 years old who had nursed the infant George Washington, had brought the budding showman what had seemed a small fortune. But this was all lost when he invested it in a small business making the peculiar combination of boot blacking and cologne and his partner departed with the takings. Now he was to sample the delights – and the perils – of the rolling circus.

An important lesson he learned at an early stage in his showman's career was at the hands of his partner Aron Turner. They pulled into a small town and during a chat in the local inn discovered that a particularly brutal murder had been committed in the neighborhood. An inveterate practical joker, Turner decided that this was too good an opportunity to miss and gave Barnum's description as the man they wanted. When Barnum, all innocence, came to join the party, he was immediately set upon. They were about to bear the showman off to the nearest tree to hang him when a timely explanation from Turner saved his neck. But Barnum had been badly frightened. When he challenged his partner about the joke which had nearly gone too far, he was greeted with the bland reply, "All we need to ensure success is notoriety. You will see that this will be noised all about town – and our pavilion will be crammed tomorrow night." Aron Turner was proved right; it was a lesson Barnum never forgot. He declared that the public like to be fooled – to his dying day this was to be the philosophy of the self-styled Prince of Humbugs, the supreme master of the art.

Another who found himself more and more closely concerned with the circus was Seth B. Howes, younger brother of "Uncle Nate" Howes of Old Bet fame. Aged eleven, he had accompanied his elder brother on a tour of Maine with the elephant and his taste for the showman's life never waned. Perhaps the first American Master Showman, Seth B. died in 1901 aged eighty-six having made himself a fortune in the circus world.

Both Turner and Seth B.'s circuses had their winter quarters in Putnam County, New York, and from here the two vied with each other to produce a bigger and better show – with an amity which was remarkable. Turner created a stir with his four wagons, nine horses and, wonder of wonders, a real band which made his street parade a sensation. Seth B. introduced a Round Top with a diameter of no less than sixty feet and tiered seats. Admittedly there were only four tiers and the tent only seated a few hundred people, but this was something new and New Yorkers flocked to see the show, which was also advertised by a billboard for the first time. Turner countered Seth B.'s efforts with a ninety-foot tent, plus seats, plus baggage wagons around the tent walls for further seating, while his sons widened their repertoire to include fancy riding and vaulting. Their chief innovation was a Grand Ethiopian Entertainment – a minstrel show.

In the 1830s and 1840s the American rolling shows became bigger and bigger, and the small township of Brewster's Station, which was Seth B.'s home town, went quite circus mad. Money would be contributed by anybody and everybody for the circus which dominated their lives. Circus wagons moored there during the winter, harness makers were kept busy, wagon builders drove a thriving trade, tent makers and repairers flourished and strange animals became a common sight in and around the little town which had so taken the circus to its heart.

The circus was thriving in America, and so were the menageries. The first elephant had come to America in 1796 preceding the famous Old Bet by nineteen years and was advertised as "the largest of quadrupeds. The earth trembles under her feet. She has power to tear up the largest of trees." She was an instant sensation wherever she went and was shown all along the eastern seaboard – no one seemed to have minded that this particular specimen measured a bare four feet in height. The first camel made its way to the United States in 1721, and the first tiger in 1789. But it was really James M. June's brother, sent off to Africa by the Flatfoots, who returned with a wealth of exotic animals, including another giraffe or camelopard, as the beasts were often known, which became centerpieces for their menageries.

The menageries and static or rolling shows had proved immensely popular. But it was the grand spectacles which had developed from the bare beginnings like Astley's, Hughes's Royal Circus, the Franconi's and other establishments which were the chief attractions. The Grand Equestrian Gallopade Entrées, as they were often billed, thrilled audiences on both sides of the Atlantic. For the most part these were hippodramic events, for horses were still the principal feature. The Tailor in its many guises was now matched by other sensations. Most were designed to show off the superb horsemanship of the principal actors, and none was more talented than Andrew Ducrow who had taken on the Astley mantle.

Andrew Ducrow had first appeared in Astley's show at the age of seven, driven there by a cruel and merciless father, a strongman of international fame known as the Flemish Hercules. There can be no denying that the young Ducrow was brought up the hard way – with belt and stick. On one occasion the boy fell off his horse and the audience was astonished to hear howls from the wings where father Ducrow was beating his son – despite his having broken a leg in the fall. Hard school though it was, Andrew Ducrow turned out to be the supreme equestrian of his age, and some say of any age. He was a brilliant mime, comic and dramatic actor, and a highly talented theater manager. But it was as an innovator of entertainment that he should be best known, for he possessed the true showman's touch – the unerring instinct of knowing what his audience liked, and would pay to see. Not content with the almost pure horsemanship of many of the Astley shows, Ducrow was one of the first to introduce full-length clowning features although horse acts still predominated and four-legged actors often indeed assumed the star-roles.

Another innovation of Ducrow were his "Poses Plastiques," the Grecian Statues or Living Statuary, which were to send circus audiences into raptures at the mere mention of his name. Clothed in an appropriate costume, he would pose as the great characters in history or mythology, motionless upon his galloping horse – a spectacle which once moved a Cockney to exclaim, "His Mercury's beautif', but his Gladiawtor's shooblime!" If London loved him, Paris adored him, for Laurent Franconi, son of the great Antoine, had spotted Ducrow when he was in Brussels with his performing horse, Jack, and brought them both to the French capital. Living Statuary were an instant success in

JOHNSON & C
Will Perform at Reading
Doors open at 1½ and 7 o'clock, P. M.
ADMISSION 25 CENTS. NO HALF-PRICE.

THE NEW YORK HISTORICAL SOCIETY, NEW YORK CITY

Horsemanship was the mainstay of early circus programs. Johnson & Cos. Circus of 1852.

Andrew Ducrow in one of his famous scenes, The Indian and Wild Horses.

New York too. The act was revived in the early years of this century, but people's tastes had changed and the attempt fell flat.

Ducrow and other London theater managers were by then employing casts of upward of 150 people at times together with numerous animals in their more elaborate set-piece dramas. Small stuff by comparison with some of the enormous spectacles put on by Barnum and others later in the century, but impressive enough in the climate of the times. In Paris though, the Franconi were already employing casts of about 400 in their more grandiose spectaculars when, religiously, night after night, in a special chair, old Antoine Franconi, founder of the dynasty, then almost blind and in his ninety-eighth year, would watch his family and others doing their acts, particularly the brilliant riding of little Mlle Minette Franconi, La Fille de l'Air, who was the talk of Paris. The old man was to die in 1835 mourned and honored by all Paris.

The scale of some of these spectacles enlarged as they caught the popular imagination. The "Battle of Waterloo," a great favorite on both sides of the Atlantic, though not perhaps in France, was regularly revived until well into the 1860s. Here there was every opportunity for wonderful display, thunderous explosions and splendid conflagrations. It had a cast of over six hundred and at times fifty or sixty horses were on the stage at the same time. A mighty melodrama to be sure, but it appeared even more so as the actors, passing behind the stage, carried out a quick costume change and reappeared in different uniforms. The effect was of a constantly changing procession and the audience loved it.

At one of the last performances of this great melodrama in London, when the theater had run into lean times and could only afford one horse, the nag had to stand as mount for both Napoleon and Wellington. And when the Iron Duke appeared riding the same horse that the Emperor had been astride in Act One, the gallery in unison shouted "Where did you get that horse?" Napoleon when his turn came around was not to be defeated and after giving a stirring harangue to his army, on foot, concluded his oration with the words, "But what I am most proud of in ye is, that by the prowess of your glorious arms, ye have rescued from the hated thraldom of the blood-thirsty British soldiery my favorite charger, who has on so many occasions carried me – and ye – to victory!" With that he produced the charger amidst thunders of applause and kept the animal for the rest of the evening.

Les Gloires Militaires, as they were known in France, were immensely popular, especially in Paris. Incidents in the Napoleon story gave ample opportunity to the ingenious, and there was none more ingenious than the Franconi in their Cirque Olympique, the home of the massive military spectacles which so stirred the patriotic hearts of all true Frenchmen. Austerlitz, Pultawa, the Crossing of the Mont-Saint-Bernard Pass, Marengo, Arcola, and other great Napoleonic successes - even the Retreat from Moscow, which somehow turned out to have been a victory - thrilled Parisian audiences. Murat, Lannes, the incomparable Ney and the Emperor's other marshals strode the stage of the Cirque Olympique and "Napoleon" himself could not pass in the streets without being mobbed. Truth to tell the stars did little to dissipate the illusion. When Napoleonic extravaganza were playing in no less than five separate theaters across Paris in the 1830s it was recorded that M. Cazot, perhaps the cream of the "Napoleons," was heard to mutter to his tailor as he pinched his ear when bending to measure him, "*Soldat, je suis content de vous.*" While another, M. Gobert, would stroll the streets with knitted brow and hands behind his back.

These warlike spectacles were almost as successful in England, after one or two patriotic adjustments had been made to the original, but chauvinistic fervor of Paris was never quite matched. So realistic were these stage battles considered that some "Cossacks" refused to fight against their "Emperor" and had to be bribed to perform with a salary of 1.50 francs per day compared with the 1 franc paid to "loyal" troops. For a touch of realism, genuine officers sometimes commanded the troops on the stage; a spectacle which prompted *Punch* to write, after commenting that the real battle cannot have been half so good as the imitation, "We can hardly imagine Lord Raglan galloping backwards and forwards on Astley's stage, or H.R.H. the Duke of Cambridge dashing up a platform on his richly caparisoned steed and exhorting six mounted supernumaries to follow him through the Upper Entrance to death or victory."

This referred to a performance of "The Battle of Alma," the opening contest of the Crimean War in which the French and English routed the Russians. Within weeks of the great victory, The Battle of Alma was being performed before rapturous audiences who cheered to the echo every patriotic allusion – and there were plenty. *The Times* was particularly loud in its praises as their war correspondent was depicted as laying low a Russian adversary with his umbrella! Four hundred real soldiers were used in the production, which had its problems as the Guards, long used to holding their fire until the last minute, waited until their adversaries were literally upon them before loosing off a withering volley which literally laid many an "enemy" low, as the wadding, normally quite harmless at a proper range, tore into the ranks of the advancing "Russians."

Gunfire, burning houses and gory battle scenes predominated in these productions, and cavalry charges in the confined space of the stage, were always rapturously received. "As complete a representation of confusion and horror as we ever saw on the stage," described one paper, "the falling and crashing of ignited timbers, the shrieks of the women, the conflicts of the soldiers, the galloping of the horses through the rains; the noise, confusion and explosion, all unite in imparting so strong an appearance of reality to what is going forward, that it is difficult to resist the illusion."

In these great melodramas the horses were considered as part of the general tableau and did not receive the attention afforded them in the true hippodrama. But they had their moments as when a Napoleon was taken ill at the last minute and an understudy brought in who had never ridden a horse in his life. All went well until the time came for him to mount the beast and after delivering a stirring speech to his soldiers the Emperor duly approached his horse, placed his right foot in the left stirrup and ended up facing the animal's tail – to the huge delight of the audience.

The "Battle of Waterloo" was performed on many occasions in New York and in 1863 Franconi brought over his hippodrome, which also received a warm reception. By then another institution had appeared on the scene and was drawing ever-growing crowds, its fame had spread far beyond New York. This was Barnum's Great American Museum.

With his small rolling show in abeyance, a brief attempt at selling books proving unproductive and uninteresting, Barnum started looking about for another outlet for his copious energy and enterprise. His eye hit upon the edifice called The American Museum, well sited at Broadway and Ann Street in New York City. For a number of years this

VICTORIA AND ALBERT MUSEUM

P. T. Barnum, King of Humbugs and master showman.

place had been in the possession of a family named Scudder who now wished to sell it. The site was perfect, the building ideal – a five-storied marble palace with lots of space – but inside was a moldering hodge-podge of curiosities collected over the years and arranged with no eye for the public and with no attempt at making the best use of their "draw." Barnum acquired it, on credit, and immediately transformed the place. On New Year's Day, 1842, The Great American Museum duly opened; within two years he had paid off all he owed. Now the name of Barnum had become widely known. For the first time he had true scope to exercise his remarkable talent in manipulating and exploiting public taste. "The Shakespeare of advertising," as a distinguished professor has dubbed him, was now in his true element.

At first he had to make use of the Scudder family's motley collection of ancient relics, stuffed and live animals, and a few aged and peeling dioramas, but the Barnum hand soon showed through. The great hall of the building was transformed into an ice-cream parlor, and "educated dogs, industrious fleas, automatons, jugglers, ventriloquists, living statuary, tableaux, gypsies, albinos, fat boys, giants, dwarves and rope-dancers were brought in," as he wrote in his equally famous publicity stunt, an autobiography called *Struggles and Triumphs of P.T. Barnum.* On one occasion he

The Feejee Mermaid. "A repellent and shrivelled object some three feet long thinly covered with black hair," but one of Barnum's greatest successes.

brought in a tribe of Indians from Iowa who had never before tasted civilization: they set up camp on the top floor and became an instantaneous success. In his insatiable search for new "features and curiosities," he scoured the country for fresh talent. From a dusty, dingy mausoleum, The Great American Museum was transformed into a place of excitement and carnival, the fairyland of New York – and all through the genius of P. T. Barnum.

Shrewdly assessing that the city needed a place where sober, God-fearing citizens might bring their wives and children without fear of molestation or offense, he turned one room into a lecture room. Here expurgated Shakespeare and "refined amusements and moral dramas" were performed on its stage, and just as he had intended, the Lecture Room became "one of the most commodious and beautiful amusement halls in the city of New York."

But it was the Feejee Mermaid which was to bring Barnum the notoriety – but always good-natured, decent notoriety – that he sought. He had inherited from the Scudders a bewildering collection of stuffed and bottled curiosities, but he was always on the lookout for more. Thus when the showman read of a real mermaid being exhibited in London by a Boston sea captain and attracting crowds of onlookers each day, he was instantly intrigued. The captain returned to Boston and died shortly afterward; his son, uncertain of what to do with such a peculiar creature, sold it to the proprietor of a museum in Boston, but the latter, afraid of the ridicule he felt sure would fall on his head if he exhibited such a freak, brought it to Barnum. Barnum had been taken in once already, by Joice Heth who had been no more 161 than he was then himself, so he exhibited a quite uncharacteristic caution. Not until he had called in a distinguished naturalist – who found no flaw in the creature, nor how it had been made, if indeed it had – did Barnum acquire it. Then began the elaborate build-up which was to precede its astonishing appearance before the public. Over the following weeks odd snippets of information about a remarkable curiosity in the possession of a Dr. Griffen of the "Lyceum Museum of Natural History" in London, began to appear in the press. First mention was from Montgomery, Alabama, then from South Carolina, and so the news items crept nearer and nearer New York. Finally, like a bombshell, it was announced that the distinguished doctor would be making a brief appearance in the city prior to boarding a boat for England. Fortunately no one saw through the disguise of Mr. Levi Lynan, a crony of Barnum's, who was posing as Dr. Griffen and whose hotel was besieged by reporters. Then it was announced that "For One Week Only" the remarkable mermaid was to be shown to the lucky public – at the Concert Hall on Broadway – another touch of the Barnum genius, for having prepared the build-up behind the scene, he was

MUSEUM OF THE CITY OF NEW YORK

avoiding being outwardly associated with the mermaid at all. Now Barnum sat back and waited. The mermaid was an outstanding success, and then she was transferred to The Great American Museum. No one seemed to pass any remarks at all about that, it seemed a natural enough solution. Nor is it ever related if the gullible public, avid to see a real-life mermaid, were satisfied with the repellant and shriveled object some three feet long which was "Thinly covered with black hair" and possessed a countenance with "an expression of terror, which gives it the appearance of caricature of the human face. The ears, nose, lips, chin, breasts, nipples, fingers and nails ressemble those of a human figure. . . . From the point where the human figure ceases, which is about twelve inches below the vertex of the head, it ressembles a large fish of the salmon species." It had canine teeth like those of a dog and one would imagine it was a monkey torso sewn on to a fish's tail.

It is hard to tell how much of the ballyhoo which surrounded Barnum's many "features" was believed. Certainly those visiting New York City from country districts or further afield for the first time may have believed everything they heard or saw. Barnum's genius lay in the fact that even if they did not, the skeptical too would come to see what he had dreamed up next – and they never went away disappointed, for if less than impressed by the special offer, they could never but be amazed at the industry and enterprise of the incredible Mr. Barnum. If the Feejee Mermaid was a hoax – although Barnum swore to his dying day that he believed the creature genuine – the next Barnum sensation was quite real, though very small.

Giants he had in plenty, dwarves and freaks of all sorts peopled The Great American Museum, but when Barnum, on a visit to New Bridgeport, Connecticut, heard of a miniature man in the neighborhood, he decided he must see for himself. He was captivated. As he wrote, "He was two feet high; he weighed less than sixteen pounds, and was the smallest child I ever saw that could walk alone; he was a perfectly formed, bright-eyed little fellow, with light hair, and ruddy cheeks, and he enjoyed the best of health." He was called Charles S. Stratton, and Barnum named him General Tom Thumb after a midget who had appeared on the New York stage during the previous century.

General Tom Thumb and his mother came to New York and on December 8, 1842, he was introduced to the public. Then started a career which was to last until the then portly, mustachioed General, forty-one years old, three feet four inches in height and seventy pounds in weight, died after a stroke. One of the most attractive things about the Tom Thumb episode, which was to introduce the amazing Mr. Barnum to Europe, was that throughout their long association, Tom Thumb always looked upon the showman as a benevolent godfather. From time to time they had their disagreements, but these were always transitory affairs. Barnum may have exploited Tom Thumb, but they remained firm friends to the last.

In December 1844 Barnum and the General departed for England. With careful newspaper presentation, he reached London a sensation and a three-day appearance at a theater there strengthened the impact. The General's fame spread far and wide, soon members of the nobility were calling on the little man and departing quite captivated by his charm, good manners and sophistication – Barnum had trained him well. But the showman was not satisfied. Like Astley he knew that to gain the most impact he must aim for the highest, and he used all his impressive powers of suggestion and persuasion to gain audience at the Palace. At length, exhausted by Court recalcitrance, he let drop word that he was shortly proceeding to France and had had it on the best authority that he was to be granted an audience by the French royal family. The gates of protocol were lifted and on March 23, 1844, General Tom Thumb and Phineas Taylor Barnum were graciously received in audience by Her Majesty Queen Victoria. The showman was now truly an international figure.

Two more visits to the delighted queen followed, and then a trip to Paris took place where the General was received with equal acclaim. The high point of his visit took place a few weeks after his arrival, when with royal approval "General Tom Pouce" was driven in state to Longchamps races in his own diminutive equipage. It had been built for him by Queen Victoria's carriage maker in London and was twenty inches high and twelve inches wide, furnished with yellow silk. Tom Thumb's coat of arms, devised by Barnum, showing the Goddess of Liberty and Britannia in a double shield supported by the American Eagle and the British Lion, was emblazoned on the carriage door. Four Shetland ponies with harnesses of black leather with silver mountings pulled the little carriage and two dwarves, who acted as coachman and footman, wore sumptuous blue liveries trimmed with silver.

Numerous individual acts and actors found their way to the Great American Museum in its heyday, and many a circus performer of a later date owed his first success to Barnum. One of the more established performers who did appear in the early days of the museum's fame was the American comedian, strongman, circus proprietor, successful owner of a one-horse show, and folk hero, the versatile Dan Rice.

Rice, his real name was McLaren, had started his career as a professional jockey, until driven by overweight to other pastures. His first circus adventures were as strongman and juggler, then he became owner of a performing pig, which he called Lord Byron and brought to The Great American Museum. In his time, Rice performed at Barnum's

Tom Thumb in England. The little man in two of his characteristic roles.

THEATER ARTS MAGAZINE 1941, HARRY T. PETERS COLLECTION

The immortal Dan Rice as Uncle Sam.

Museum on several occasions, until one memorable day. The great artiste was by then a star able to draw a salary of $1,000 a week from more than one employer – despite his well-known habit of chucking contracts when the mood suited. On this occasion Dan Rice was doing a strongman act for Barnum in which he bore on his broad back an immense barrel of water. As he was heaving and straining, his neck sinews standing out like iron rods and with the sweat pouring from him, while the audience was hushed and apprehensive lest the great barrel should bear him down to the stage with its sheer weight, he deliberately dropped it and the half bucket of water it contained poured onto the orchestra. Barnum never forgave him.

Despite having offended and spited proprietor after proprietor, abandoned contract after contract, proved the most temperamental of stars and having a strong taste for alcohol, Dan Rice was still avidly sought after as the first entertainment star on the circuit, the First Clown in America. When he was playing in Washington, D.C., a recess was declared in both Congress and Senate so they could attend his performances and he was reputed to command a greater salary than the president himself. His repartee was nationally famous, his withering, devastating verbal attacks on the unfortunate ringmaster, his butt, were widely quoted. It was Rice who introduced the Pete Jenkins act to the American circus – that of the old tramp who sits in the audience, comes out of the crowd, divests himself of his tattered clothes and performs like an angel on horseback. He also cultivated an impressive pair of side whiskers and a red, white and blue suit, becoming the prototype of Uncle Sam.

The story goes that when Zachary Taylor was running for the presidency in 1848, Dan Rice suggested by way of a bit of publicity for the candidate that he and his party get on his circus bandwagon and parade with him. On arriving at the center of town Dan Rice stopped his parade, stood up on his seat and gave a moving speech in support of Taylor, whereupon the crowd shouted "Look, Dan Rice is on Zachary Taylor's bandwagon." So another expression found its way into the dictionary.

By the middle of the nineteenth century the circus as an attraction was everywhere making sweeping progress. In America and England, rolling or tenting shows crisscrossed the two countries. Most cities had their permanent halls or amphitheaters where circuses and melodramas or hippodramas were regularly performed. In Paris by 1850 there were several such theaters, in other cities across Europe circus dynasties and circus families were spreading far and wide. There was a thriving international currency of circus acts and individual artistes. Germany had a number of circuses and the art was also strongly established in Scandinavia.

Gradually too the Russian circus was coming into being. Many of the early European traveling circuses had been French and during the period from 1830–1850 circuses under the direction of Tournaire – who had first toured Russia in 1815 – and others, came to be established in that vast country. Under this impetus the indigenous skills of clown, acrobat and funambulist which had been fostered by Peter the Great in the late 1600s, were matched with the imported equestrian turns of such as Charles Hughes. The ancestral origins of the great Soviet circus of today had been founded.

THE GOLDEN YEARS AND AFTER

One day in the early 1830s a small boy by the name of George Sanger was taken by his father to see Andrew Ducrow at Astley's. Open-mouthed and wide-eyed, he watched the performance; he gasped at the incredible feats of daring equestrian skill, laughed till his sides ached at the antics of the clowns and wondered how it was possible to train animals to do such remarkable tricks. As he watched, he marveled at the spectacle and breathed in the unique atmosphere of the circus. He said to himself, "One day Astley's will be mine." So recounted the supreme English showman "Lord" George Sanger – as he came to be known and loved throughout Britain and the Continent.

The Sangers claim that in the dim past one of their forebears had traveled to England and became court jester to King John, who died in 1216. But a nearer influence was George Sanger's father, James, who at an early age had been pressganged into the navy from which he had been honorably discharged after the Battle of Trafalgar in 1805. He brought with him knowledge of some rudimentary tumbling, a few conjuring tricks and some sound advice about hanky-panky – as the art of showmanship in the fairgrounds was termed – picked up from a couple of shipmates. James Sanger also possessed a pension of sevenpence a day from the grateful government and a parchment headed "Royal Prescription" which he wore around his neck in a bag. This entitled its owner in perpetuity to carry on any lawful trade without restraint, as well as giving him freedom to travel where he would. It was a priceless document which was to save the young showman's skin on more than one occasion.

For these were days when showmen and fairground performers were classed as "rogues, vagabonds and deceivers of the peace." Despised, disliked and distrusted, they were frequently a target for abuse and often violence. In Scotland

VICTORIA AND ALBERT MUSEUM

An evening at Astley's.

the sort of show James Sanger put on was likely to be classed as the work of the devil and the showmen branded as servants of Satan and driven from the burgh. Under the law, anyone could be charged with vagrancy if they slept out, and as the showmen had nowhere else to sleep, they were wholly at the mercy of any disagreeable magistrate. Their lives were a continual battle against the law, against the weather and against poverty. It was a long time before the traveling showman was granted any degree of respectability.

Wearing a white frock coat, beaver hat, knee breeches with stockings and buckled shoes and carrying on his back a large box – a peep-show – James Sanger trudged his way round Britain. In winter he and his wife returned to London and sold fish, fruit and candied apples to keep alive. Through hard work and perseverance he prospered and soon the family graduated to a caravan. This was the atmosphere in which young George and his two brothers, Will and John, were raised and introduced to circus training, showground life and fairground ways.

Soon the young Sanger brothers had their own show.

A traveling showman.

GUILDHALL LIBRARY, CITY OF LONDON

George's task was generally to look after the entertainment while Will was responsible for money matters, together with any painting and carpentry, and John ejected the undesirable and looked after what is known as the "front." George was no mean acrobat himself, a conjuror and a trainer of small animals – performing canaries and white mice were his first ventures. He then graduated to a tame hare and some fish which were tied by strings to little boats and with these he would display the most stirring fleet actions. But the Smoking Oyster routine was an immediate draw wherever they went. This consisted of two suitably large oyster shells and a clay pipe stuck between them. It was connected to a long tube on the other end of which a small boy, hidden under a table, puffed on command.

In 1850 George Sanger married Ella Chapman, the Lion Queen of Wombwell's Menagerie – one of the biggest in the country – and gradually, from these humble beginnings grew Britain's largest and most impressive circus.

In winter the small Sanger show was in London. Summers would find the circus – although a single caravan and a few animals hardly justified the title – on the road. 1851 was the year of the Great Exhibition in Hyde Park and the showmen, among them George Sanger, determined to make the occasion a gala such as London would always remember. From far and wide, traveling booths, hanky-panky merchants, shows of all shapes, sizes and nationalities converged on Hyde Park. The place began to resemble an enormous showground, with signs and smells and sounds in such quantity and splendor as London had ever witnessed. The eve of the opening was upon them, and then the Heavens opened. Little business could be done on the first day, and even less on the second. With a couple of days of fine weather everyone's spirits rose, but then came the rain again. The colors on the bright awnings ran and faded; the canvas itself grew so sodden that stakes could no longer support it and everything subsided into the mud; performers were soaked and their props, so carefully prepared over the previous months, were ruined, while the carts, caravans and stalls sank deeper and deeper into seemingly bottomless mud. Dripping wet, the showmen gave up in disgust and determined to pull out. But how? For by then the carts were axle-deep in the mire. Two hundred men were employed in batches of fifty or sixty with as many horses, and slowly and wearily the wagons were extricated from the mud to wend their damp and weary way from what would have been the greatest fair London had ever seen.

This was the start of a period of bitter years and hard times for George Sanger. Soon after the Hyde Park fiasco his baby son died in their caravan and the miserable couple had to bear his little body with them to the next town where they could earn enough money to see him decently buried.

In 1854 came the turning point. In that year, the great aggregation of Seth B. Howes and Cushing's American Circus came to England, and by flagrantly plagiarizing and out-advertising the advertisers, Sanger at last saw success – so much so that the American show decided to adopt his name to take with them back across the Atlantic. Thus Sanger's London Show came to America and for many years was known in the eastern states, although the owner of the title never came too, nor was he ever paid royalties for the use of his name, a subject which rankled all his life.

Triumph followed triumph for George Sanger and within half-a-dozen years Sanger's was a name known throughout Britain. With his reputation secure, Sanger reckoned it was time for him to bring a full-scale circus to London.

The 1860s were peaceful enough in Britain which, under Queen Victoria, grew in greatness as the British Empire rose toward its zenith. But in America all was confusion, for 1861 saw the outbreak of the Civil War. Circuses and other entertainments were hard hit. Performers left their jobs and

The mighty Floating Palace.

CIRCUS WORLD MUSEUM, BARABOO, WISCONSIN

moved as their consciences dictated. Purely Southern shows like that of Ol' John Robinson, which was to have a long and distinguished life after the Civil War was over, remained untouched, but others, caught in the South, especially when they numbered Yankees in their troupe, were less lucky. Hardest hit of all were what had become known as the Boat Shows.

With the roads hazardous and rough in much of eastern America in the middle years of the nineteenth century, whenever possible the showmen took to the rivers (as indeed was also being done on the great rivers of Germany and eastern Europe). By the 1850s many troupes moved solely by boat up and down the waterways of Ohio, Indiana, Kentucky and farther west and south. Most used the rivers purely as a means of transportation, piling their animals and their tents on steamboats, stopping at likely halts and pitching their Big Tops on any convenient open space near a town. It was a Dr. G. R. Spaulding who was to see and realize the great potential these waterways afforded the traveling circus.

G. R. Spaulding – the "Doctor" he owed to his

profession as a pharmacist – had come into circus life after lending money to a small circus owner who appeared likely never to repay it. He was possessed of a highly original and inventive mind, and is credited with being the first man to introduce quarter-poles. Set between the king pole in the center and the sidewall poles, the quarter-poles not only gave additional height to the tent above the seats, thus giving the tent a much flatter appearance, but also increased its stability in high winds. Spaulding also invented special runways for circus wagons to board flatcars for the first circus railroad train – yet another innovation of his – while his parade was enhanced by the presentation for the first time of the Forty-Horse Hitch. Pulled by horses harnessed four abreast, this enormous equipage was driven by a single man. The use of oil rather than candles to light the circus is also attributed to the versatile talents of the "Doctor."

Of all his accomplishments, though, "Doc" Spaulding is best known for his vast flat-bottomed floating amphitheater. Christened the *Floating Palace*, this great boat was launched with a duly impressive ceremony and on it Spaulding's circus

THE NEW YORK HISTORICAL SOCIETY, NEW YORK

On board the Floating Palace *was accommodation for artistes and animals, while performances were held in the huge amphitheater which seated two thousand spectators.*

made its way up and down the rivers of the central states. The vessel had no power of its own and relied on tugs to drag it from place to place but it was wholly self-contained, except for food and water. Sunken below deck and roofed with timbers, was a huge amphitheater – and a gallery with more seats; in all the *Floating Palace* had seating for two thousand. There was accommodation below deck for animals and troupers and the vast amounts of forage and provisions that were required. His troupe and animals lived aboard, while his advance publicity teams went ahead to advertise the coming of the mighty boat. Others followed the "Doctor's" lead until show boats became frequent sights on the rivers.

When war broke out in 1861, Spaulding and his entourage were at New Orleans, and stranded because the *Floating Palace* had been commandeered to become a hospital for Confederate wounded. Not wishing to spend the rest of the war in the South, the troupe rented a steamboat and made their way slowly northward, although they now called themselves Castello's Great Show as Dan Castello, their dancing and leaping clown, had toured the southern states for many seasons and was widely known and loved.

As Earl Chapin May put it in his book *From Rome to Ringling*, "Slowly working up the Mississippi, Castello's Great Show flew the Palmetto flag and its band played *Dixie* religiously. . . . After it reached the clear Ohio, Castello's co-operative circus literally played both sides. In a Union town they hoisted the Stars and Stripes to the top of their center pole; for they were forced to exhibit under canvas after their Floating Palace was seized. In Union towns the band feelingly obliged with *Yankee Doodle*. On the southern and eastern shores of rivers they found the Palmetto banner and strains of *Dixie* more inducive to friendliness and patronage." On the whole they showed the right allegiance at the right time and eventually sailed clear of war and back to the North.

It was while working around Chicago after this adventure that Castello met a retired showman, reluctantly turned farmer, called W. C. Coup and together the two put on a show which worked the Great Lakes. It was these two, many years later who were to draw Barnum into the circus.

In 1855, with his Great American Museum in a flourishing state and Tom Thumb the talk of two continents and envy of the civilized world, Barnum seemed on the crest of an ever-rolling wave. He decided to retire, and at the age of forty-five, he withdrew to the remarkable, oriental-style pile called Iranistan which he had built at vast expense at Bridgeport, Connecticut. It was modeled after the Royal Pavilion at Brighton – which he had seen and admired on his visit to England – with a number of bizarre, vaguely Turkish, vaguely Byzantine, vaguely nightmarish embellishments of his own.

Barnum had been involved in writing his autobiography since 1854. At last the great work was finished and Barnum prepared to bathe luxuriously in the fame which he had now recorded for posterity. But he was in for a cruel disappointment for the book revealed to a startled and incredulous

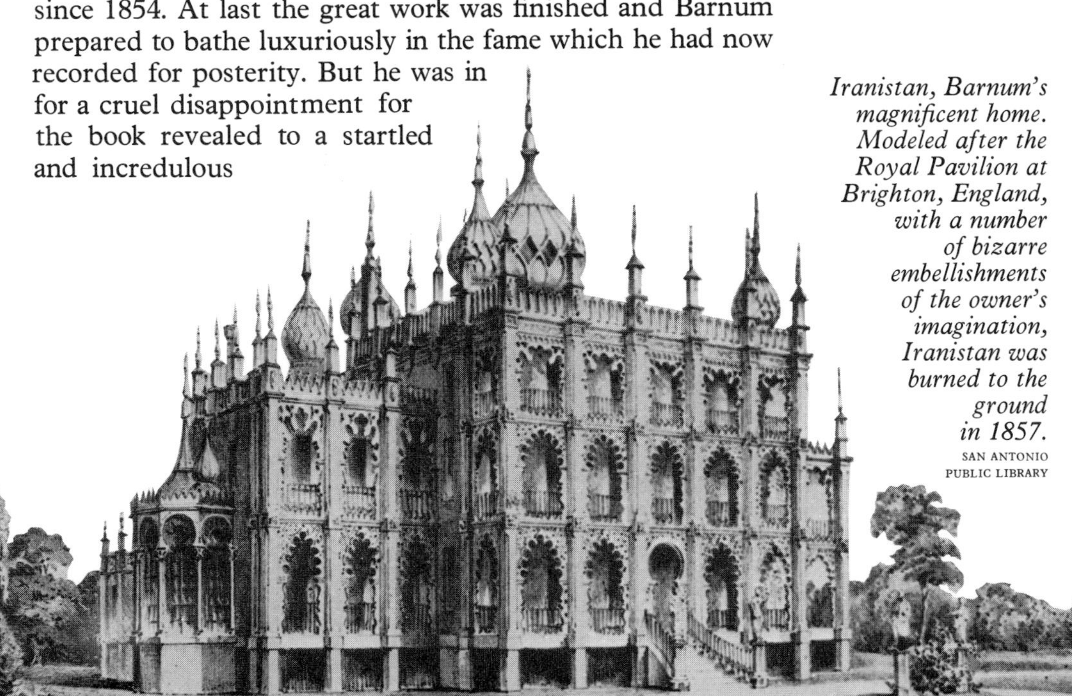

Iranistan, Barnum's magnificent home. Modeled after the Royal Pavilion at Brighton, England, with a number of bizarre embellishments of the owner's imagination, Iranistan was burned to the ground in 1857.
SAN ANTONIO PUBLIC LIBRARY

THE NEW YORK HISTORICAL SOCIETY, NEW YORK

The Great Fire of 1865 which destroyed Barnum's second museum.

public that their hero had been, and was, nothing less than . . . a crook. Berated by reviewers, he was described as a rogue exulting in his roguery, a confidence trickster who would dupe them for his own malevolent ends. Barnum was flabbergasted, and appalled. Self-justifying the book certainly was, but it had been written also in high good humor and although, inevitably, mocking the public's gullibility, it was never with malice, disdain or contempt. Nevertheless, the book was wholly misunderstood and those who had taken Barnum at face value were outraged. Worse was to follow: he had been dabbling in the affairs of an ailing clock company and suddenly found that through extreme carelessness he had agreed to guarantee its debts. Disowned by the public, *his* public he had always thought of them, and condemned by them as a cheap scoundrel, he was now hounded by creditors. The inevitable happened – the great Barnum, the unassailable Barnum went bankrupt.

Luckily the Museum was in other hands – but his wife's possession of the lease left him with an intimate interest. His beloved Iranistan had to be closed down and many of his erstwhile friends deserted him – which hurt him more than anything else. Then to crown all his misfortune, Iranistan was burned to the ground. A few years later, in the biggest fire New York had seen for ages, the Great American Museum suffered the same fate. Within minutes the fruit of genius and the labor and love of years was a blackened ruin of smoking rubble – although fortunately all the animals and many of the exhibits were saved. A lesser man would have given up, but Barnum carried on, buoyed by the encouragement of his few true friends – and none more loyal than little Tom Thumb, who wrote offering any help he could give, while an editorial by his old crony Horace Greely of the *New York Tribune* must have proved a heart-warming encouragement to the desolate Barnum now down on his luck.

Greely wrote the day after the tragic fire: "We mourn its loss, but not without consolation. Barnum's Museum is gone, but Barnum himself, happily, did not share the fate of the rattlesnakes . . . . There are fishes in the seas and beasts in the forest; birds still fly in the air and strange creatures still roam in the deserts; giants and pigmies still wander up and down the earth; the oldest man, the fattest woman, and the smallest baby are still living, and Barnum will find them."

And find them he did. White whales, Indian chiefs, a dying handler of grizzly bears and a baboon which posed as a gorilla, brought Barnum back to his feet. A respected member of society again, the showman was elected to the Connecticut state legislature. He founded the New American Museum in New York, bought a menagerie, and seemed set once more for prosperity. Then, again, fire was to prove his undoing. In 1868 the New American Museum joined the fate of its greater ancestor and was burned to a cinder – this time with almost total loss of the animals he had so painstakingly collected. The fifty-eight-year-old Barnum at last had had enough; he decided to retire again, and for the last time. Or so he said. Two years later he burst on the scene – to run now, of all things, a circus. The wheel of Fate had turned full circle, conceived by adversity out of perseverance The Greatest Show on Earth was about to be born.

Barnum always persuaded himself, and tried to persuade others, that it was he rather than Coup and Castello who conceived the great idea of a giant circus. But whoever was responsible, the show opened in Brooklyn on April 10, 1871 with Coup as general manager, Castello as equestrian manager and Barnum's son-in-law as treasurer and the great man's representative. Success was instantaneous, and a tumultuous reception greeted the circus in a tour which ran from New England to California. Every day, except Sunday, there were two performances and a street parade; sometimes demand was so high that three performances were given. Receipts that first season reached $400,000.

Novelty followed novelty; attraction succeeded attrac-

SAN ANTONIO PUBLIC LIBRARY

Barnum rises again. An early Barnum poster.

tion. This was circus in the grand style and they treated their stars to match. With a roll of the drum, a great artiste would be driven into the ring by coach, and a groom would bow him or her out. When the act was over, amid rolling applause, the great ones would make a coach-driven exit, bowing and acknowledging the plaudits of the crowd as they went. In all this Coup was the inspirational and driving force. Barnum was now comfortably in his sixties; he lent his name and his experience and from time to time pleaded caution to his younger and now more adventurous partners. It was Coup who decided that road days were too arduous for a circus of their size, and took to the railroad. It was Coup who invented and perfected an improved method of loading circus paraphernalia onto flatcars – a method to which military men were to pay particular attention, in the years to come. It was Coup who introduced half-rate circus-excursion trains to bring in people from outlying districts, and he seemed, to the bemused Barnum, to go mad in his advertising displays which reached an intensity even Barnum had never envisaged. But one must suspect Barnum's hand in the theme which was – and still is – the watchword for The Greatest Show on Earth. This was what he called a Sunday School Show, a moral show, a children's show and as his lavish programmes expounded: "No expense or effort is spared to ensure them a regular, out-and-out fairyland frolic, and an uproariously lavish and spicy, yet entirely wholesome and harmless, feast for the eye, heart and mind." The result? Takings of $1 million in six months.

After differences with his partners, Barnum bought them out. Coup left to take on the New York Aquarium, which he was later to lose on the toss of a coin. And old Barnum, having married his second wife – an ebullient English girl forty years his junior, seemed to take on a new lease of life. The last seventeen years of the old showman's days were to be the happiest and most triumphant of all.

His two-ring shows were vast – they were using over three acres of canvas now – and nothing seemed to satisfy the old man's insatiable appetite for new attractions. His circus went from strength to strength. A merger with a rival concern, the International Allied Shows, brought Barnum into partnership with the thirty-three-year-old James A. Bailey. This union with the brilliant little self-effacing circus organizer, really put The Greatest Show on Earth on the road. Soon the running costs of Barnum and Bailey's, as it was affectionately known across America, had reached $5,000 a day and he was drawing huge crowds. His Congress of Monarchs – a show he bought as it stood from George Sanger – attracted an audience of 10,000 people at a performance in New York City.

Perhaps the crowning point of Barnum's many achievements was in the vast Olympia in London in 1889.

The Greatest Show on Earth. A poster of 1894.

CIRCUS WORLD MUSEUM, BARABOO, WISCONSIN

"Positively Exhibiting in London Only," read the bills, "P. T. Barnum's Greatest Show on Earth. America's Truthful, Moral, Instructive, Grandest and Best, Largest Amusement Institution. And Imre Kiralfy's Original Stupendous Historical Spectacular Classic Drama of Nero or the Destruction of Rome." It was a massive assemblage employing 1,200 people and 380 horses. "A Real Hippodrome. Millionaire Menageries. Prodigious Museum. Performing Caravans. 100 Chariots and Dens. Beautiful Ballets. Trained Animals. Supernatural Illusions. Triple 100 Act Circus. All kinds of Thrilling Races. Wondrous Mid-Air Feats. Monster Elevated Stages. Stupendous Spectacles. Gladitorial Combats." But to all those who beheld this incredible circus, the high point was before the performance actually began when Barnum, in an open carriage, drawn by two horses with coachman and footman in full livery, would drive round the ring from time to time calling on his carriage to halt and standing up to bellow, "I suppose you come to see Barnum, didn't you? Wa-al, I'm Mr. Barnum." They had. They were impressed, and they loved him for what they thought of as a bit of Barnum ballyhoo.

Barnum was now nearing eighty, a much-loved personality. Even Barnum was not immortal – although at one time he had seriously thought he might be. In 1891, a few weeks after reading his own obituary which he had summoned from the editor of the local newspaper, Barnum died in his sleep. The Greatest Showman of them all, the Prince of Humbugs, the Child's Friend was no more, and his death closed a chapter in circus history.

As long ago as 1843, Barnum had presented what he chose to call a buffalo hunt to a credulous New York audience. "Great Free Show," thundered the advertisements, "For the first time a Genuine Buffalo Hunt." A crowd estimated at twenty thousand flocked across the Hudson River to Hoboken in New Jersey to see the great event. They were greeted by the spectacle of buffalo all right, but not by the great beasts, "the Monarchs of the Plain," they had been expecting. Rather, there were a dozen buffalo calves not much bigger than large dogs and a good deal less fierce. The grand buffalo charge turned into a gentle amble across the roped-in arena as the bewildered animals sought a way out, and when one calf bolder than the rest broke into a trot it was duly lassoed in true western style to thunderous applause. As a spectacle of animal fury, Barnum's buffalo hunt was a fiasco, but it had been free and no one minded being taken in. Free indeed it had been, though it transpired later that Barnum had taken all the rights on the ferries over the river that day for a paltry sum, and had turned over a tidy profit.

Now, shortly before Barnum died, the crowds were to be fêted with a spectacle with all the tang, all the excitement and not a little of the danger of the authentic Wild West. For a new showman appeared on the circus scene. Of all the great Indian Scouts and western heroes "Buffalo Bill" Cody (he had been christened William Frederick) stood alone and preeminent. William Cody's father had been brought up on a farm near Cleveland, Ohio, but being of a restless spirit – a trait which he passed in full measure to his celebrated son – he turned pioneer, Indian trader and even farm manager at one stage. When the boy William was nine years old, the family decided to move to Kansas, which was then near the border of mid-western development. In a leisurely way they made their way to the West and here father Cody settled down and his son acquired the many skills which were to make his exploits legendary in the breaking of the West.

Pony express rider, guide, friend of the Indian, deadly shot and "Champion Buffalo Hunter of the Plains," Bill Cody soon became known across the continent. In 1880 he turned his hand to acting. Although no Irving, his presence and reputation attracted full houses wherever he went. Most expected something rather special in the way of entertainment

CIRCUS WORLD MUSEUM, BARABOO, WISCONSIN

Colonel W. F. Cody, Buffalo Bill.

– they were rarely disappointed. It was in *Scouts of the Prairie* that Cody achieved acting fame, of a sort, a "play" which one critic said could "have begun in the middle and gone forward or backward just as easily as the way it was written." Another said: "Everything was so wonderfully bad it was almost good. The whole performance was so far aside of human experience, so wonderful in its divine feebleness that no ordinary intellect is capable of understanding it." It was meat such as the critics had not been allowed to eat for years and they made the best of it. The leading lady – a sloe-eyed Indian maiden – was said to have an Italian accent and a "weakness for Scouts." Another alleged that the more refined easterners referred to Cody as "Bison William." Another called the principal actor "a beautiful blonde." It was a comedy show which played to huge houses but it was not to the liking of another great hero of the West, "Wild Bill" Hickock, who skipped for home as soon as he could.

Despite the dramatic fiasco of Cody's acting, it gave him a taste for riches and titillated his appetite for drama. In 1883 he realized an ambition which had been germinating for a long time – he staged a Wild West show. He chose Omaha, Nebraska, as his teething ground.

Over the years the concept behind the Wild West had been evolving in Cody's mind. He wanted something which would show a new dimension in horsemanship – practical horsemanship, he called it; something too which would bring to the easterners the spirit of the real Wild West, not the glamorized version which had so captured the imagination of America – not least through the medium of his own adventure stories which had taken the pulp book trade by

"Four hours of such entertainment, action and sustained drama as the world had never seen before." The Wild West, Buffalo Bill's new dimension in practical horsemanship; and showmanship of a very high order.

CIRCUS WORLD MUSEUM, BARABOO, WISCONSIN

storm. His was at first a raw, untutored idea, the ingredients of a truly great show were present, but they needed a managerial hand to bring out their full potential. That hand was provided by Nate Salsbury, the outstanding actor and actor-manager of his day, who was to remain the steadying influence during the great days of the Wild West show.

In 1884 a much-enlarged Wild West show emerged. Over one hundred Indians were now employed – including

Sitting Bull, almost as great a legendary figure as Buffalo Bill himself; Captain A. Bogardus, a fabulous rifle shot; Buck Taylor, a champion rider and lasso thrower; and animals – bears, elk and buffalo. And of course, there was the legendary Deadwood Stage. Built at Concord, New Hampshire, this famous coach had been shipped to California. It first operated on the line from Northwood into Oregon, but with the building of the Central Pacific Railroad across the Rocky Mountains, it was sent into service in Utah. 1876 found it abandoned on the trail from Cheyenne to Deadwood, and Cody, realizing that here he had a winner, duly acquired it.

With this aggregation, Cody and Salsbury toured the Middle West, attracting huge crowds and refining the show as they went. New Orleans then drew the Wild West and while journeying south the steamboat carrying the circus was in a collision and sank, carrying all their ammunition, animals and equipment to the bottom of the Mississippi River. Only the horses and the famous stage were saved.

With disaster staring him in the face, Cody telegraphed Salsbury, then acting in Denver, asking what he should do. Salsbury promptly cabled him some money, the show was saved. And it never looked back from that moment on. By its own later standards it was a crude, rip-roaring assemblage of talent. Those who knew the show in those early days were amazed, not so much at the skills of the performers – although these were considerable – but by the sheer stamina of the cast. "You've got to stay awake for twenty hours out of twenty-four for weeks on end," commented one – although he wasn't complaining – for the early Wild West was one continuous party. When they moved by train, one of their sixteen cars was devoted solely to liquor. When a show was over, they drank until it was time to move or to prepare for the next one, yet the performance rarely suffered – some reckoned it was all the better for a bit of drink.

By now the show had taken on the broad form it was to retain throughout its long life, of a fast-moving, hard-hitting spectacular. Four hours of such entertainment, action and sustained drama as the world had never seen, and was never to see again. Confident now of their strength, in 1886 the Wild West invaded the East and showed in Staten Island, New York, for a five-month season. Ever conscious of the importance of publicity, Cody was an enthusiast for press parties. On the eve of the great ceremonial opening in New York the Wild West invited the press to a feast. According to The *Dramatic News*, the menu was as follows:

Soup: Whisky with water Fish: Whisky Straight
Entrée: Crackers with Pepper, Salt and Whisky
Roast: Chunks of Beef Ribs, Timber Sauce
Salad: Tomatoes au Naturel Dessert: Watermelon Beer
Lemonade Whisky Champagne *Ambulances to Order*

This unusual meal may have helped, for in that season they played to over one million visitors and grossed $100,000.

In the winter they moved to Madison Square Gardens and staged a show called The Dream of Civilization. The Wild West was now truly established, and Cody and Salsbury decided that the time had come to try their hand in Europe. Buffalo Bill's Wild West show was on the eve of international greatness.

By now the British and Continental circuses were facing increasing competition from across the Atlantic. The indigenous shows, for the most part dwarfed in size and competing with circuses which had the immediate attraction of coming from a different country, found themselves hard-pressed. But there was one doughty adversary, in particular, who could contend with any transatlantic invasion – Sanger, or rather the Sangers, for the brothers George and John were still together at the time, but Will had dropped out of the partnership. As Barnum's, in its many and various forms was to become the greatest name on the American circus scene, so Sanger's was to do the same in Britain in that golden era.

Each spring the Sanger show would go on the road. In an average year they would travel over two thousand miles in their nine-month touring season, visiting over two hundred towns and giving two shows a day – Sunday excepted. Their road-train was impressive with a two-mile long column of about seventy horse-drawn wagons, including twenty which carried the wild beasts. The most valuable horses were hitched behind, but romping about at the rear of the procession would be a herd of over a hundred Shetland ponies. In a separate and more stately procession the fourteen elephants and eighteen camels made their way at their own speed toward the next stop.

"Lord" George Sanger, the great British showman, from The Sanger Story *by John Lukens (Hodder & Stoughton, 1956).*

Presiding over it all was the slim, elegant figure of George Sanger – immaculately dressed in a black frock coat with a high white collar and black tie in which he always wore a diamond tie-pin – a present from his Queen. He was rarely without his glossy top hat, and when he doffed it he revealed an almost totally bald head – save for a side fringe which he kept black by the liberal application of what he called his "gip." His moustache and beard were as original as the man and were cut in the shape of a ring around his mouth. He had a pleasant voice and a quick, and at times, devastating wit.

Sanger's move to London proved the greatest step in his career. After performing at the Agricultural Hall in 1871 he bought Astley's – and so his boyhood dream was realized. Throughout this time the two brothers, so different in both appearance and temperament, had been in partnership. But George Sanger was not the sort of man who could ever be in partnership with anyone for long, and so the two decided to part company and split the circus properties. An embarrassing, painful process, one might be inclined to think. But the division passed off with the utmost friendliness. As one lot was put forward a coin was tossed and the winner had the choice of either taking the property or of paying half its value to his brother. In a matter of a few hours the circus, conservatively valued at £100,000, had been divided amicably between the two. Once this was done, John Sanger toured England, while George crossed the English Channel on a worn-out cattle-boat with a troupe of over two hundred, with eleven elephants and 160 horses, and sought fresh fields to conquer on the Continent. For eleven years, from 1874 to 1885, George Sanger toured Europe in the summer, returning each winter to Astley's. His brother had now brought his sons into his circus and his wagons were emblazoned with the title "John Sanger and Sons." Not to be outdone, George Sanger, with equal flourish, painted on his: "George Sanger and Daughters."

It was at Astley's that George Sanger put on his most impressive spectacles. He was using a three-ring circus by this time, having first experimented with the idea in 1860 when his young circus was performing on Plymouth Hoe. That must have been quite a gathering as Sanger, remembering his early struggling days, had let it be known that he was offering free ground space to any showman who came along. Over one hundred accepted the invitation. The grand fair on top of his own three rings and two platforms all going together must have created a memorable sight. For some years Sanger clung to this pattern, although he was later to discard it as being too cumbersome and, in his view, not suitable for showing off the individual skills and artistry of his performers to the best advantage, as well as being bewildering to the audience.

But it was for his colossal spectacles and melodramas that Sanger became best known. One of the biggest was Gulliver's Travels where, disregarding the locations of Gulliver's likely ports of call, the cast included emus, ostriches, pelicans, kangaroos, reindeer, deer, Brahmin bulls, buffalo, chamois and mouflon as well as thirteen elephants, fifty-two horses, two hundred men, three hundred women and two hundred children. A stickler for perfection in all he did, George Sanger would personally preside over rehearsals – immaculate in his customary dress, the effect only slightly marred by the horse hairs which clung to his clothing.

His horses, in which he took a particular interest, were renowned for their impeccable grooming and beautiful conformation, and so, as a rule, were his supporting cast. On one memorable occasion, though, one of the girls proved to be downright plain; worse, she also had a pronounced squint. On the night of the performance a real stream would be flowing along the side of the stage, but for rehearsals a chalk mark denoted where the banks would be. The girls were asked to walk along the "bank" to take their places at the rear of the stage, but somehow the plain one could not get it right. George Sanger appeared to take it manfully, saying not a word, but those who knew him felt the inner volcano which was about the erupt. Finally, the band struck up Sanger's favorite tune – "The Girl I Left Behind Me" – and the girls set off on their way. Those beside him heard Sanger singing to himself: "First the right foot, then the left." Then, out loud so the girls might hear him, "And make your footsteps shorter." Finally, he bellowed, "and can't you see, you cock-eyed cat, you're walking in the water!"

Water shows were, in fact, a favorite with Sanger. His aquatic spectacles, in which practically everybody became soaked, were monster attractions. One of the high points in most of these spectacles was the presence of the policeman, whose waistcoat inflated when, as inevitably happened, he fell into the water. The only trouble was that the waistcoat was not self-righting and if the unfortunate man happened to fall in the water face down, there he stayed in imminent danger of drowning until someone came along and put him right side up. There seemed no end to George Sanger's ingenuity. In a spectacle called North Pole no less than seventy-six polar bears were used, an elephant, which had geographically strayed, dived down a shoot into the water, while trained cormorants had been brought over especially from China with their helpers, and "unique" diving horses from Texas nightly jumped from a great height into the water below.

Sanger was never at a loss for new or borrowed ideas and, getting to hear of the Wild West which was by now an established part of the American circus scene, he promptly pirated it. Thus "Indians," "Cowboys" and a Sanger version of the Deadwood Stage became part of British circus history. Two years later, Cody brought his own show over with him to England and discovered what Sanger had been up to. He took legal action and won the day. Sanger was furious. He had been dwarfed in the witness box by the tall, handsome American with his flowing locks and soft drawl. But worse, Buffalo Bill, because he was a member of the Nebraska state legislature, was called in court and referred to in the press as the Honorable William Cody.

Supper in the Sanger household that night was a somber affair. No one spoke and seeing the scowl on George Sanger's face was enough to make the bravest member of his family quail. Then, as Sanger's grandson, George Sanger Coleman, recalled: "I remember well how the silence was at last broken. My grandfather banged his fist on the table with a force that made all the cups rattle, and exclaimed: 'The Honorable William Cody! If that Yankee . . . can be an Honorable, then I shall be a Lord.'" And from that moment he was never known as anything but "Lord" George Sanger.

A few years later, after a performance before Queen Victoria, Sanger was presented to the Queen. For once in his life the great showman was embarrassed. The Queen soon set him at his ease. "George Sanger, we believe?" George Sanger bowed his head. "'Lord' George Sanger," she added with a twinkle. "Yes, Ma'am," the showman replied, red to the roots of what little hair he had left. "We hear," the Queen continued, "that you bear the title with distinction." From that moment any qualms, if qualms he had, vanished and he bore his self-appointed title with dignity to the day of his death. Others followed suit, including his nephew John who had by now succeeded his father in ownership and referred to himself as "Lord" John Sanger, while a descendant of old Thomas Taplin Cooke called himself "Sir" John Henry Cooke, and a rival with roots of almost equal antiquity in circus history called himself, as do his descendants, "Sir" Robert Fossett.

With the death of Barnum, Bailey, his partner, had become the undisputed Circus King of America – although he still called his show Barnum and Bailey. A small perfectionist, he never showed anger and never raised his voice. His supervision of his show was minute, and he was an indefatigible taskmaster. He hated to see anyone idle and people not actually doing anything would give James A. Bailey as wide a berth as they could, while he took a particular delight in rousing his staff on Sundays and getting them working. He appeared never to be still and would perpetually play with a pencil and a silver dollar in his pocket; when irritated he would chew rubber bands. An immensely shrewd little man, he would look at people through his glasses which hid a pronounced squint and as a showman with a high regard for quality, he would hire more acts than he needed and weed them out ruthlessly. People may have loved Barnum, but they greatly respected Bailey, not just for his business and administrative skills, but for his utter honesty. When he died they discovered just how much his unassuming presence and quiet authority had meant in their lives.

For five years his show toured the states while its manager perfected the huge aggregation. In 1897 he set forth on a European tour which was to cover many countries and to last for five years. In France he received nothing but the warmest cooperation and The Greatest Show on Earth performed in the old Roman amphitheaters at Nîmes and Arles – the most spectacular of settings. Their tour in Austria the following year was an even greater success, but in Germany the parade had to be cancelled, for the Germans, reckoning that they had seen everything, stayed away from the performances. In 1903 Bailey returned in triumph, to find that a new circus constellation had been discovered in his absence.

For many years Bailey had considered the eastern

The brilliant circus organizer, James A. Bailey.

SAN ANTONIO PUBLIC LIBRARY

seaboard as his special sphere of influence – although his hold must have been rather tenuous since there were then more than fifty rolling shows in the United States, of a considerable size – and when he left for Europe he felt confident that the smaller Forepaugh Circus, which he had owned for a number of years, would be able to look after his interests. Imagine his surprise when he returned to find that in his absence his supremacy was being challenged by some upstarts who had their origins in the small town of Baraboo, Wisconsin.

These newcomers on the circus scene who were to dominate the American circus – and whose name still does so – were christened Rungeling, although they are better remembered as the Ringlings, an anglicized version of the name which they adopted soon after taking up show business. Father Rungeling was a Hanoverian saddlemaker who had come to America around the middle of the century and when the story starts in 1870 he had five sons: Al, then aged eighteen; Otto who was thirteen; Alf T. who was seven; Charley who was six; and baby John, then only four years old. The family had recently moved to McGregor, Iowa, and it was here on a fateful summer evening that the Rungeling brothers first saw a circus – a boat show run by old Dan Rice.

So began a circus saga which lives on today. To most Americans the circus means Ringlings, which was immortalized by Cecil B. de Mille in the epic film *The Greatest Show on Earth*. It is now a colossal business concern with its circus divided into two huge groups. The Ringling tenting circus toured the States until 1956 when it was decided that tenting was no longer possible, and that in any case most cities possessed a stadium which could hold The Greatest Show. So the great circus rolled no more – and the ghosts of Astley, Ricketts and the other early circus performers who had delighted audiences in permanent buildings for so many years found themselves at peace again.

But those days were far off for the five boys from Baraboo. Although many circus artistes who become circus proprietors have been highly versatile performers themselves – there can have been few who combined the collective all-round skills of the Ringling Brothers. Gradually, from a panorama show, an old goat and a disreputable pony, in 1882 the Ringling Brothers Classic and Concert Co. was founded. "A Refined and High Class Entertainment," their primitive bills proclaimed, "Containing Many of the Most Prominent features of the Musical and Comedy World." Snowstorms, opposition and extreme skepticism dogged the redoubtable brothers during that first season, but they persevered. Otto was their herald, paving the way for the troupe, walking between towns to save hard-earned pennies and distributing handbills about the forthcoming attraction about to hit the unsuspecting townsfolk. Alf T. wrote the sketches, and

The Ringling Brothers. Trademark of their great circus until it was discontinued on the death of Otto.

doubled with Charley in the musical numbers; Al was plate-spinner and balancer supreme; and John was the comedian, as much at home playing an Irishman as a Dutchman – and they were all actors in the stage dramas.

From these rudimentary beginnings they progressed to the Ringling Brothers Carnival of Fun, and in 1884 they joined Fayette Lodawick (Yankee) Robinson, a venerable old trouper, and Yankee Robinson's Great Show, Ringling Brothers' Carnival of Novelties and DeNar's Museum of Living Wonders took to the road with their first real circus. In 1885 they had fourteen ponies and . . . a hyena; in 1887 they had two elephants. The boys from Baraboo had arrived.

The Midwest was their hunting ground. Throughout the seasons that followed their first successes, the Ringling Brothers were flexing their muscles. An old established circus, the Sells Brothers, provided their first real opposition in Texas. The rivalry was bitter, more often than not ending in blows and a violent poster war with torn sheets and bruised heads. The departure of Bailey for Europe gave the Ringlings their chance. Moving into New York and those towns in New England which had previously been the strongholds of the Barnum and Bailey group, the Ringling Brothers thrived.

When Bailey returned from his highly successful tour in Europe in 1903 it was to find that the Ringlings not only matched him for size, and almost for reputation, but that they had stolen a march on him. Instead of a ponderous, unwieldy circus, theirs was a highly mobile show with new railroad flatcars, a large menagerie and magnificent tableaux and parade equipment. What was it to be? War or merger?

Good sense prevailed. Bailey was now getting on in years. The responsibility of handling the Barnum and Bailey empire, with the Forepaugh-Sells operation as well as the Buffalo Bill Wild West show which now comprised the great circus empire of the slight showman, weighed heavily upon him. He passed a half share in the Forepaugh-Sells operation and its management, over to the Ringlings, and within a year the other half followed. The pattern of the great American circuses of the twentieth century was becoming clearer.

These were the golden years of the circus. There was no serious rival in sight. It was decades before the cinema was to make its revolutionary impact on the entertainment scene. Serious drama, vaudeville and the music halls were restricted to the big cities. In the country areas and smaller towns and cities the circus had the field to itself – and the great showmen of the day proved that they were equal to the challenge.

To those who recall that wonderful era, it is not the superb performances in the ring, or the dazzling spectacles, the stunning melodramas – with no expense spared – which they remember most vividly. Instead it is the great parades, which transformed the drabbest streets with their humdrum

CIRCUS WORLD MUSEUM, BARABOO, WISCONS

ABOVE: *"Large streams from little fountains flow, tall oaks from little acorns grow." In 1923 the Ringling Bros. and Barnum & Bailey combined shows needed 100 railcars to move their vast aggregation.*
OPPOSITE, ABOVE: *The Grand Parade.*
OPPOSITE, BELOW: *The Golden Age of The Circus. The Adam Forepaugh and Sells Brothers Combined Shows' street parade at the pinnacle of their fame.*

wagons and carts – for this was still wholly the era of the horse – into a fairyland of blare, glitter and glamor. Circus proprietors spent thousands on producing a finer, larger, more spectacular street parade than their rivals. One of the biggest circuses was reputed to have spent $50,000 on a ten-minute grand entry and had sent to France for six hundred yards of tapestry for the horses as well as ninety thousand rhinestones for the costumes of the seventy-two women in the parade. These were literally glittering cavalcades as the great tableau wagons were liberally coated with gold paint.

Astley may have given up the parade early in his career and pronounced that "he never more intends that abominable practice," but for many circus owners the parade was the only means of advertising their coming. Newspaper coverage in the large cities was easy, and any new and exciting events at the great theaters and hippodromes could be announced in advance with reasonable chance that most people would either read about or otherwise come to hear about them. But in the more remote country districts it was different. Posters and billboards duly announced the coming of the great event, but it was the parade through the center of the town which spoke of the actual arrival of the show.

Long past were the days when the mud shows would stop and clean their wagons at a nearby creek before making a ceremonial entrance into town, with their small bands blaring

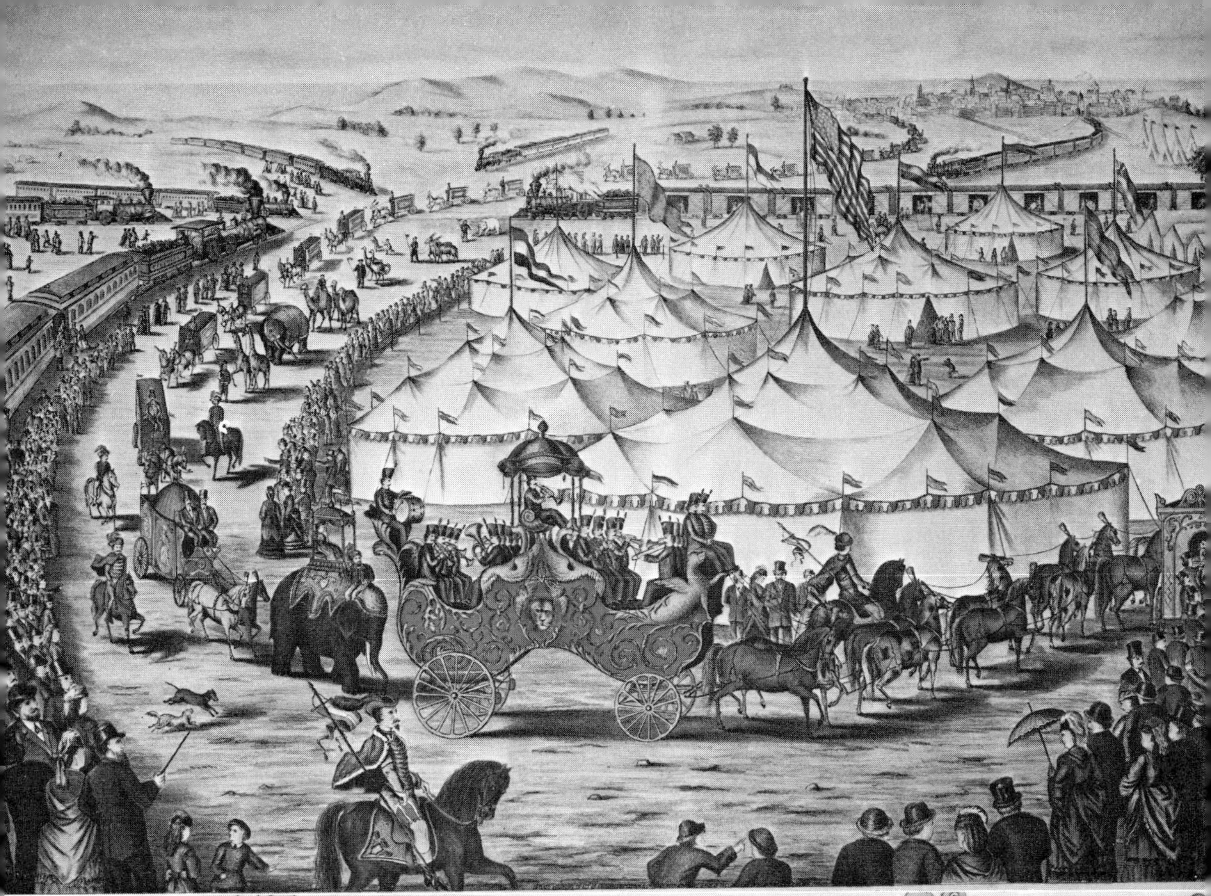

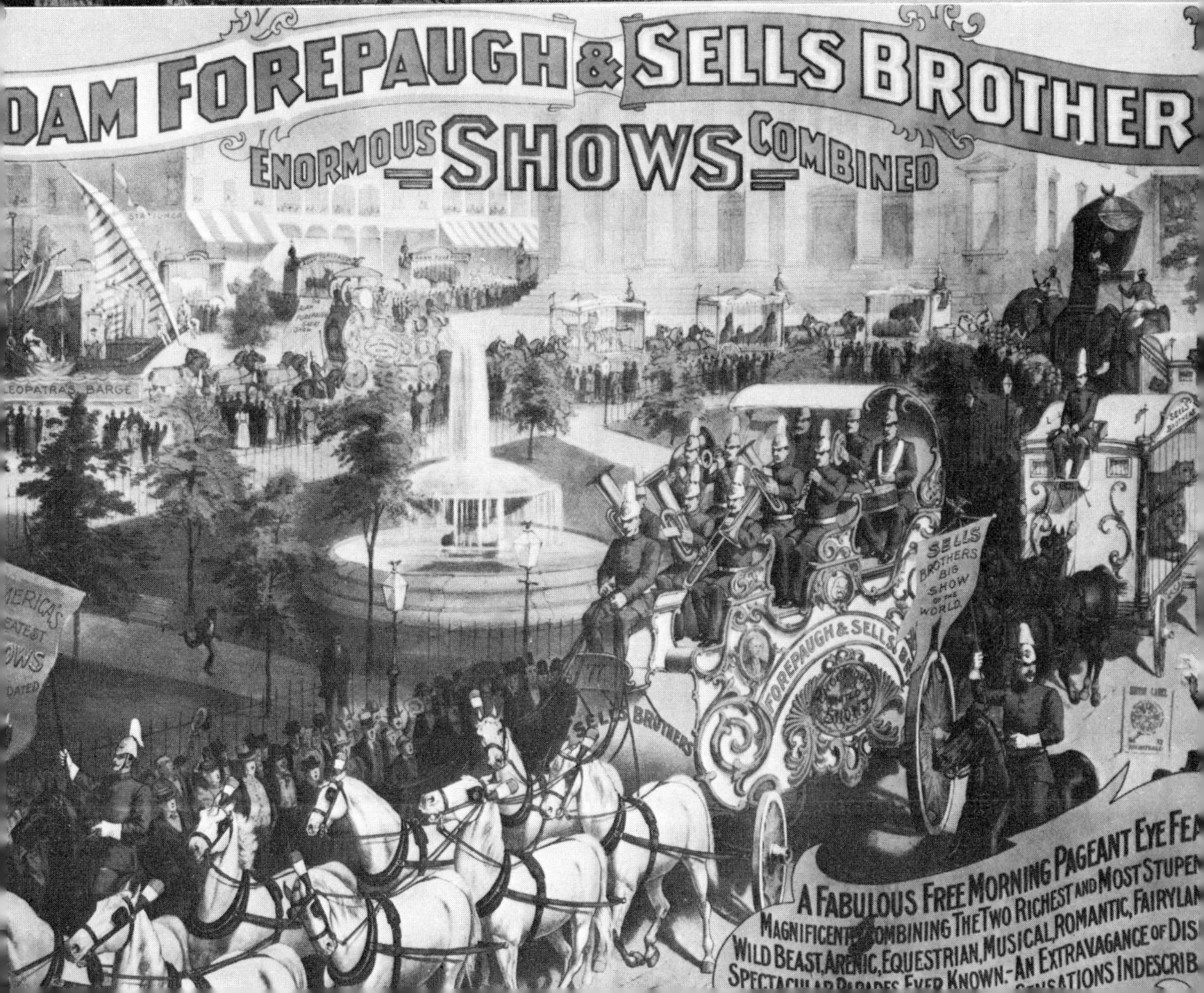

DAM FOREPAUGH & SELLS BROTHER

ENORMOUS SHOWS COMBINED

SELLS BROTHERS BIG SHOW OF THE WORLD.

FOREPAUGH & SELLS

SELLS BROTHERS

A FABULOUS FREE MORNING PAGEANT EYE FEA

MAGNIFICENTLY COMBINING THE TWO RICHEST AND MOST STUPEN

WILD BEAST, ARENIC, EQUESTRIAN, MUSICAL, ROMANTIC, FAIRYLAN

SPECTACULAR PARADES EVER KNOWN.-AN EXTRAVAGANCE OF DIS

SENSATIONS INDESCRIB

OPPOSITE, ABOVE: *One of the Ringlings' great tableau wagons, a feature of their mighty parades.* CENTER: *The Five Graces bandwagon. In Greek mythology there were only three Graces but five seemed to fit better on this fabulous float – so five there were.* BELOW: *The steam calliope. Bringing up the rear of the parade, the steam calliope gave out an unearthly sound, described by some as musical, which could be heard up to five miles away on a still day.*

and trying to make their paltry collection of animals seem bigger than it was. Although the little mud shows still tried to ape their larger brethren, in their own earnest way, it was the great parades of the circuses which now caught the public imagination. Barnum's pride was his great Two Hemisphere Wagon with elaborate decoration, drawn by four magnificent heavy Shire horses. The largest wagon of all was the Chariot of India which had been brought over from Europe in 1866. A popular number at any time was the Wagon of the Graces. The Greeks, with a woeful lack of publicity sense, had only created three Graces, Barnum reckoned five was a better number and the naming of the other two was a pleasant, if ribald occupation for many an agile mind in those wonderful years of the circus.

Bandwagons, beast wagons, beautiful matching teams of peerless horses, Indians, cowboys, "Indian" lancers and any other equestrians the agile minds of the showmen could devise, delighted and amazed the onlooker. "Fixers" would ride on the flank of the great parade to discourage trouble-makers and frighten off small boys who thought it fun to throw fireworks under elephants, and to warn of the elephants themselves who exerted an unholy fear on horses not used to them – "'Old yer 'Osses, here come the Elephunts," was the war cry of the circus. Bringing up the rear of this mighty procession was the incredible steam calliope which emitted extraordinary high-pitched howls, an unearthly sound said by some to be musical, and which could be heard up to five miles away on a still day. One thing was certain; the old circus parades never passed unnoticed. And there were the animals: elephants, docilely moving along at their own pace, each tail firmly grasped by the trunk of the animal behind, or else moving with stately solemnity with trunks swinging from side to side; the horses, ridden with skill and style by beautiful equestrians and equestriennes; the lions looking ferocious and wicked in their great barred wheeled cages; and more, much, much more.

Everyone took part, from the most magnificent – and most expensive – artiste to the meanest tentman. Costumes were lavish, and bore no relation to anything whatever. Eighteenth-century heroes might ride beside the latest military conqueror; cavalier would ride near cowboy – and with no incongruity. The whole was preceded by the bandwagon with musicians blowing as though their lungs would burst. They may have played a tune, but no one noticed, it was noise and spectacle and razzmatazz that mattered. Interspersed among this great procession were the tableaux, the great wagons with their intricate carving and rich colors. Bringing up the rear of Sanger's show was always the Queen's Tableau, a massive wagon in three tiers, topped by Britannia holding her trident, on one side a live lion, on the other an equally live lamb. The lamb, which soon became a full-grown

CIRCUS WORLD MUSEUM, BARABOO, WISCONSIN

CIRCUS WORLD MUSEUM, BARABOO, WISCONSIN

CIRCUS WORLD MUSEUM, BARABOO, WISCONSIN

ram called Billy, was by far the most ferocious of the two, and, brought up with the lion ever since it had been a cub, the two were fast friends. But when Billy died and a substitute put in his place, the newcomer lasted a matter of seconds before he was devoured.

Come the twentieth century and the circus was still in its heyday. But the giants were dead; Barnum had died in 1891, Bailey died in 1906; even the apparently indestructible "Lord" George Sanger was no more, although not from natural causes – he died as the result of an attack by a crazed employee in 1911. After Bailey's death the Ringlings took over the Barnum and Bailey Circus. The brothers were now undisputed kings of the circus and owned the two largest shows in the world. But they were not personally to enjoy their preeminence for long.

First Otto, "The Little King," the banker of the family to whom economy in the circus had become a way of life and who frowned on pomp and waste, died in 1911. Then Al, the eldest of the five, boss of the show, who had devoted his whole life and considerable energies to make Ringlings preeminent in the circus world, passed away five years later. This left just Alf T., Charlie and John of the original five brothers, and Henry, youngest of all, who had never owned any of the circus until he inherited half of Otto's portion. By then the First World War had broken out, and although foreign acts were impossible to use as most were European and Europe was in turmoil, the circus continued to thrive in the United States.

With the death of Henry in 1918, and Alf T. no longer the force he used to be, the time had come, the surviving Ringlings felt, to combine the two huge shows of Ringling Brothers and Barnum and Bailey which had operated as separate entities for so long. At the conclusion of the 1918 season, therefore, both shows made their way to Bridgeport, Connecticut. There the two massive organizations became one and the following season set out bearing the name which is still used today, Ringling Brothers and Barnum & Bailey Combined Shows. It was an enormous aggregation employing 1,500 people, using a tent with seating for 10,000 and needing ninety railroad cars to shift it – in 1922 they achieved their ambition. With one hundred cars it was the largest circus train ever.

Death continued to whittle away at the brothers, for the year after the great merger, Alf T., master organizer, the planner supreme of the grand spectacle, the choreographer of the Ringling circus, who even, sometimes, wrote the music for the performances, also died. This left Charlie and John.

A greater contrast between two brothers it would be hard to find. Charlie was the most even-tempered, the most tender-hearted and generous of all the brothers. He was the man with the soothing word, the calming touch. But John was the master. To most Americans Ringlings meant John Ringling. His very style and appearance breathed power. A dark man, physically very large – all the brothers had been big men, except for Otto, but John had towered above them all physically and metaphorically. He had the constitution of an ox and loved luxury. He lived only for the best, but he was prepared to work for it and the night hours he kept wore out more than one employee. John did things in the grand style; he had a siding for his special railroad car, while a 125-foot houseboat was moored in the private yacht basin near his fabulous Florida home, "Ca' d'Zan" at Sarasota where he established the Ringling circus empire and winter home. He owned a ranch in Montana and other property in many parts of the country. In his heyday John Ringling, the unassailable Circus King of America, was one of the richest men in the United States.

While Charlie Ringling saw to the day-to-day running of the circus, John Ringling's was the master showman's touch. Together they built up The Greatest Show on Earth until it dwarfed rival circuses. It was a highly efficient organization, it was also a courteous one which built up good will wherever it went. This was an asset which was to prove of priceless value as the "Roaring Twenties" were followed by the great slump.

The First World War was a watershed in circus history, after it things were never quite the same again. The horse-drawn era was now over for good. The richer shows were able to convert to the mechanical age, but many of the smaller ones could not, and foundered. Parades soon became much-mourned relics of a past age and the old tableau wagons which cut into the asphalt covering most roads were either given pneumatic tires and hitched to tractors – which lost most of the glamor – or found their way to museums. Many towns and cities banned parades as authorities were less than enthusiastic about the disruption brought about by a couple of miles of razzmatazz – especially as tram cables made the use of the tallest tableaux impossible.

Now two other attractions started to cut into circus audiences. Radio was still a novelty and had made little real impact. However, the advent of the cinema was to prove the greatest threat. The early 1920s had seen the first real inroads of the silver screen as the silent movies attracted attention everywhere; when from 1928 the talkies began to appear in quantity, the circus was in a state of real crisis.

The smaller shows, having struggled through the immediate post-war years, had insufficient financial backing to continue. The gold paint was peeled from their tableau wagons, their stock and props were sold to the highest bidder – and there were not many of them coming forward – and the artistes found themselves looking elsewhere for jobs. Many a fine circus, which in its own small way had meant an evening of entertainment which those who had enjoyed it would remember all their lives, vanished into oblivion. The maligned music halls and vaudeville proved the salvation for many artistes; at first they drifted there in the long winter months when the circuses were still, but later they sought employment on stage and in carnivals the year round.

In Europe, none was so hard hit as the Russian circus, which rocked on its very foundations. Not because of rival entertainments, but because a remorseless deadening hand descended on Russian drama in all its forms. Instead of the fine, traditional and well-balanced performances enjoyed before the Bolshevik Revolution, the audience was treated to hour after endless hour of tumblers and acrobats. Gone were the animal skills of old Russia, the clowns and comic men of the ancient fairs with their origins in Byzantine times, the equestrian prowess taught by Charles Hughes and others – these were prohibited as being reactionary, and thus worthless.

However, the Russian circus gradually emerged from the wilderness into which the Revolution had thrown it. The circus was soon accepted as a pure art form which owed nothing to theatrical make-believe and was in keeping with the philosophy of the machine age. The circus was found to be an ideal weapon to influence the masses and help correct deviationist thought. This was particularly so at the hands of the clown – the "Fool and His Majesty the People," as he was billed – who was permitted to poke fun at the regime and was allowed a satirical license reminiscent of that given to court jesters in the Middle Ages. But many years passed before the Russian circus attained the eminence it now holds.

Elsewhere in Europe people started to think again of circuses as soon as the war was over. Many of the brighter young stars were no longer young, and war had stripped others of their sparkle, but slowly the circus started to come wearily to its feet. In Britain even the bigger circuses were finding conditions hard but struggled on against steadily falling gates, as other attractions lured away their audiences. It was a period of depression for the circus, but there was a man equal to the occasion, one who was prepared to take on the challenge of the growing competition which assailed the circus from all sides. His name was Bertram Mills and his was a remarkable act of faith. As the name of Barnum was synonymous with the circus in America in the latter years of the nineteenth century – and as Ringlings is today – so the name of Bertram Mills *was* the circus to countless thousands of Britons from the 1920s.

The Mills family had owned a successful firm of undertakers during the nineteenth century and from these beginnings a prosperous sideline in coach-building developed, first with carriages and later with the bodies of automobiles. Bertram Mills's abiding passion was horses. He was a fine judge of horseflesh and a noted whip in the horse show ring,

Bertram Mills, the great British circus proprietor and showman who dominated the circus world in Britain from the 1920s to his death in 1936.

knowledge which was to stand him in good stead when he came into the circus world. However, after the First World War, when business was slow to pick up, and looked like remaining so for some time, the then proprietors of the massive Olympia in London suggested that Mills might care to run the place for them, and they mentioned that they wanted a circus. So Bertram Mills arranged for John Ringling, whom he had met on a visit to America, to bring over The Greatest Show on Earth. But no shipping could be found. There were only six months to the opening date, and Bertram Mills knew nothing about a circus, indeed his only known utterance on the subject was when the Olympia owners had taken him to see one and he had commented that if he could not put on a better show himself, he would eat his hat! He had no performers, no props, no experienced team of advisers to call upon, but he did have boundless energy and determination to match. They wanted a circus. A circus they would have.

It is difficult now to appreciate the audacity of the operation. The whole circus world in Europe was in the doldrums. The war had almost sounded the death knell of the circus, and rival attractions were taking away audiences everywhere. Yet an unknown – a "josser," as they call someone outside the circus world – was having the temerity to put on a huge show in the enormous Olympia – for which a total of 350,000 seats needed to be sold for the short five-week program. It was a problem of daunting proportions.

The Great International Circus, as it was called, opened on December 17, 1920, but it was preceded by something which was a revolutionary twist in the history of circus advertising. A circus parade through London would be quite impracticable – even if permission were granted, which was unlikely – besides they had no tableau wagons and at such short notice a scheme of this nature would add an impossible dimension to a task difficult enough already. Mills felt that the only way to attract people to his circus was through the press, and accordingly he decided to give them lunch before the opening performance. The idea was a roaring success, but the praises which cascaded down from all sides were earned by much more than a good lunch. "Great Circus Revival," trumpeted one. *The Times* referred to "The Big Circus – Enraptured Audience." But the significance lay deeper than mere entertainment, of however high an order, for Britain was then a weary nation struggling to find an identity in the aftermath of the most catastrophic war in the history of mankind. The British needed an act of vision, and they found what they unconsciously sought in the perfection of the performance, and the comedy of the circus. It was an outlet for the shriveled sense of enjoyment which for many had perished, seemingly forever, in the mud and blood of the trenches in Flanders. Astley would have approved, so would Barnum, and London loved it.

From the beginning, quality was what counted. The proud name Mills gave his circus – and no one disputed it, was the Quality Show, and these high standards were maintained throughout the forty-seven years of the circus's existence. Trust, strict fairness and unswerving loyalty to whomever worked for him were the keynotes of Bertram Mills' reign as showman, as they were for his sons who succeeded him. Circus artistes the world over respected him.

His circus was to be run on strictly business lines, incorporating the atmosphere, the spectacle and the glamor of the old circus, but with a hard-core of level-headed business expertise behind its every activity. Fòr Bertram Mills knew that in those days only a sleek, efficient machine could ever pay its way. Old circus hands shook their heads sagely. "It cannot work," they said, but work indeed, and triumphantly, it did.

Over the years, Mills developed his celebrated lunches to embrace the notability as well as the press, until well over a thousand people were present at a sitting. The lunches became one of the most sought-after events in the social calendar and Bertram Mills' Circus – which it became in

1923 – flourished. A fun fair was added and this soon became almost a greater attraction than the circus itself – and provided a happy hunting ground for sharp-practice merchants and touts of all sorts until they were sent packing. For this too was a Sunday School show. In 1930 a tenting show was started, at first by road and later by rail; by then Bertram Mills' Circus had become a much-loved national institution.

Bertram Mills remained the presiding genius over the circus, although his two sons, Cyril and Bernard, soon joined him to help run the operation. Mills was a shortish, thick-set man, always impeccably dressed, a presence to command respect, but it was more than just respect that his employees had for the man they knew as the Guv'nor. He was renowned the circus world over as a man of his word. He was an administrator, organizer and business man of the highest order, but this josser from the horse world also had the true showman's touch, he knew what his audiences wanted and he knew how to give it to them. It was a sad day for the British circus when the Guv'nor died in 1936.

By a coincidence, John Ringling died in the same year. The financial and other shadows over "King" John's last years, his overbearing manner and ostentatious life style are apt to lead one to forget the true showman's genius that John Ringling possessed. Although by then he was no longer in control of the circus empire he had created, when he died it was the end of an era in American circus history. Two years after his death, the Ringling empire was taken on by the great man's nephews, John and Henry Ringling North, and during the years of World War II the circus carried on under their management and with special dispensation from the president to help keep up home-front morale. The European circuses were not so lucky. Wartime stringencies saw the death of those on the Continent, and many in Britain. After the war, the old staff came dribbling back but it was clear that a new era in the circus had started with challenges not only from radio and the screen but also, most threatening of all, from television and the mobility which people now accepted as normal. In Britain the Bertram Mills Circus, faced with the expiry of its lease on Olympia and prohibitively rising costs, and refusing to compromise those high standards which had been the byword of the Mills Circus since its inception, sadly and reluctantly closed down in 1967. Eleven years earlier, on July 16, 1956, Ringlings, now able to make use of the many huge permanent arenas which had mushroomed across America since the end of the war, gave up their tenting circus. The Big One – as it was affectionately called – would play under canvas no more. That same year the Ringling Brothers and Barnum & Bailey Circus came under new management when the Feld Organization, the acknowledged leaders in arena presentations, purchased the huge business.

Sadly, the Big Top has now virtually vanished from the American circus scene. Although there are still about twenty tenting circuses, only four or five are large shows, the seventy or so other circuses on the circuit all use permanent stadiums. Few now give independent performances for, with very few exceptions, American circuses are sponsored by one organization or another. In most cases this sponsorship covers 90–100 percent of all performances in the year, though one or two circuses work to a lesser degree. Ringlings is an exception, in every way. They now own the only circus trains on the circuit and they are by far the largest circus organization in the country, employing about 400 people. In 1969 the aggregation was divided into two units, the Red and the Blue. These are carefully routed so that 90 percent of the American population can see The Greatest Show on Earth. Between them the two units give over one thousand performances annually in seventy different cities, playing to more than six million people and covering a phenomenal thirty thousand miles or so to do it.

The other great circus producers on the American circuit are the Shrine circuses which play in over five hundred cities each year. With 176 Shrine Temples across the United States, this near relation to masonry is the largest philanthropic organization in the world, maintaining twenty-two Shriners Hospitals for Crippled Children and carrying on a wealth of other charitable activities. The Shriners take on almost all the activities of the circus except the actual performance itself, thus costs and overheads can be kept to the minimum. Shriner Nobles undertake the advertising, the booking, the voluntary labor to get the show off the ground. For these workers it is a labor of love and a way of showing their community spirit. Some will take their vacation during circus time, others will give uncounted free hours to help make their circus the greatest possible success. The profits are divided between Shrine and circus, sometimes the former getting up to 75 percent to enable them to keep up their colossal charitable contributions.

European circuses are, on the whole, smaller than their American counterparts. It has been a European circus tradition to rely on finesse rather than sensation and mass spectacle, hence the single ring has always held sway where the prowess and skill of the individual performer may be seen to the best advantage. The best European circuses are very good and can stand comparison with any in the world and some can trace their ancestry back for centuries.

In Russia the circus has gone from strength to strength since it was given equal standing with the opera and ballet in the art world of the Soviet Union. The famed Moscow Circus School was founded in 1926, and many of its graduates perform in the hundred or so circuses across the country. It is estimated that there are fifteen thousand people closely concerned with the circus in Russia, of which half are actual performers. It is little wonder, given such support and with such a wealth of trained talent to choose from, that the Russian circus has attained the status it enjoys today.

In Britain there are today about a dozen large circuses and as many small ones. Some are resident circuses which perform under roofs during a summer or winter season, but the rest are tenting circuses and the sight of a Big Top in Britain is by no means as rare as it was once feared it would become. Many of the old names continue. The Chipperfield family, as well as running a number of safari parks, still have their own circus – theirs is a showman tradition which goes back three hundred years to an ancestor who set up a booth on the River Thames during a period of great frost. Another family with roots in antiquity are the Fossetts, whose members, as well as performing in individual troupes in many circuses and in many lands, also have three circuses tenting under a Fossett banner: their origin can be traced to one Robert Fossett who traveled the land as a one-man band, with a concertina in his hands, a drum on his shoulders and cymbals on his ankles. The brightest and the most exciting constellation in the British circus firmament today is the Gerry Cottle Circus which started in a small way in 1971. It is becoming renowned for slick performance, tradition and an endless search for new ideas. It was the Gerry Cottle Circus which made recent history when the entire show was flown to the Middle East for a four-week season.

That the circus is an international entertainment and a source of international amity could not be more clearly demonstrated than by the success of the Festival International du Cirque. This festival is the brain child of Prince Rainier of Monaco and it attracts forty or fifty of the best acts in the world. To be invited to Monaco is the accolade above all others for an artiste; to be chosen for one of the two final programmes is the achievement of a lifetime; to win one of the coveted prizes is an acknowledgment of greatness. The festivals started in 1974 and proved an instantaneous success, popular with performer and audience alike. Never before have the *crème de la crème* of the circus profession been gathered together in this way, and if ever one was to doubt that the circus is still thriving there is no need to look further than the list of talent from fifteen to twenty different countries which each year come to Monaco. The legacy bestowed on the world by Sergeant-Major Astley is very much alive.

HORSES

A crowd had gathered in the market square, for the reputation of the Englishman Banks, and his magic horse, Morocco, had preceded him to France. All Orléans wanted to see the man and his wonderful animal. Could it be true that this amazing beast could count, tell the time, pick out coins, cards and dice? Surely no animal was so intelligent that it could return belongings to their owners or pick out in a crowd the most righteous person present? They had heard that Banks had been imprisoned in Paris for practicing magic, but had been released. Why? If this man was devil-inspired and the horse the devil in disguise, what had become of their brothers' faith? They would show what piety in Orléans really stood for; the devil could expect no mercy here.

With curiosity and a tingle of excited anticipation, the crowd gathered around the showman and Morocco. Banks was a tall man with a neatly cropped beard; the wonder horse a middle-sized bay gelding some fourteen years old, or so they had heard. There was nothing remarkable about the animal, except the bright look in its eye, or could it be devil-made cunning? Hastily the most pious crossed themselves.

Banks began his act. First he made Morocco kneel and bow obeisance to the audience. Then he made him perform tricks. The audience gasped at the animal's cleverness – and they studied Banks minutely to see if he made any movements which could act as cues to his horse – but they saw none. When asked the time, the horse pawed the ground to tell the hour; when bade to pick out the numbers on dice he was unfailingly right. The cries of astonishment gave way to sullen murmurings of anger and disbelief. What they had heard was right; this was the devil, no real animal not inspired by Lucifer could do these things.

The climax came when the horse, confronted with a number of objects, returned them all to their rightful owners.

GUILDHALL LIBRARY, CITY OF LONDON

Banks and his wonderful horse, Morocco.

The crowd broke into uproar. What they had seen before could have been trickery, but this, this was assuredly magic. A man elbowed his way forward and confronted Banks demanding that he do something which would show beyond any doubt that what they had seen was not indeed Hell-sent magic. If he would not, he would be consigned to the flames as a wizard and heretic – and Morocco would go with him.

Throughout the angry scene, Banks had remained imperturbable, as though he had experienced it all before. Now he stepped forward and told the crowd that his was no devil show, and he would prove it. With this he told them that Morocco would go to a man whom he had seen wearing a crucifix in his hat. Morocco did as he was bid. The horse knelt down before the burgher as though asking for a blessing and when he rose to his feet again the animal brushed the crucifix with his lips. The anger of the crowd changed to expressions of wonderment, Banks and Morocco went on their way unmolested.

There had doubtless been other Moroccos before this but Banks and his horse, which he had showed at the Belle Sauvage Inn in Ludgate Hill, London, in Shakespeare's time, was the most famous. To the ignorant and superstitious the "talking horse" must indeed have appeared magic. Yet the three movements in the act – the nod, the shaking of the head and the counting or pawing of the ground – are simplicity itself and easy to teach. All are derived from a

A medieval performer; a drum-kicking horse.

horse's actual actions. Study a horse in a field for a while and soon enough you will see it brush a fly from its withers with a quick jerk of the head – that is "no." A lunge with its head is "yes." Every horse paws the ground, it can be in irritation or it can be because it wants to soften the ground for rolling – this is the "counting" which perhaps amazed Bank's audience more than anything else.

Had the crowd that day in Orléans been more observant they would have been able to spot his cues. It is sometimes forgotten that a horse has considerable side vision, and an animal can be facing the audience yet still see the trainer at its side making a slight movement of hand or arm and telling it what to do. To get the animal to paw the ground it may at first be necessary to point the whip at the leg, but later this can be accomplished merely by making a slight bow from the waist, then the whip may be discarded. The bow indicates the moment to start pawing, when the trainer stands upright again the animals knows it must stop. This is the secret behind the calculating horse; but whatever happens the trainer must not lose count himself.

As Astley was the father of the circus, he was also a foremost authority on the training of horses, and his advice is as sound today as it was then. "Judgment, Temperance and Perseverance are indispensably necessary to bring the brute creation to a proper sense of duty," he wrote in his treatise on horsemanship which ran to no less than seven editions. Bertram Mills said the secret was "Patience, Understanding and Carrots." The essence of Astley's horse training, as he describes it, was the combination of the hope of reward and a sense of fear, although he temporizes on this for he adds "through perseverance you will dissipate all their apprehensions." "Your chief endeavours must be directed," he continues "with easy and deliberate approaches to convince him, that neither you, nor your assistant is his enemy; to do this effectually, you are to encourage him by words such as 'So, So! So, So!', endeavouring always to imitate the same TONE OF VOICE, which he will very soon comprehend in a MOST EXTRAORDINARY MANNER; and more particularly, if you do not CHANGE THE SOUND; also rubbing him, and wiping his eyes

ASTLEY'S SYSTEM OF EDUCATION

A. Cavesson and Cord.
B. Snaffle-reins, intended to adjust the given point, or exact position of the Horse's head.
C.D. The breast-plate, appertaining to the buckle-surcingle, bearing-rein, crupper & etc., and intended to keep the whole secure.

No. 1. Professor in the act of working the Horse; circle to the left.
No. 2. His assistant, in each hand a pistol, waiting for the signal from the Professor.
No. 3. The position of the Horse's head.
No. 4. The cavesson-cord; two small rings thereon.
No. 5. A small hand-line (passed through two small rings to keep it steady), occasionally used to refresh the Horse's mouth, and to render it sensible to the motion of the hand, when the Professor judges proper to ease him and reward his labor.
No. 6. The leather buckle-surcingle, communicating with the breast-plate, crupper, bridle-reins, bearing-reins, etc.
No. 7. The chambrière.
No. 8. A basket containing (the supposed) rewards, viz. corn, carrots, apples, pears, etc.
No. 9. A drum, for the familiarizing a Horse to it, when wanted.
No. 10. A flag, used for the like purpose.
No. 11. A trumpet to sound on similar occasions.
No. 12. Fire-works of different explosions, intended to be let off at the will and pleasure of the Professor. . . .
No. 13. Sketch of a bag to be filled with any given weight of sand, the more effectually to habituate the Horse to bear his rider, and which the Author buckles round the Horse for such a purpose.
No. 14. Sketch of a spur-stick, six feet long, used on various occasions, also to accustom the Horse to the use of the spur, previously to his being mounted.
No. 15. The assistant's dog, which he occasionally causes to bark at the pleasure of the Professor.
No. 16. A small hand-whip, hung on the pillar for the use of the Professor.

and nostrils with your handkerchief, giving him to eat a small piece of carrot, or a slice of a good sweet apple, and other similar inducements, by WAY OF REWARD." But Astley was no fool. By way of warning he adds "Be not too familiar with him before you have some domination over him, but he should strike you with his feet."

Astley's would appear to be the first book which dealt with the training of circus horses. He used a drum and would lead his animal round in a walk and stop it on a drumbeat. "Convince him," he wrote, "that it is not meant to hurt or terrify him, but as a kind of language by which he is to understand your desires."

Astley's famous horse, Billy, the Little Military Learned Horse, was nothing if not versatile. He could undo his saddle, wash his own hooves in a bucket of water, remove a kettle from the fire, make tea and act as a waiter at a tavern, and when out of the ring would romp and play like a puppy. His counting and "thought reading," were nothing short of remarkable, so they said, and Billy could correctly strike the hour of the day and the day of the month with his hoof. The highlight of his act, which always raised a patriotic cheer, was to feign death when told he must go away and fight the Spaniards, but to jump to his feet and fire a pistol when told that he was after all to join the army with his master and his regiment.

It is related that some time after Philip Astley's death, Billy, or more likely, Billy's successor, was lent to a traveling salesman who sold the horse to settle some heavy debts. Several years passed and two of the performers at Astley's were one day walking along the street when they saw a horse which they were sure they recognized. They asked the tradesman who owned him how he had acquired the animal and to their delight heard that the honest fellow called the horse Montebank as he was always playing tricks. With their hopes high they looked again at the horse and then one of them clicked his fingers – the signal to which Billy had been used to work in the old days – and to their utter delight the old circus horse performed such capers that he all but turned over the cart he was pulling. They bought him back on the spot and so Billy returned again to Astley's where he remained for many more years, a much-loved veteran. Eventually the horse, now considerably old, lost all his teeth and had to be fed on bread soaked in water, but he still performed and evidently relished his particular act as Fire Horse where he would mount a platform and stand contentedly and quite unmoved while a barrage of fireworks was set off all round him. At the ripe old age of forty-two, Billy died. To perpetuate his memory, his hide was made into the skin for the thunder drum. This remained at Astley's until the theater finally closed down, and then the last relic of old Billy disappeared.

There were other "clever" horses, evidently just as versatile as the famous Billy. Rickett's Cornplanter would also undo his own saddle, then take it off his back and had been trained to pick up handkerchiefs and other objects from the ground. Poole, probably the first American-born equestrian, displayed a trick horse in New York in 1786 which lay down and groaned when commanded to do so and would then sit up like a lap dog and "make his manners to the ladies and gentlemen."

Astley's animal care was as advanced as his animal training. What he stressed on the treatment of tired horses is as true today as it was when he wrote it. For "if you force him to repeat his lesson whilst he is panting for breath, you will

Riding airs; Monsieur Pluvinel instructs the King of France.

INVARIABLY TEACH HIM THE MOST VICIOUS AND PERVERSE HABITS AND DESTROY HIS EMULATION." His treatise was also full of useful tips for horsemen, and Astley recommends washing the feet of a tired horse in mild ale and then stuffing them with cow dung to relax them after a long day's journey. When breaking a horse he would use a sandbag to get the animal accustomed to the weight of a human, and then would let a "rough-rider" mount and exercise him.

Sadly, Astley was an exception to the rule among circus-horse trainers. Sanger used a pin on his horses in the initial stage of training them to do tricks. When he stuck it into its flank the animal pawed the ground; soon the pin could be dispensed with altogether and the slightest movement of the hand which had once held the goad would get the horse to react. When he was training a horse for the great hippodrama Mazeppa, which was to be the rage on both sides of the Atlantic in the later decades of the last century, he would stick a pin sharply into the animal's withers causing it to rear up. A few caresses and a reward when the animal obliged and soon by the merest tap of a finger he had a "fiery, untamed steed" at his command.

There are three principal types of circus horse act; the high school or *haute école*; liberty horses, of which the calculating horse is one; and voltige, the resinbacks – the bareback and jockey acts.

"Whenever he himself chooses to show off before horses, and especially before mares, he raises his neck highest and arches his head most, looking fierce; he lifts his legs freely off

Haute École in the nineteenth century.

VICTORIA AND ALBERT MUSEUM

the ground and tosses his tail up. Whenever, therefore, you induce him to carry himself in the attitudes he naturally assumes when he is most anxious to display his beauty, you make him look as though he took pleasure in being ridden, and give him a noble, fierce and attractive appearance." These words were written by Xenophon the Greek historian, philosopher and soldier in the fourth century, B.C., and describe what is the essence of the *haute école*, the ultimate in horsemanship.

Who has not thrilled to the *entrée* – the word itself derived from a royal entrance into a captured town – of the majestic *haute école* horses? To most people *haute école* means one thing – the Spanish Riding School in Vienna, a place of pilgrimage for all horse lovers and home of the incomparable and beautiful snow-white Lipizzaners, many of which have delighted circus audiences the world over with their grace and regal bearing. The breed itself – and the Lipizzaner starts life an undistinguished brown, not until between the seventh and eighth year does it begin to assume the characteristic snow-white color – is descended from Andalusian and Moorish barb stock. With the passing of the age of chivalry, brought about by the advent of the gun, the knight in armor, who had held sway on the battlefield for so long, became an anachronism. Armor was of little use against ball and shot, but mounted soldiers were still needed and so started a revival of the art of unarmored horsemanship which found its origins in many ancient civilizations but had seen its acme in classical Greece. The Renaissance in Europe, and particularly in Italy, saw a revival of horsemanship as an art,

SUSAN CRAWFORD AND THE TRYON GALLERY, LONDON

The magnificent Lipizzaner. A recent picture of Colonel Handler of the Spanish Riding School by the outstanding horse artist, Susan Crawford.

and it rapidly became apparent that the great horses which could carry a knight in armor were too ponderous for the lithe cavalry of the day; something lighter, something more manageable was needed. So more suitable breeds were sought for the formal aristocratic riding schools of the sixteenth and seventeenth centuries, and none seemed better than the barb which the Arabs had brought with them to Europe from North Africa – "A little horse, but swift" and renowned for its longevity – and the native Spanish Andalusian strain – the "breeding Jennet, lusty, young and proud."

The Holy Roman Empire embraced Spain and much of Europe at that time. Although the spread of the Empire was vast, communication was close. In 1570, when the emperor, Archduke Charles, founded a stud in the small village of Lipizza in rough, limestone country near Trieste, he acquired breeding stock from Spain, together with a small nucleus of Spanish horses which his father had introduced some years before to another stud in Bohemia. Through the centuries, triumphantly overcoming a number of vicissitudes and surviving many wars, the Lipizzaner has flourished and the Spanish Riding School in Vienna maintained its international reputation and preeminence in the horse-training world.

The Lipizzaner is ideally built for the role of an *haute école* horse. It is a stronger animal than the Arab, with weightier bone and more massive quarters – which is important, for it is principally the forelegs which execute the movements, so strong, driving hindlegs are essential. It is possessed of an even temperament but has plenty of spirit and is endowed with a naturally high action, which looks good in circus or show ring. Not until the animal is four years old does training begin, and the course takes three years. The curriculum for an *haute école* horse embraces the most elementary exercises to the most advanced airs. Cadence is a word frequently heard in *haute école* circles. In the dictionary cadence means rhythm, but to Astley it meant more: "Cadence means the agreeable equality of the walk, the trot, the gallop, as also the various artificial paces of the horse," he wrote. "I conceive the rider may be said to be in cadence when his feat on horseback is strictly agreeable to the eye. Cadence also, in my firm opinion, is the very essence of regulating not only the horse's natural paces, but also his artificial airs." Astley's own favorite air was the pirouette, which he calls the "*ne plus ultra* of pure cadence."

Obedience on the long rein is the first lesson for the *haute école* horse, and from there the animal is taken by easy stages – never, never hurried – at a steadily increasing pace through the walk and the trot to the canter, by which time it has reached the second year of training. This next year is devoted to making the animal more supple and to laying the foundations for the more advanced airs of the *haute école* proper. Not until his third year of training is the young horse introduced to the memorable and beautiful airs of the piaffe, the passage or Spanish walk, the pesade, the croupade, the balotade and the exquisite cabriole, derived from the Italian word capro, a goat, and emulating that animal's leap.

These airs look contrived, yet each is derived from the perfectly natural movement of the horse. Observe young horses at play and it is easy to see from where the great airs of the *haute école* have come. And it should not be forgotten that each air has been created for the needs of war – the pasade and balotade protected the rider from a frontal shot; the cabriole could prove lethal both before and behind in close combat. But the true art of *haute école* is in getting the horse to produce these movements at the will of the rider, and in displaying a perfect harmony between mount and rider.

There are two divisions of the high school today; the classical *haute école* which requires the highest standards in walk, trot and canter, but frowns on any air which is regarded as unnatural – such as the Spanish walk when the horse proceeds with a jerky motion like an automaton each foreleg in turn stretched out to its fullest extent; and the modern *haute école*, whose advocates have no such susceptibilities – it is usually the modern school which is displayed in the circus. But in both the rider must appear as one with his horse, his movements of hand and leg must be imperceptible, his seat impeccable, the horse on the bit the whole time and showing

BLACKPOOL TOWER COMPANY. PHOTOGRAPH BY BARNET SAIDMAN

Circus riding. Ingrid Schickler at the Blackpool Tower Circus, one of the permanent British circuses.

eagerness to go forward. For, again in the words of Xenophon, "What a horse does under constraint, he does without understanding and with no more grace than a dancer would show if he was whipped and goaded. Under such treatment horse and man alike will do much more that is ugly than graceful. No, a horse must make the most graceful and brilliant appearance in all respects of his own will."

France, and Paris in particular, was the center of the *haute école* in the circus. In the middle of the nineteenth century under the hand of the Franconi and other circus proprietors, enthusiasm for *haute école* as the epitome of horsemanship reached a height it has never attained since. This was less so in England, largely due to the fact that the circus was then considered as essentially an entertainment for the masses which the nobility avoided, an attitude which remained until Bertram Mills persuaded them otherwise. In Paris, though, the great equestriennes of the *haute école* were the rage of Paris, fêted richly, they became the darlings of Paris.

"A course of wild horses . . . with the wildness with which they would rush through their native plains, uncurbed by the hand and power of man," was how Ducrow described what was one of the first liberty horse acts in circus history. It was evidently rather more untamed than liberty acts are today, and it is a sad reflection of the times that the huge liberty horse acts, using a dozen or so horses and which so thrilled audiences in the past, are becoming fewer and fewer as the costs of training, keeping and exhibiting such acts rise astronomically. Nevertheless, Ducrow's wild horse act was a great step forward in the story of the circus horse for until then there had only been either demonstrations by calculating horses, or the voltige of the great circus riders of the day.

The methods Astley adopted in training his horses bear a marked resemblance to those employed today, yet it is curious that with all the old soldier's flair for showmanship he never exploited the spectacle of what we now understand as a liberty horse act. This act, when well performed, transcends all others for grace, beauty and animal mastery.

To watch a liberty horse trainer at work with his horses is a privilege given to few of us, but it is one of the most thrilling experiences in the circus. Magnificent animals, impeccably groomed, alert and eager, their bearing reins giving them an air of grace and a fine crest – and there is more than just appearance behind the bearing rein, for its restriction prevents the horse from moving his head freely and thus helps keep him under control and forces attentiveness. In each hand the trainer holds a whip. In his right, he holds a long one with a thong – the ring whip. This is not for chastisement, it is used as a pointer, an extension of the arm, and with it the trainer governs the movement of the hindquarters and can urge the animal to move forward. In his left hand is the guider, a shorter, thicker stick and without a lash. This is used to govern the forequarters and with it the trainer can slow down or halt the animal, or direct it in whatever direction he wishes. If you watch carefully you will see that the trainer barely ever touches one of his horses, and if he does so it is with what one authority calls a caress.

This is the bare equipment of the liberty horse trainer. His technique is by a gradual association of ideas and constant practice to indoctrinate and develop habits in the animal; for horses are creatures of habit. They soon learn what is their musical cue; and when the band strikes it up, woe betide anyone in the way when what could be called a controlled cavalry charge into the ring takes place. The actions of the liberty horse are no less natural than those of the *haute école*. The clever sitting horse is a horse which, by training, has been frozen in the act of rising from a lying position. The kneeling horse, one caught in the act of getting down; and from there it is a simple matter to persuade the horse to lie down on command. Horses used in films are liberty

SWISS NATIONAL CIRCUS KNIE BROS PHOTOGRAPH BY CHRIS KRENGER

A well-matched team is essential. Three Lipizzaner stallions trained and presented by Fredy Knie Sr. at the famed Swiss circus Knie.

horses in another guise, and there can be few dry eyes in the cinema when the touching scene is enacted of the master's horse nosing among and turning over the corpses on the battlefield until it comes upon that of its beloved master. It is less poignant when one realizes that this remarkable feat is achieved by the liberal use of lumps of sugar hidden in the "corpse."

A well-matched team of horses is essential – in color and conformity, of course, but also in temperament and

intelligence, for an animal that is not even-tempered or is more stupid than the others will completely mar a troupe of liberty horses. At first they must become used to their names, which must be short and sharp and as different from the others in the troupe as possible – and they must become accustomed to their place in line, for liberty horses, like elephants, are taught their positions at the start of their training. Once selected, named and numbered, they must always be kept in the same rotation in the ring, their entrance must always be in the same order, their harness carefully labeled and kept apart, for routine is the first essential. At the beginning all is quiet, for no distractions can be permitted to interrupt training, but as school continues – and it will take all of nine months to perfect a liberty act from scratch – more and more noise is not only permitted but obligatory. An advanced training session of a liberty horse act must be as near a modern Bedlam as it is possible to devise. Circusmen, onlookers, anyone hanging around with nothing to do is brought in to make as much noise as they can. Arc lights sweep down and all but blind the horses, tin cans are beaten, blank cartridges are fired off, people jump up and down and wave programs or newspapers. Throughout the racket the horses must remain oblivious to the din around them, giving their full attention to their trainer as he gestures with his whip and guider.

Liberty horses at London's Bertram Mills Circus. A typical example of the Mills's showmanship genius.

The best age to start a liberty horse is from four to seven years, as by then their muscles will be fully grown. At first they will be taken singly into the ring and lunged on a long rein, and the trainer will try to discover each horse's individual characteristics, its aptitudes and what disturbs it. In short, he will get to know his horse, and it is a mutual process. Then more and more of the troupe will be brought into the group until the full number of eight, twelve or sixteen, or whatever, are working together.

The true art of the liberty horse is more profound than just displaying beautiful and well-trained horses; presentation is vital. The horse master, as he holds his whip high to get his horses to stand still to order, is like the conductor of an orchestra, but his task in presenting his act is that of a choreographer of a ballet as he blends together music, lighting and above all the harmony, the tempo, the cadence of his act. It is a genius given to very few, but when it comes off there are few finer or more satisfying acts in the circus. Spare a thought for the bandmaster. The horses do not keep in time with him, he keeps time with them!

The third main group of circus horses are the voltige – the ring-horses or resinbacks as they are variously called. They must be "bomb-proof" animals, as the expression goes, for unless the horse's back on which the rider stands is completely steady, disaster will inevitably result, for this is a

dangerous act. The voltige horse must never shy, change pace or change legs, nor must it "hump" when the rider alights for that will throw him or her off balance, and the voltige rider relies solely on a sense of balance. A fairly thick-set, heavy, slow-moving horse is best, usually not more than fifteen hands high; solid, stolid and above all reliable. Its pace must be unvarying, it must have a controlled canter – which is none too easy to obtain – with short, even strides and it must remain quiet whatever happens either on its back or near it. Check reins are used in training to keep the animal's gait steady, but in work it must be immediately responsive to command and be able to slow or quicken speed on a signal from the trainer. The perfectly trained resinback, as it moves imperturbably round the ring, might be likened to a moving mountain.

A resinback training session is as noisy as that of the

A lady circus rider of the last century.

liberty horses, but the significance is far greater, for should a voltige horse falter or shy an accident, and quite possibly a fatal accident, will result. Considered by some as the greatest equestrienne of modern times, the little May Wirth was one day doing some of her tremendous tricks when a dog escaped from the crowd and yapped at her horses legs. She was thrown and hit the ringside, but was not badly hurt. The inimitable Ella Bradna was once performing in Paris when her horse shied and she was thrown bodily into the crowd. But this accident had a happy ending for she fell into the arms of a young German cavalry officer who later married her and became famous in circus circles as probably the greatest ringmaster the circus has ever known – Fred Bradna. But others have not been so lucky.

Voltige equipment consists of the "roller," a leather pad which crosses the horse and is secured behind the withers. On either side is a leather-bound handle, on the top another. After dusting the broad back of the voltige horse with resin, and the rider's shoes with more, one is ready to begin to try the voltige.

Learning to ride on the knees is the first lesson; from there the next step is to attempt to stand on the back of the

OPPOSITE: The Vaulting Master *by William Stokes. "Your horse ready, and your gentlewoman seated, leave the raines of the bridle on the neck of the horse, then fixing the left hand on the fore pummell mount, clapping the right hand on the hind pummell, but be sure the right leg move at the same time with the right hand, that so you may readily motion the right thigh towards the gentlewoman's lap, and then reverse the same leg over the fore pummell into the saddle, without molesting her" – and easier said than done.*

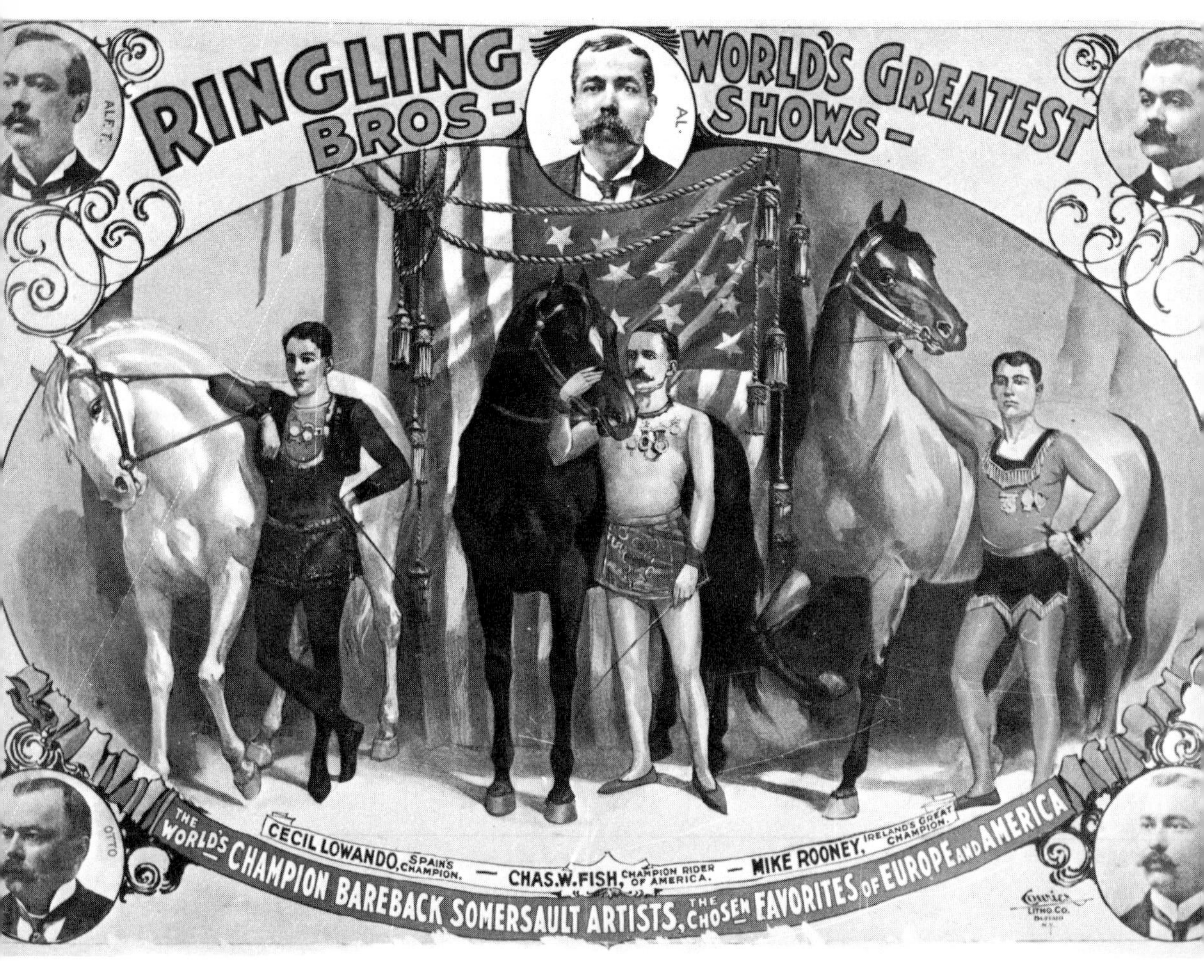

ABOVE: *Champion bareback riders of a former age, with the celebrated Charles W. Fish in the center.* OPPOSITE, ABOVE: *The Mechanic. A riding lesson at Sanger's circus.* FAR RIGHT: *James Robinson, the wondrous bareback rider. A poster from 1865 advertising "The Champion Bareback Rider of All the Earth."*

moving horse, and learning to fall. For a fall will inevitably occur sooner or later, and it is essential to know how to minimize the effects. It is a wearying business, taking a heavy toll on the legs, particularly on the knee joints. For sheer athleticism it is hard to beat, for a good rider can vault on and off the horse four times in one circuit of the ring, and that takes skill, superb timing, agility and a lot of courage.

The voltige riders, the somersaulters and trick equestrians, and later, equestriennes, were the cream of the circus world and the highest-paid stars in the middle of the last century. The successors to the Astleys, the Ricketts and the Ducrows of a former era were such men as James Robinson, Charles Fish, James Hernandez – billed as Young Hernandez who had "an elegance approaching poetry" in his performance – and Levi J. North; these were the men crowds came to see perform. The backward somersault on a horse, then the forward-forward somersault – a more difficult feat, finally a backward-back – in which the artiste faces the animal's tail – the most difficult of all as the rider cannot see where his feet are alighting and he is liable to be thrown backward on landing – all became part of the repertoire of

the skilled voltige rider. Charles Fish could do eighteen somersaults through hoops – "balloons," in circus parlance – and land on one foot on the horse's back after each, whereas his great rival "Jimmie" Robinson once turned twenty-three consecutive somersaults, alternately backward and forward. Fish was no match for Robinson in looks and he was once described with unkind candor as looking like the "breakup of a hard winter," whereas Robinson, who called himself "The Champion Bareback Rider of all the Earth," was more frequently likened to Apollo, and he wore his uniform of short jacket, knee breeches and stockings with immense grace. A favorite trick was to stand on a horse's rump on one leg with the other straight up by his ear as he galloped round and with amazing quickness would turn a "twister" somersault, alternatively facing first the animal's head and then its tail. This was a particular risky maneuver, but Robinson was philosophical about his work as a voltige star. "I take the law of averages," he would explain. "It has always been in favor of the performer. He bites the sawdust many times but he generally dies in bed."

At first there were no equestriennes in the ring to succeed Mrs. Astley and Mrs. Ricketts. For years it was considered too dangerous for a lady to accomplish or even try to do what Fish and Robinson did every night. In fact, they may never have found the limelight had it not been for a gentleman by the name of Spencer Quinn Stokes who invented the Stokes Mechanic – a form of gibbet which revolved round a center pole and on which was a swivel through which a rope was run. One end was held by a man on the sawdust, the other was attached to a belt fastened round the rider. By pulling before the rider crashed to the floor, it was possible to prevent a fall. It is an essential aid in learning to balance on the back of a cantering horse.

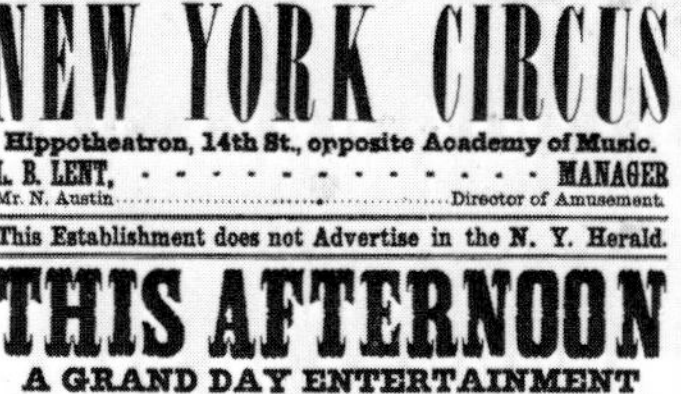

NEW YORK CIRCUS

Hippotheatron, 14th St., opposite Academy of Music.

L. B. LENT, ... MANAGER

Mr. N. Austin . . . . Director of Amusement.

This Establishment does not Advertise in the N. Y. Herald.

THIS AFTERNOON

A GRAND DAY ENTERTAINMENT

When will be given when

The Daring Robinson

And the Entire Strength of the

NEW AUGMENTED TROUPE

WILL APPEAR.

Wednesday Afternoon & Evening, Dec. 5

The Entertainments will commence with the Grand

Star and Waltz Entree

Produced with New and Magnificent Costumes and Trappings.

James Robinson

The Wondrous Bare Back Rider,

Who stands without a rival, either in Europe or America, will appear in his GRAND PRINCIPAL ACT, invariably received with the most Tumultuous Demonstrations of Astonishment and Delight. During each performance MR. ROBINSON will introduce his Infant Son,

Little Clarence, the Baby Wonder,

Only Five Years of age, the Smallest, Youngest and Prettiest Child ever brought before the public in an Equestrian Act.

ALL THE GREAT RIDERS AND GYMNASTS

In an infinite variety of ASTOUNDING FEATS, together with pleasing and Extraordinary Performances by

DANCING AND TRICK HORSES

AND EDUCATED MULES.

Clowns to the Arena . . . . Messrs. N. Austin and W. Conrad

Riding Master . . . . Mr. R. ELLINGHAM

MATINEES

For the accommodation of Juveniles and Family Parties will be given WEDNESDAY and SATURDAY, commencing at half-past 2 o'clock When ROBINSON WILL RIDE, and All the Great Attractions of the Establishment will be brought forward.

PRICES: Dress Circle 50 Cents; Children under Ten, 25 Cents. Reserved Seats, 75 Cents; Children under Ten, 50 Cents. Amphitheatre, 35 Cents; Children under Ten, 25 Cents.

TIME: Doors open at 7 1-4; Performance to commence at 8 o'clock. For the Matinees; Doors open at 1 1-2; Performance to commence at 2 1-2 o'clock.

3 Performances Thanksgiving Day,

Commencing at 10 1-2 A. M., and 2 1-2 and 8 o'clock, P. M.

Clarry & Reilley, Engravers and Decorative Steam Job Printers, 12 & 14 Spruce Street.

SAN ANTONIO PUBLIC LIBRARY

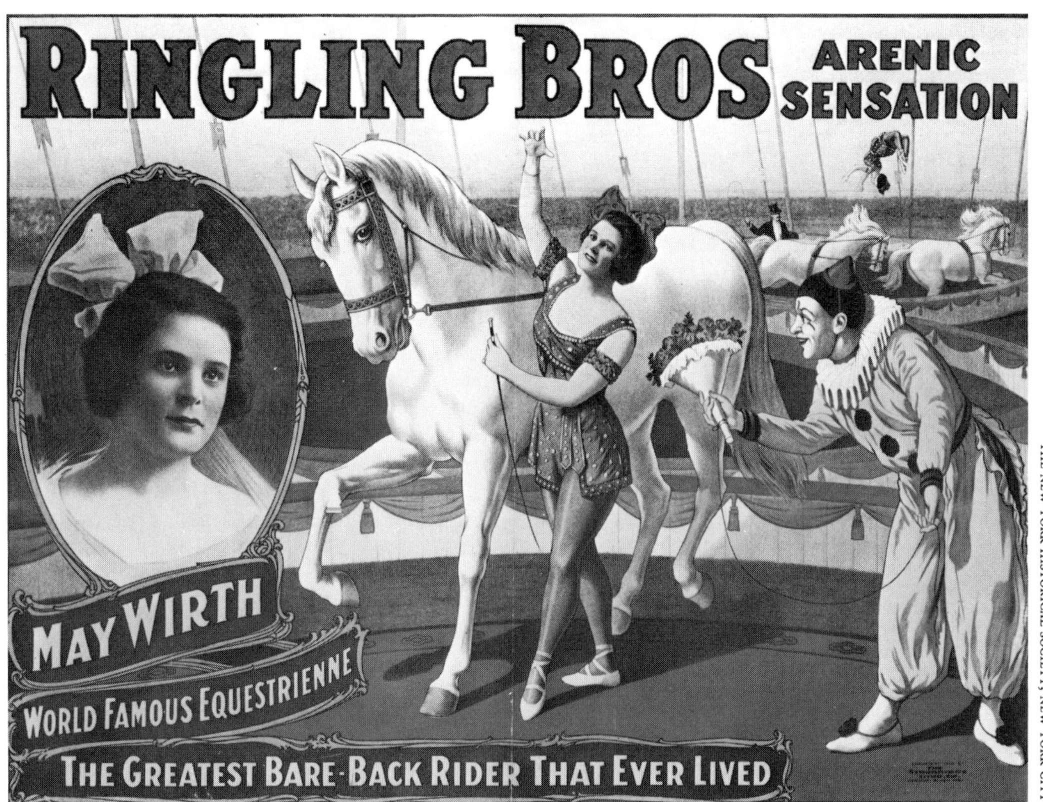

THE NEW YORK HISTORICAL SOCIETY, NEW YORK CITY

The fabulous little Australian, May Wirth, who some consider the greatest equestrienne of all time.

In the days when equestriennes were real news, the same Stokes introduced to the circus scene a fabulous new star, Ella Zoyara. "A very graceful and accomplished rider, very femininely pretty and winning," described The *North American*. She was an instant success when she toured England and Europe; everyone marveled at the way she "rode upright on her horse while it jumped hurdles and flew through fifty balloons before performing an aerial walk to the throne of fame." Her dressing room was besieged after every performance, and she was courted assiduously by the rich and titled. In 1857 she was performing in London; in 1860 she was in New York. When there, rumors were circulating that another Ella Zoyara was riding in Philadelphia, and to everyone's astonishment a third Ella Zoyara turned up, also in Philadelphia. This was too much for the credulous public. Investigation ensued and it was discovered that the first Ella was a proud husband and father – to the considerable consternation of those who had courted her so assiduously in many countries – one of the Philadelphia Ellas turned out to be a hermaphrodite and the other prudently disappeared.

With the departures of the Ellas from the scene, the way was clear for the great equestriennes of the circus ring. The pictures of the period showing the delightfully graceful ballerina-like figures balancing on one foot on the back of a heavy horse are charming, but give no true idea of the sheer

SAN ANTONIO PUBLIC LIBRARY

The famous Cristiani Troupe.

grace which a talented voltige rider can display. Those who had the good fortune to see the little Australian, May Wirth, in her heyday were in no doubt that they were privileged to see the supreme artiste of their generation. The Wirth Circus in Australia was not only the first circus in that country but by far the largest, and the Wirth circus dynasty one of considerable renown. May Wirth started her circus career as a child rider and a contortionist with the family circus – in the days when a young man called Will Rogers performed as the "Cherokee Kid" with a lariat in his own version of the Wild West. A tour with the Downie Circus in America at a then fabulous salary set her on her way to stardom. And like all great stars of the period she found her way to Ringlings where her superlative performances were the talk of the circus fraternity.

Another outstanding voltige star was Ella Bradna who had fallen into the arms of her future husband during a performance in Paris, she too occupied the center ring –

CIRCUS WORLD MUSEUM, BARABOO, WISCONSIN

Cristianis in action. Backward somersault from one horse to another.

always the place of honor in the three-ring circus – for many years at Ringlings.

The most renowned modern voltige riders are the Cristianis, a circus family of Italian descent who for a while ran their own circus in America. It is as voltige riders that the Cristianis are best known, but other members of their vast clan have also been preeminent artistes in almost all branches of the circus. The Cristiani story goes back to the 1840s in Italy where a certain Emilio Cristiani was blacksmith to the royal stables. At length he retired from his job and with his pension set up a blacksmith's shop of his own. With thirty people working for him, he found time heavy on his hands and so Emilio, by no means a young man, took up tumbling as a hobby. One day a circus was playing nearby and Emilio's son, Pilade, himself a noted strongman, went to watch, fell in love with one of the riders, married her and went off with the circus. From these beginnings the Cristianis and the circus were inseparable. By the early 1900s the Cristianis had their own small circus – tumbling was still their forte, but they also introduced horses and a dog. The 1930s found the Cristianis playing in Scotland, England and Belgium, and it was while touring there that an agent of John Ringling spotted them and persuaded them to come to America – and America has been their home ever since. From 1951 to 1961 they were highly successful circus owners.

"The somersaulters supreme," they have been called, and with great justification. The full-twist somersault

Mr. DUCROW as the COURIER of ST. PETERSBURGH.

The Courier of St. Petersburg. Andrew Ducrow's celebrated act.

from one horse to another, and sometimes to a third horse in line, is an outstanding act. It is no ordinary somersault for the rider pirouettes in the air before alighting as softly as a feather on his chosen horse. The rightly called "suicide" trick is another Cristiani speciality. In this, three of the family are standing on the backs of three horses one in front of the other. At a signal they all turn a backward somersault through a hoop to alight on the horse behind – the last one landing on the ground. It is a fabulous trick requiring perfect timing, coordination and remarkable agility.

Voltige had a firm place in the dramas enacted in the early days of the circus, and was never better displayed than in Ducrow's celebrated Courier of Saint Petersburg. The story behind this dramatic spectacle is of a courier bearing precious dispatches who risks death in many forms before he successfully and loyally triumphs over all threatened disaster and completes his mission. It was the sort of plot beloved by the authors of the period and gave huge scope to the scene designers and effects men to exercise their talents in "scientific" works of remarkable ingenuity. The star in this impressive spectacle enters the ring standing on two horses, he is astride a third and can be controlling anything up to seven more – a modern version of the Courier has twelve horses galloping round at the end. Other artistes could do the same, but evidently none with the consummate skill and expressiveness of Ducrow. From time to time the Courier was revived, in many countries, sometimes under the title of *Les Relais de Longjumeau*, or *La Poste Royale*.

Horses in drama had come a long way since Astley's "Formidable Jack" was trained to resist any horseman dressed as a tailor and would set upon him, kicking and rearing, tearing his coat and wrenching his whip away with his teeth. It was Ducrow who really gave the horses the star role,

Cossack riding in the Moscow State Circus.

NOVOSTI PRESS AGENCY

he was the originator of the expression "Cut the dialect and get to the 'osses," and he seems to have carried out his own advice on every occasion. In one of his dramas, Blue Beard, sixteen horses were borne up into the flies "with inconceivable velocity," and one reporter complained that the dressing rooms of the "new comedians," as he termed them, were immediately beneath the orchestra so that those in the first rows of the pit were treated to a smell so abominable that they "might as well have sitten in a stable." As star actors, though, the horses might have been allowed some consideration, for nightly they "knelt, they leaped, they tumbled, they danced, they fought, they dashed into water and up precipices in a very superior style of acting." Others "climbed up walls perpendicular or scampered longitudinally, and leaped through breaches with the greatest ingenuity."

Dick Turpin, the highwayman, was another character to catch the public imagination, though people were more impressed by the performance of his horse, Black Bess than the man himself. There were few dry eyes in the theater when the faithful Black Bess, having gallantly delivered her out-and-out scoundrel of a master to safety from his pursuers, collapses on the stage and just has strength enough to stretch up ger head to kiss Turpin – and to get a bit of sugar if the truth be known – before she falls "lifeless" and lets herself be borne away without so much as a twitch of her tail. One critic wrote that the only skills the human actors needed in their roles were "steam-engine lungs, limbs of adamantine, and toes proof against the hooves of horses." There was little speech – scrolls with the words written on them sufficed – just mime and spectacle. And what spectacle!

Of all the great dramas that thrilled audiences on both sides of the Atlantic during the middle of the nineteenth century, it was a piece called Mazeppa or the Wild Horse of Tartary which proved the all-time favorite attraction. The story was broadly based on Byron's poem of the same name which tells of a young man, Mazeppa, who falls in love with the wife of a Polish nobleman who catches the couple *in flagrante delicto* and as punishment has the errant youth tied to the back of a wild steed captured only the day before and driven into the wilderness. The animal with his strange burden heads for home ranges and for the next two nights and days Mazeppa is rushed through rivers, over mountains – "upwards ever upwards" – and past the drooling fangs of packs of wolves, until the horse dies of exhaustion and our hero is rescued from an unpleasant death at the beak of a vulture by a conveniently passing band of Cossacks. Mazeppa eventually comes to lead the Cossacks into an attack on the castle of the barbarous prince, to find the tyrant's wife, and there true love meets its mate. These are the bare bones of the story, but it had all the potential for the wildest of super-colossal melodramas imaginable – especially the thrilling and highly perilous ride of Mazeppa bound lengthwise along the back of the horse.

Mazeppa in various versions had appeared in Paris and London from time to time, but the production which was to take London by storm had its opening on Easter Monday, 1831. Writing of the dash of the "wild" horse the *Morning Chronicle* said, "There was something almost terrific in his first start with the victim lashed to his back; and the way in which he bounded up the different platforms . . . gave no faint idea of the speed with which the real steed might have dashed along precipices and mountains." For the occasion there was a narrow pathway disguised by scenery to denote a rocky path which zigzagged ever upward to the very flies. This was rightly considered too dangerous to risk an actor's life, and so another "untamed steed" was docilely waiting in the wings with a dummy Mazeppa bound to its back.

The first production in America was in April, 1833, in New York City and in the same year two further versions were put on in Philadelphia. Soon Mazeppa was as popular across the Atlantic as it had proved in England and on the Continent. But in the United States there was no question

OPPOSITE: *The inimitable Adah Isaac Menken.*

of a dummy being borne upward to the flies; as a matter of honor a live actor performed the feat. Then it was conceived that the role might more fetchingly be performed by a woman, suitably and provocatively clad and so, after a rehearsal during which she and her horse fell off one of the platforms, one of the great entertainment stars of the era first appeared before an audience. This was Adah Isaacs Menken, who was to achieve international fame as the Naked Lady of Mazeppa, a title which owed more to the imagination of the producer and the public than real fact, as Menken invariably appeared in what today would be considered a highly decorous costume.

Menken came to England in 1864 amid waves of publicity. Weeks before the gala opening of her Mazeppa she was to be seen in Hyde Park driving in a landau, wearing a flowing crinoline with sleigh bells on her carriage announcing her coming. Her debut at Astley's, so carefully built up, was a sensation. For weeks London had been talking about nothing but the Naked Lady, alluring and suggestive posters displayed what lay in store for the lucky audience. For the opening night on October 3 there was not a seat unsold, and this was to be the pattern throughout her ten-week season.

No one seemed to mind that the real Menken bore remarkably little resemblance to the picture on the posters. Her costume, described one paper, consisted of loose folds of white linen which extended "only slightly towards the knee and left the upper limb exposed," but "not indelicately," the correspondent hastily added. Menken was the toast of the country; there was even a popular song written about her which included the lines "The classical style of her dress does *not* much trouble the sewing-machine!"

Menken was half Irish, half Creole. The pictures of the period reveal her as a decidedly dumpy figure with short black hair curled close to her head which gave her a boyish appearance. She had dark eyebrows, dark eyes and a positively firm set to her mouth and chin. Not by the wildest stretch of the imagination could she be called beautiful, yet the Menken was to become the first outstanding sex symbol of the circus. London went Menken-mad; girls dressed their hair à la Menken – in a fuzz. "Cleopatra in crinoline," one writer dubbed her; another called her limbs "statuesque," a third said that she was shaped for loving. She was a generous warm-hearted soul who would give away handfuls of coins to beggars or other actors down on their luck. To the terror of management she was also an inveterate smoker – in the days when smoking by a woman was unthinkable – and at Astley's a small boy would follow her wherever she went with an ashtray for the cigarette stubs.

She had four, some say five, husbands and a number of romances including one with the elder Dumas and another with Swinburne, the poet – an affair which shocked all Victorian England. From time to time the Menken assumed

"Again do I stand erect, again assume the God like attitude of Freedom and of Man"

Rousing Roman Races at Sells Brothers enormous united shows.

pretensions of being an actress – and of being a poet, which was worse – but managements soon became wise to this and were usually able to trim any lines she had to speak to the absolute minimum. Wilson Disher, the finest of circus writers, refers to her as "an actress who could not act, a poet who never wrote poetry, and a nudist who always, in public, was decently clad." A little unkind, for despite her failings, Adah Isaacs Menken made the role of Mazeppa her own, and from the moment she made her appearance on the stage, no man could ever perform the title role with the same effect.

Menken's success was as great in Paris as it had been in London. She toured Europe and 1867 found her in Vienna performing before enraptured audiences but the following year, while rehearsing in Paris, she was taken ill and died a few days later. She had started a fashion which was to be copied everywhere hippodrama was performed. Her imitators prospered. The Naked Lady became gradually more naked and the Wild Horse of Tartary, with its gallop to the flies, continued to draw audiences until hippodrama died.

Other attempts to bring the horse into circus drama had been tried on both sides of the Atlantic. After his successful representation of "The Battle of the Alma," William Cooke – another descendant of old Thomas Taplin Cooke – started putting on performances of Shakespeare on horseback. Some plays, particularly *Richard III*, which was a "natural,"

BUFFALO BILL HISTORICAL CENTER, CODY, WYOMING

A striking poster of Buffalo Bill's Wild West during the show's tour in France.

were more suited to this type of presentation than others. But in their day they achieved wide popularity. However, in 1845, Laurent Franconi introduced horse races and Roman chariot races in an outdoor hippodrome behind the Arc de Triumphe, and they were a great success. Others in many countries copied his example and the chariot races of old became a vogue. The arenas they performed in were considerably smaller than those in ancient Rome and to keep the chariots from straying too wildly off course the inside wheels were heavily weighted. These were dangerous sports, spills were frequent and sometimes injuries were severe. Eventually the chariot race went out of fashion, but by then the Wild West had stolen the horse limelight with a display of speed, glamor, noise, excitement and sheer riding and other skills which have never been surpassed.

Successful as Buffalo Bill Cody's appearance in New York had been, it was his subsequent trip to England and Europe which was to secure his reputation and make him a legendary figure in circus history. Embarking, appropriately enough on the *City of Nebraska*, in early April, 1887, Cody's whole troupe crossed the Atlantic without trouble. The Indians, who had a superstition that anyone crossing the ocean would die, were the worst off and the weather did its best to prove the legend true as the ship ran into a fearsome storm soon after leaving. The show he brought over consisted of eighty-three saloon passengers, thirty-eight more were in steerage and there were no less than ninety-seven Indians, one hundred and eighty horses, eighteen buffalo, ten mules, ten elk, five wild steer Texas steers, four donkeys, two deer and, of course, the famous stage coach.

To the strains of the "Star Spangled Banner," the *City of Nebraska* arrived at Greenwich and three special trains drew the show into London and to the Earls Court arena where a track one-third of a mile in circumference had been laid out. All London turned out to see the great show arrive, the Indians were a special attraction and the opening night was awaited with an eagerness London had not experienced for years. Buffalo Bill's Wild West was part of a great American Exhibition in honor of Queen Victoria's Golden Jubilee, and the rest of the exhibition must have been more than a little overshadowed.

As rehearsals continued and the troupe became accustomed to the arena and to London, particles of information about the treat that was in store for them seeped out to the waiting Londoners. Hoardings everywhere proclaimed the arrival of the great show, as if everyone didn't know that already. The *Globe* summed it all up:

> I may walk it, or 'bus it, or hansom it; still
> I am faced by the features of Buffalo Bill.
> Every hoarding is plastered, from East-end to West,
> With his hat, coat and countenance, lovelocks and vest.

On May 9, 1887 the gala opening took place. The show was an instantaneous success. London took the Wild West to their hearts, and Queen Victoria saw the show three times – and unprecedented royal accolade. As the queen wrote in her journal:

> Hurried back & took a cup of tea before to Earl's Court, where we saw a very extraordinary & interesting sight, a performance of "Buffalo Bill's Wild West." We sat in a box in a large semicircle. . . All the different people, wild, painted Red Indians from America, on their wild bare backed horses, of different tribes – cowboys, Mexicans, & Co, all came tearing around at full speed, shrieking & screaming, which had the weirdest effect. An attack on a coach, & on a ranch, with an immense deal of firing, was most exciting, so was the buffalo hunt, & the bucking ponies, that were almost impossible to sit. The cowboys are fine looking people, but the painted Indians, with their feathers, & wild dress (very little of it) were rather alarming looking. . . A young girl, who went through the "haute ecole", certainly sat the most marvellous plunges beautifully, sitting quite erect, & being completely master of her

ARY OF CONGRESS

An action-packed poster of Buffalo Bill's Wild West and Congress of Rough Riders of the World.

horse. There were 2 other girls, who shot with unvarying aim at glass balls. Col. Cody "Buffalo Bill," as he is called . . . is a splendid man, handsome, & gentlemanlike in manner. He has had many encounters & hand to hand fights with the Red Indians. Their War Dance, to a wild drum & pipe, was quite fearful, with all their contortions & shrieks, & they came so close. . . .

In the spring of 1888 the show had returned to the United States and was performing in New York. Cody and Salsbury put their heads together to ponder on ways to strengthen the presentation and to broaden its aspects. Still thinking along the lines of the whole field of horsemanship, it was decided to introduce other horse acts, and so, to give the show its full title, "Buffalo Bill's Wild West and Congress of Rough Riders of the World" was born. With a huge cast of 640 members, it now included twenty members from regular cavalry regiments of the United States, German and British soldiers, Cossacks, Argentinian gauchos, Mexican vaqueros, cowboys, cowgirls, a thirty-seven-piece cowboy band and a hundred Sioux Indians, who had now succeeded the original representatives of the Arapaho, Brule and Cheyenne tribes.

1889 found the Wild West en route to Paris for the Grand Exposition and from there a glittering tour followed across the rest of France, Spain, Italy and Germany. By 1893 Cody was back in America with a show of unprecedented size and variety which he decided to play at the World's Columbia Exposition in Chicago. To advertise the event, a Grand Race was organized to exhibit the resilience of the western horse – a thousand-mile cowboy race for a prize of $1,500. The conditions stipulated that it was to last no more than thirteen days (an average of twenty-seven miles a day) and that each rider could have two horses and no more. In the event there were ten entrants, half of whom finished the course. But Cody had his publicity; the show attracted an astonishing six million people and profits were in excess of one million dollars.

A glance at the program of the Wild West indicates what a remarkable array of talent each performance displayed:

1. Grand Processional Review.
2. Entrées – Introduction of Individual Celebrities, Groups, etc.
3. Race between Cow-boy, Mexican and Indian on Ponies.
4. Pony Express.
5. Rifle Shooting by Johnnie Baker, the Cow-boy Kid.
6. Illustrates an Attack on an Emigrant Train by the Indians, and its Defence by Frontiersmen. After which a Virginia Reel on Horseback by Western Girls and Cow-Boys.
7. Miss Annie Oakley – Wing Shooting.
8. Cow-Boys Fun. Throwing the Lariat. Picking Objects from the Ground while Riding at Full Speed. The Riding of Bucking Ponies and Mules by Cow-boys.
9. Lillian Smith (The California Girl) Rifle Shooting.
10. Ladies Race – by American Frontier Girls.
11. Attack on the Deadwood Stage Coach by Indians. Their Repulse by Scouts and Cow-boys, Commanded by Buffalo Bill.
12. Race between Sioux Indian-boys on Bareback Indian ponies.
13. Race between Mexican Thoroughbreds.
14. Horseback Riding by American Frontier Girls.
15. Phases of Indian Life – Nomadic Tribe Camps on the Prairie. Attack by hostile Tribes, followed by Scalp, War and other Dances.
16. Mustang Jack – the Cow-boy Jumper.
17. Buffalo Bill (The Hon. W. F. Cody) America's Practical All-Round Shot.
18. Roping and Riding of Wild Texas Steers by Cow-boys and Mexicans.
19. Genuine Buffalo Hunt by Buffalo Bill and Indians.
20. Attack on Settler's Cabin by hostile Indians. Repulse by Cow-boys under Leadership of Buffalo Bill.

CUS WORLD MUSEUM, BARABOO, WISCONSIN

Cody's was not the only Wild West on the circuit. Pawnee Bill's Show, along with others, attempted to rival Buffalo Bill's magnificent performances.

Cody's entrance was a heart-stopping moment and one to get the show off to a rousing start. At full gallop Cody would enter the arena, pulling up at the last moment in a cloud of dust before the center of the expensive seats. With a flourish he would remove his hat (on one memorable occasion he removed his wig as well, and from that moment, however sparse it was becoming, he wore only his own hair) and announce: "Ladies and Gentlemen. Permit me to introduce a Congress of The Rough Riders of the World."

For fifteen years Buffalo Bill's show thrilled and delighted audiences over two continents. Those who were privileged to see it felt that they never again saw anything to compare with it. It was a spectacle which could never be forgotten, one of breath-taking daring, non-stop action and incredible skills. In 1908 the Wild West joined with a show run by Pawnee Bill – who had started his showman's life, and collected his name, when he was in charge of the Pawnee

Indians attached to the Wild West in the early days. They chose to name it "An Ethnological Congress of Strange Tribes, Clans, Races and Nations of Peculiar People." The combined shows came to be known affectionately as The Two Bills' Show. Four years later Buffalo Bill, then aged sixty-six, gave up his own shooting acts which he had done since the very beginning. He called himself an all-round shot, a "man of deadly aim in any emergency, with any weapon – a small Derringer, a Colt's, a shot-gun, a carbine, a blunderbuss or a rifle – at any foe, red or white; and at any game – chicken, jack-rabbit, antelope, deer, buffalo, bear or elk; at the swiftest birds or soaring eagle; on foot, in any position; on horseback, at any speed."

In 1914 the Wild West failed and was sold to the Sells-Floto Circus, and in 1917 Buffalo Bill Cody died. With his death the legends which had surrounded him all his life became history, in many instances inaccurate history.

There were other Wild Wests before, and during Buffalo Bill's reign – and there were to be more after – but none could touch the authentic one in sheer excitement, glamor and action. The pale pretense of the so-called Wild West, which is a frequent act in smaller circuses, should be called the Deep or the Far West, or perhaps the Old West, or even the New West, but never the Wild West for in the story of the circus, the biggest, the best, the most authentic and true-blue Wild West was Buffalo Bill's. It had been a glorious era, and one which showed a different and wholly practical side of horsemanship. And the theme behind Buffalo Bill's old show can still be found in the rodeo of today.

A modern Wild West.
Circus World.

FILMS CORPORATION AND NATIONAL FILM ARCHIVE, LONDON

ANIMALS

There is a fascination about the unusual members of the animal kingdom which has prevailed with man since he first began to walk upright. Ancient Egyptian, Assyrian and other civilizations show captive and exotic animals in the friezes they carved to celebrate their great victories. Visiting potentates would present prize animals to their hosts. Zoos and menageries and collections of wild beasts were created in many countries. But the reputation for the most lavish and the most brutal of animal displays must be reserved for ancient Rome. The Circus Maximus and other arenas were the stage for some of the most gruesome spectacles ever perpetrated by man on animal – they were called the *venatio*, hunting games. On many occasions wild animal fights acted as the *hors d'oeuvre* to gladiatorial contests; wild bulls would be pitted against elephants, lion against lion. The dictator Sulla injected a spice of extra excitement when he matched javelin men against one hundred fully grown lions. The sheer elemental blood lust which could tolerate the slaughter of five thousand tame animals and nearly as many wild ones – which happened at the consecration of the great amphitheater of Titus – is too incredible to contemplate.

There has never been any attempt to emulate these horrifying spectacles of mass slaughter on such a scale, but from time to time, until as recently as one hundred years ago, there would be attempts to pit wild animals, or particularly ferocious tame ones, against their own kind or against dogs. Cock-fighting and bear-baiting are good examples of such entertainment. Therefore, during the early years of the nineteenth century, when brute tamers first appeared on the circus scene and traveling menageries were being built up in many countries, it was spectacle and controlled ferocity for which the audience craved. The subtleties of animal training were lost on them. They wanted to see an animal

The Association's Celebrated and Extensive

MENAGERIE AND AVIAR

FROM THEIR

ZOOLOGICAL INSTITUTE

IN THE CITY OF NEW-YORK,

acing all the Subjects of Natural History, as Exhibited at that Popular & Fashionable Resort during the Winter of

YAL TIGER AND TIGRESS.

CAPE LION, LIONESS, AND TIGRESS.

LION, LIONESS, AND PAIR OF LEOPARDS.

YOUNG LION, LEOPARD AND

E KEEPER WILL ENTER THE CAGES TO THE ABOVE ANIMALS AT 3 O'CLOCK P.

CAN OSTRICH. THE EMEU. ELEPHANT WITH SADDLE. ELEPHANT JULIET. CASSOWARA. AFRICAN PEL

THE ANIMALS WILL BE FED IN PRESENCE THE AUDIENCE AT 4 O'CLOCK, P. M.

Will be Exhibited in

Admittance, including the Addition, only 25 Cents, Children under the age of 10 years h

Hours of Exhibition from O'clock to O'clock, AFTERNOON.

Unicorn: or One Horned Rhinoceros.

MALE ZEBRA. BUFFALO. THE ALPACHA. DROMEDARY. QUAGGA. THE GNU OR HORNED H

ATIC LEOPARDS. PAIR OF KANGAROOS. HUNTING LEOPARD. PORCUPINE. BENGAL TIGER. JAGUAR AND

LEOPARD. ICHNEUMAN. SEMIA TRIBE. PUMA. AFRICAN PANTHER. JACKAL. BRAZILIAN T

goaded, they wanted to see it cowed and subdued before them, they wanted to see man the master. But if man occasionally happened to lose out to animal, so much the better. During the Middle Ages people thought trained animals had been taught by witches. The uncanny ability of certain people to be able to communicate with animals gave rise to innumerable instances of unfortunate showmen with their performing beasts being looked upon as guided by Satan. Banks and his famous horse Morocco traveled in peril of their lives, and they were by no means alone.

It is evident that many animals in those days were abominably treated by their owners, but it is a comforting thought that some trainers of animals, wild and tame, wiser than their rivals, knew that their livelihood depended on the well-being of their charges, so saw them groomed and fed. Their training, though, was never less than harsh in the extreme.

Bears would be made to stand on their hind legs by burning their front paws. They would be taught to dance by placing hot plates under their feet. They were cowed into submission with red-hot pokers and they were led with a ring through their noses, a muzzle on their mouths and a chain attached to a collar. To make them fierce and irritable they would be goaded with sharp sticks, and the reflex action when they naturally flinched against such treatment was turned to good account in their training. Bears weren't alone as candidates for this treatment; one showman had some clever dancing geese. They danced because they were standing on a metal plate under which someone had lit a fire.

But the performing horses, those steadfast companions with so many uses, were for the most part better treated. It would have been unthinkable for Astley to misuse one of his horses as it would be for the Schumanns, the Althoffs, Alexis Grüss, John Herriot or Trevor Baleor, some of the acknowledged maestros of the modern horse world. Even nowadays well-meaning busybodies fulminate about cruelty to animals in the circus, a campaign which infuriates circus folk today as it did their forebears. These people should ponder on two things; first, whether a lion or tiger would ever tolerate really bad treatment without turning on its trainer – only a thin stick separates trainer from animal in the ring; and second, would a circus ever risk the loss of such expensive animals through carelessness or cruelty?

As gypsies, mountebanks, jugglers, tightrope artistes and itinerant showmen of all sorts traveled Europe, often accompanied by trained animals, an increasing audience became introduced to strange, "exotic" and "outlandish" creatures. In 1640 the camel came to England from Grand Cairo in Egypt. This creature, the advertisement stated, "is twenty-three years old, his head and neck are like those of a deer." Doubtless it created as great a sensation as did, a year

An early stage animal act. Captain Midnight's Animal Comedians, reminiscent of some of the Russian small animal acts of today.

later, the first chimpanzee whose gentle, almost human ways delighted all who saw it.

The first camel did not appear in America until 1723 when a note in a Boston newspaper talked of it being seven feet long and twelve feet high. Another was in New York in 1739: "A very wonderful and surprising creature to all persons in these parts of the world; and it is in Scripture the very same creature which is there called a Cammel." The *New York Gazette* wrote, tantalizingly, "It is impossible to describe the creature; and therefore all persons of ingenious curiosity have an opportunity of satisfying themselves." Already a strong leaning toward the Scriptures can be seen in animal advertising, a trend which was to reach satiation point at the hands of Barnum in later years.

In 1733 another animal was evidently responsible for this letter in the *Boston Weekly News Letter*:

> Whereas I the Subscriber . . . have preposed a voyage to another part of the world; and I thought I could not do less (in point of honour) than acknowledge the many civilities I have received by the visits of many good people of this and the neighbouring towns; and, to the credit of New England be it spoken, I never was in

CIRCUS WORLD MUSEUM, BARABOO, WISCONSI

more perfect health and better case in my own country; my cloaths that I brought with me, I have outgrown, and have now a clean white suit that fits me to a hair. I design to sail for Europe in the first ship, so that I desire all persons with whom I have accounts open to bring them in and settle by next week, and all those from whom I have received favours, I should be glad to shake a paw with, and take my leave of at my lodgings nigh Mr. Clark's wharff.

It was "Dated from my Den, Boston, April 19, 1733" and signed "Ursa Major or the Great White Bear."

These were all individual animal exhibits. The first British traveling-menagerie owner is believed to have been one Polito who took to the road in 1758 and his show was still going strong until it was lost while crossing the sea to Ireland in 1836. It was evidently quite a show according to the *Nottingham Journal* of September 1805:

During the fair only. The largest travelling collection of the known world, to be seen in six commodious

A more modern menagerie poster. Forepaugh and Sells Brothers, 1903.

caravans, built for the purpose and all united (which together provided one of the noblest views of the wonderful production of nature ever beheld) in the market place. Polito's grand pleasing assemblage of most rare and beautiful living birds and beasts from the remotest parts of the known world; among which are a noble lion from the Tower of London (where was the first zoo in the country); a striped Bengal Tiger and Tigress, commonly called Royal Tigers, acknowledged to be the first ever seen in the kingdom; four of those singular quadrupeds, the large kangaroos from Botany Bay, males and females; noble male and female panthers from the River La Plata, South America; the most industrious of all animals, the beaver; remarkable handsome leopard and leopardess, the finest ever seen in the kingdom and male and female wolves from Thibet, commonly called Muscovy cats; a large satyr or Ethiopian savage; the opossum, the wanderoo, and upwards of fifty other quadrupeds.

Another menagerie, which was to become as well

known to British audiences as the Zoological Institute of the Flatfoots was to Americans, was run by George Wombwell. An eccentric little man "undersized in mind, as well as in form, a weazen, sharpen-faced man, with a skin reddened by more than natural spirits," was how one of his erstwhile employees described him. Nevertheless, he was a skilled manager and Wombwell's menagerie had a great reputation and attracted huge crowds. He was also a skilled vet and the story is related that after employing his skill in the service of Prince Albert, the Prince Consort, he was asked what he would like in payment. He replied that he particularly wanted some planking from the old man o'war, the *Royal George*, which had recently been recovered from where she had sunk. It transpired that this was for a magnificent coffin which remained as the principal piece of furniture in his house until it was finally transferred to other accommodation in the nearby cemetery.

These were the great menagerie owners, but showmen in fairs across many countries were finding that exotic animals were a ready draw. Typical was the itinerant showman at Bartholomews Fair who was heard to describe his wares: "Valk up, Valk up, Ladies and Gemmens, here's the most vonderful bird, fish and vild beasts and beastesses ever was in the world from Vest Indies. Alive! Alive! Alive!"

Of all the "vild beasts and beastesses" that have fascinated man, the lion seems to exert a magic of its own. "He is not only the largest and most noble, but the tamest and most beautiful creature of his kind, that has been seen, he grows daily, and is the wonder of all who see him," said a Boston paper of what is assumed to have been the first lion in America. Eight years later "The Lyon," which is probably the same animal, was being referred to as being "strikingly majestic, his figure is respectable, his looks are determined, his gait is stately, and his voice tremendous," and throughout his career he was bombarded with rhapsodies on his strength, his courage, his noble mien.

Even allowing for the love of the macabre by the average Englishman in Queen Victoria's time, many must have thought it was going too far for a writer to describe a lion who had mauled his trainer the previous evening and to whom crowds flocked next day as "The principal actor – I mean the lion – expressed no remorse for what he had done the previous night, his face was calm and even benignant and he was clearly getting the utmost relish from the scene," as indeed, quite clearly was the author. But those were the days when lions were cheap, animal trainers cheaper still, and all the latter had to do was to rouse their charges into sheer, unbridled fury. The animals were shown in ordinary beast wagons lit on every side by guttering torches which produced a foul smell, a pall of smoke and an atmosphere of mystery. If a lion was stubborn it would be prodded from outside with an iron bar; inside, the tamer operated with a whip and heavy club. Simulated savagery was the perennial theme and accidents were faked to add realism. Near the end of the act the smoke would be increased and when the tamer was hidden from view, blood would be poured over him to suggest that his charges had attacked, an effect strengthened by some blood-curdling yells. Then, to tumultuous applause the brute tamer would stagger from the wagon, while his charges, goaded by more prods with iron bars, growled and snarled hysterically. It was bloodthirsty, it was exciting, but if the audiences craved for blood then it was less harmful than the Roman spectacles of old.

This was the world of which a remarkable man called Isaac Van Amburgh was to make himself king in the 1830s and 1840s. We have no clear idea of his method of training except that initially he cowed his beasts by sheer force – with the aid of an iron bar. It would seem too that the iron bar was never too far away and that he used it liberally whenever the need arose. But his was more than just another of the brutal shows which the crowds then loved and which makes one sick to contemplate nowadays. For Van Amburgh was clearly one of those people with that strange, almost mystical mastery of animals, and he taught them tricks which required from his beasts a docility such as wild animals had never before displayed in public. He may have used cruelty initially but thereafter he employed his remarkable instinct and power over animals to get them to do what he wanted.

His background had been far from usual. One day, in far-off Kentucky around the middle of the eighteenth century, a settler of Dutch descent was saved by an Indian after wounding a bear which had turned on him. The settler invited his rescuer back to his cabin, and there began a romance between the settler's daughter and the Indian. Eventually the two married and, deserting his tribe, the Indian turned to other ways. In due time a son was born who kept his mother's name, and after the passage of years the settler's daughter and the Indian found themselves with a grandson. Although not a particularly smart lad, young Isaac did have one remarkable attribute – his uncanny gift for dealing with animals. From a tender age he could manage the most unruly horses, often he would be found in the farmyard sharing his bread not only with the farmyard cat and hens, but also with rats and mice, who seemed to have no fear of him, nor, when in his presence, of the cat or the family dogs. By the age of eleven his powers were well-known, and people would call in Isaac if their chicken coops were attacked by foxes or their beehives by bears. The young animal charmer would then track down the culprit, and what went on then no one knew except that the raids never happened again. It was as well Isaac Van Amburgh lived when he did, for in an earlier age he would undoubtedly have been burned as a sorcerer.

Isaac Van Amburgh, The Beast Subjugator in one of his most famous acts, The Lamb and Child.

One day Isaac was wandering in the woods near his home when he came upon two hunters leaning over an animal they had just shot. He walked over to see what had been their quarry only to discover that it was his tame bear which had been slaughtered. He lost all reason and in a blind fury felled them to the ground. Fearing he had killed them, he fled Kentucky and took to the sea. Some years later he was back in New England, and by chance he heard that the two he had attacked were still alive. Feeling himself a free man at last, he set forth from Boston to his home state.

The road was long, tedious and dusty as Isaac Van Amburgh started his walk back to Kentucky carrying all he possessed in a sailor's bundle over his shoulder on the end of a stick. It was with mixed surprise and delight that he came on a circus stopped by the side of the road feeding their animals. He approached full of curiosity and discovered that the show was owned by a man named Titus, one of the great rivals of the circuses of Aaron Turner and Hackaliah Bailey. Titus was a Kentuckian and after some conversation, Van Amburgh discovered that that very morning their lion had mauled his keeper and was now in such an irritable state that no one could go near him to clean his cage. Van Amburgh promised to tame the beast. Titus, on the look out for an outstanding animal tamer such as he had seen in Europe on his travels over the previous years and perhaps wanting to help a fellow countryman, promised a princely salary if he succeeded. And so the Lion King, as he was soon to be known on both sides of the Atlantic, had found his metier. He had never approached a lion before in his life, but within a matter of days he could lie down between the paws of the great beast.

It was in his eyes, his admirers said, that Van Amburgh's power lay. Conspiratorially, as though bearing a secret beyond price, people pointed out and whispered to each other how protruding they were. He could surely see, they said, almost all around him. And his eyes were peculiar in other ways too, for they darted about and were never still – an essential attribute for any animal trainer, one might think. And they were cold eyes, like icebergs, they said, whitish and unexpressive yet magnetic and hypnotic. Where did he get his extraordinary power, people asked? Certainly not from his father, who, so the story went, had always been scared of animals and had actually died of fright when one day he rounded a corner and was confronted by an all-too-lifelike picture of a wild boar on an inn sign.

Van Amburgh undoubtedly achieved phenomenal success with his animal training, but it is also probable that he did not always succeed. An acquaintance related how the brute tamer would sit for hours with an opossum trying to teach it to read. The schoolroom was a gum tree, here in the branches master and pupil would perch with Van Amburgh holding a copy of *Doble's Spelling Book* before the animal, trying to impress on it the importance of grammar.

Van Amburgh went from strength to strength. Soon he was able to buy and show his own menagerie. He showed in the Bowery in New York, "The most extensive collection of beasts and birds in the known world," and regularly twice a day would enter a cage with a lion, lioness and tiger all living in a perfect "state of harmony together." With this he toured the eastern states of America. But it was the Lion King himself who was the principal attraction. His audience had only one concern, they could not make up their minds about which was the more impressive or dangerous, the act when the brute tamer dipped his arm in blood and thrust it dripping into the maw of his lion; or when he placed a lamb between the lion's paws and stood a small child on the lamb, while the rest of his mixed group of tigers, panthers and more lions watched from their positions, "grouped in picturesque attitudes" – and doubtless with drooling jaws.

Like so many in his trade, the Lion King met his death in the ring. In 1846 his menagerie was in Boston. It had been a sultry day with a heavy overcast sky. People found it stifling and almost unbearable. So did the animals who fretted at the conditions, the lions pacing up and down restlessly. Then the weather cleared and an electric storm of incredible ferocity broke over the city. The atmosphere was tense too in the ring when Van Amburgh started his lion act; the big cats were still restless, something was disturbing them and they were disobedient. Van Amburgh turned to admonish one of his pets, and with his back turned momentarily, a lion rushed at him. Terribly mauled, the trainer tried to beat off his attacker, while an assistant more quick-witted than most, drove the rest of the group to one side of the cage. But there was nothing they could do to help the trainer himself, this was a battle between the two. At last Van Amburgh managed to force his hand down the beast's throat and throttle it, but by then he was within hours of death. His widow continued the Van Amburgh menagerie until eventually it became part of the Barnum circus empire.

"There is probably no sphere in which the growth of humanitarian sentiment has been more striking than in the treatment and training of performing animals. . . . Sympathy with the animal, patience with its deficiencies, has brought about a perfection of education which cruelty altogether failed to secure." So wrote Carl Hagenbeck who started a revolution in the training of animals in the later years of the last century with his "gentling" method. Animal trainers and animals trained in the Hagenbeck way have monopolized the circus animal world for close on one hundred years, and Carl Hagenbeck and his successors have done more than any other individuals to eliminate animal cruelty from the circus ring.

Under Hagenbeck and his disciples, the whole approach to animal training was transformed. The former brutal methods were wholly unacceptable; rousing the animal's temper and then thrashing him to submission was anathema. The days when the tamer – not the trainer – would play on his beast's worst traits, exploit them and keep the animal in a state of terror, revolted him. Hagenbeck's secret was to understand his animals, not to make them fear their trainer. So deep-rooted is this creed in modern animal trainers that – and it is one of the curious by-products of the training method – an animal trainer never, never blames his charges. If an incident occurs, it is his fault, not his beast's; if something goes wrong the error lies in his own behavior, not in that of the animal.

The Hagenbeck story – a story which has embraced circus, zoo, ethnological groups, animal catching and, in particular, the renowned "gentling" method of animal training, goes back to the 1840s when Gottfried Claus Carl Hagenbeck carried on a flourishing trade as a fish merchant in the busy port of Hamburg. This Hagenbeck, like his successors, must have been gifted with a highly enquiring mind, for not content with only dealing with fish, he also had an arrangement with the local fishermen that he would buy anything unusual they caught in their nets. Thus it came about that one day Hagenbeck found himself the surprised owner of six seals. His son Carl took an immediate interest in the new arrivals and, more to please him, Hagenbeck decided to keep them. They were shown locally and attracted great interest, but the burden of keeping them became too much and they were sent to Berlin where they continued to earn the Hagenbecks a pretty penny.

This was the start of the Hagenbeck business. Soon fish were forgotten and the Hagenbecks became principal suppliers of animals to the burgeoning circuses, zoos and menageries which were booming across Europe and beyond. Barnum on one of his visits to Europe bought a number of animals from Hagenbeck and soon the German firm was as well known in American wild animal circles as they were nearer home.

The young Carl Hagenbeck, who in 1866 took over the management of the business from his father, was not only interested in the commercial possibilities of shipping wild animals, he was a genuine lover of wildlife and an enthusiastic zoologist. By now he had begun an impressive menagerie of his own in Hamburg but shortage of space was to drive him to seek more room, and also somewhere to display his animals as he wanted them, in as natural a setting as it was possible to devise. The ground he chose was outside the Hamburg city boundaries in the little town of Stellingen and here he constructed what may be considered the first modern zoo with moated enclosures. The animals thrived in their new setting and thousands of people came to see the great Hagenbeck achievement.

Soon Carl Hagenbeck noticed that the more his animals came in contact with humans, the more amenable and understanding they became. A number would even do little tricks, and many had quickly learned to obey words of command. Presently he set up a training ring where the public could view what was going on – for from the very first, Hagenbeck determined that there would be no mystery about his methods, no one was going to accuse him of cruelty behind bars and it also helped to get the animals used to crowds, a very essential piece of schooling. Soon regular training sessions were instituted – and so began the famous "gentling" method of training animals.

As he explained in his book *Beasts and Men*, the key lies in the animal's personality. Animals will repay cruelty with hatred, and kindness with trust, he used to say, and this was the basic philosophy behind the work of Carl Hagenbeck the animal psychologist. Some animals, he averred, simply cannot be trained – it is essential to understand this at the outset – although the greater part can (it is interesting to note that in his first experiment with lions, out of twenty-one he found only four which seemed to have the necessary talent, but as his technique developed and improved the wastage rate dropped dramatically).

By kindness and not cruelty and by dint of vast amounts of patience, the animal's confidence may be obtained; then, by observing it at work and play, its characteristics and natural actions are turned to advantage and exploited. Animals are all different. Some are lazy, some are quick to learn, others sluggish in their actions and their responses. Animals differ in their physical characteristics and these too may be turned to advantage, for it is easier to get a short thick-set dog to do dangerous jumps than ones with long, brittle legs; a bear with short hind legs finds it easier to walk upright or ride roller skates than its longer-legged brother; small lions or tigers may jump better than their larger more unwieldy brethren.

Whatever the trained animal may turn into when its training is complete, whatever incredible tricks it may perform before an audience and appear to do so willingly, the early days of training are the most important.

It was the Hagenbeck practice to teach his pupils young; as young as is possible and practicable. They would be kept in a line of mixed cages, separated only by bars so that the inmates could get to know one another. They would be allowed to play together too, rough, tumbling puppy games, enjoyed by all – but with the ever-present possibility that someone might lose his or her temper. They would be watched so that any fomenting fight could be quelled instantly, and also so that the individual characteristics of each animal could be studied at close range. This one might be a leader, that a docile follower; that one can roll better than his sister over there, but she seems ready to stand up on her hind legs . . . ! Over the weeks and the months the steady, quiet, unemotional assessment could continue.

Gradually the trainer's soft voice would become associated with food, and also associated with kindness, and from time to time with firmness and, perhaps, gentle chastisement. A loose collar and chain would be put on, the trainer would come and sit inside the cage with his charge, petting and fondling it, until that too became a natural event. Slowly, very slowly, mutual confidence would be established. With a big cat the moment of truth would now be near, the animal is unchained, attendants are at hand should anything go wrong, the trainer walks in, only his instinctive reactions, his experience and the confidence he has built up over the weeks stands between him and a mauling, or perhaps death. The old Duke of Wellington, who was as fascinated by Van Amburgh's big cat acts as the rest of Victorian England, asked the Lion King if he was ever afraid. Van Amburgh answered, "When my pupils are no longer afraid of me, I shall retire from the wild beast line." What he meant, too, was that he must know no fear himself – for if he feels it, his charge will sense it, then his mastery of his animals will be over. He will then have lost their respect, worse he may lose

RINGLING BROS. AND BARNUM & BAILEY CIRCUS

Modern animal mastery. Gunther Gebel-Williams with one of his Bengali tigers at the Bicentennial edition of Ringling Bros. and Barnum & Bailey Circus.

his "touch" – an indefinable quality which may come only after years of experience or which may appear – as it evidently did with Van Amburgh – from the outset.

Always the trainer's will must be stronger than that of his beasts. How often has one been to the circus and suddenly felt a certain tension in the cage when a beast is proving difficult? There is clearly a battle of wills going on. The most observant in the audience will watch fascinated, the rest will sense that a moment of crisis is upon them, and the trainer must impose his will and his mastery on the recalcitrant animal. He may turn quickly upon it as though making quite clear that it has earned his displeasure, and, if not careful, will earn his chastisement; he may merely look in the direction of the animal, he may point imperiously with his whip – not that that would prove any real protection should the animal attack – it is more an instrument for instruction. And then with a snarl, or with a whimper, or with defiance, the beast will do as it should have done, and every one will sigh with relief. The battle of wills is over, man has won and the other animals in the act will be as aware of that all-important fact as the wayward beast itself.

OPPOSITE: *Vladimir Durov, the great Russian clown and animal trainer with one of his first pupils, "Bishka."*

Another man to exert a great influence on animal training, and almost contemporary with Hagenbeck, was the Russian, Vladimir Durov. Durov too, was shocked and horrified at the cruelty he saw every day in the circus rings of old Russia. Apart from his strong views on kindness to animals, he felt that with proper care and treatment they could be made to do more than had ever been achieved by even the most talented animal trainer of his day. "He who works, eats," he would say, and his training methods were a combination of playing on an animal's greed and exploiting its natural movements. He would watch an animal in the wild, study the way it moved, how it behaved with its food, what its natural aptitudes were. He saw how a hen scratched for its food, and from that he taught it to play the zither. He noticed how cranes hopped from foot to foot – he trained some to dance. His skill with animals was phenomenal. Vasilly Vasilievich the goat, Chuska the Parachuting Pig and Misha the Acrobatic Bear were the stars of his animal circus. In 1902, Durov opened his Animal House, which stands to this day as a place of pilgrimage and is known affectionately to generations of young Muscovites as Uncle Durov's House. Here the animals are the actors and in a tiny ring, bears ride cycles, dogs sing, cats instruct mice and the wolf will lie down with the lamb. A street in Moscow is named after Vladimir Durov, who died in 1934, and the Animal House is now run by his family.

There is no doubt that in the circus the big cat acts give the greatest thrill of all animal performances. Elephants are ponderous and there is a limit to what they can do and be asked to do, although they hold a very special place in the affection of all circus goers. Monkeys are fun; sea lions clever; bears look, and are, unpredictable; the other larger beasts which appear from time to time in circuses are curiosities. But true drama lies with the lions and tigers and panthers. Cat acts send shivers down the spine of many a circus goer. In the primeval way of man, secretly, never openly, not a few who are watching hope that something unexpected will occur. Not a fatal accident necessarily, that would be too bloodthirsty, but a thrill that is not billed. Only too often in circus history has their unspoken desire been fulfilled. Why? Perhaps the trainer's reactions and reflexes were too slow. Perhaps he did not notice the telltale signs of an impending catastrophe – an unfamiliar object, the presence of a small animal like a dog or a cat, the whiff of heavy oil, a sudden noise such as a shot or a clap of thunder – all these can lead to an "incident." For big cats are never wholly dependable. "Cat animals are not built that way," was the verdict of one of the greatest of cat trainers, Clyde Beatty. The trainer must exert perennial vigilance, and never appear overconfident. If he falls, then he is lost. On one occasion the great trainer Matthies, a pupil of the Hagenbeck system, was struck down by his favorite tigress. He had the presence of mind to call her name, "Julia!" Through the mists of her temper this brought her back to reality and obediently she trotted back to her pedestal, while Matthies picked himself up from the floor. Had he not cried out in time, not even the love which the two had showed to each other over a long period would have saved the man.

Nine feet long, three feet high at the shoulder, with a four-foot tail and weighing up to a quarter of a ton, the full-grown lion will eat fifteen to eighteen pounds of meat a day according to its needs. By tradition this is raw, but some trainers, zoos and menagerie owners use cooked meat with no ill effects. The lion eats no pork and little fat and fasts every seventh day, but it is inclined to become liverish and petulant, particularly in damp, muggy conditions – a complaint which was unknown in the old days of the rolling circus when the constant buffetting it received on its journey from town to town kept its liver in tip-top condition. On the whole the lioness is the more docile, but a "killer" lioness is the most dangerous of the breed. Some of the "lionesses" one sees in the ring may well turn out to be gelded lions, which, after the operation lose their manes and become as mild as big dogs.

Every lion, as every other animal, has its own personality. A lion with one famous menagerie feared nothing so long as the whip was held in the trainer's right hand, but was all docility when he carried it in his left. Another, in a different circus, hated its trainer and would never work with him if he wore a particular blue coat. Some lions it is safe to touch, others go mad when the whip is cracked. It is the trainer's unenviable task, and a challenge in which he revels, to take these idiosyncracies into account and still mold a performance around the individual characteristics of his beasts.

Never very far beneath the surface are all the elemental humors of the wild animal. The instinct of a lion is to destroy unfamiliar objects. Should the trainer fall, or one of his lions somehow knock him down, their instinct for pack hunting may bring them all to the kill. They are intelligent beasts with needle-sharp perception, and highly suspicious of anything new, be it a weakness in a cage or a man's fear. But they quickly tire and return to their natural laziness. This want of persistence has saved the life of many a trainer attacked by his charges, for as long as he can hold off the attack for thirty seconds or so, the lion will lose interest and lope away, bored with the whole affair. But note how small are the tubs the lion sits upon – rarely larger than a foot square – and much too small for a large beast. This means that it is constantly fidgeting to find a more comfortable position which takes its mind off making a meal of its trainer and makes it more eager to leave the tub when it is bidden. In nature, the lion attacks from the ground, having crouched down for the spring, something it cannot do from a small, restricting tub or

A lion cub displaying its remarkable sense of balance.

pedestal. But beware the lion on the wander, it must be brought under control and returned to its tub at once, or it may attack the trainer when his attention is concentrated on another animal. The most dangerous moment is when the animals enter the cage and go to their places. Sometimes one may turn on another in the tunnel, and a right royal battle will occur, with the other animals of the group pressing in from behind. Sometimes, through carelessness, something is impeding the way to its own tub – for they always take the same route to their tubs – or perhaps an animal gets on the wrong tub. Chaos, dangerous chaos, is never very far away. A trainer was once asked what steps should be taken if the lions get out. "Long ones," came the swift response, and never was better advice given in jest.

The trainer must know the moods of each of his animals, and the danger signs – the lie of the wrinkle about its jaw, the look in its eye, the movement of its tail, if it is more or less restless than usual. As a breed, lions are restless in the spring, and a period of intense heat makes them fidgety and more difficult to control. They are often very jealous, and more than one trainer has owed his life to a favorite lion turning on a would-be attacker. To save his master? Perhaps. Or could it be that this interloper was showing more attention to the trainer than was permitted?

These are all hazards of the profession, but the rewards are as great, and none more so than the achievement of a new act – for an animal, especially a predatory animal, will always remain unpredictable. When a success is achieved, all the danger and all the frustrations are forgotten; that is why the animal trainer considers the big cats as the true challenge of his profession. What could be more impressive than seeing a puny trainer with his head in the jaws of one of these massively powerful beasts? But trainers have

Jorge Barreda, America's young lion trainer with some charges. A regular feature with the Carden-Johnson, Clyde Brothers Circus the largest producer of Shrine Circuses.

CARDEN-JOHNSON CLYDE BROTHERS CIRCUS

different ways of minimizing the danger, some used to chew tobacco and should the lion be slightly reluctant to let go, would squirt a stream of spittle down the animal's throat. Others, when they seize the animal's jaw, take care to push the beast's lips onto its fangs so that should it try to close its jaws it will only hurt itself. Once in the mouth, by pushing back the head as far as possible, the lion cannot close its jaws and then, quite safely, the trainer can put his hands behind his back and appear at ease. Taking the head out again, though, can pose some problems and it is a great deal easier to get the head in than it is to get it out again!

He sticks his head in the lion's mouth,
And holds it there awhile,
And when he takes it out again,
He greets you with a smile.

The tale is told of one brute tamer who had a hated rival in the circus who had sworn to kill him. The years passed and his enemy seemed to have forgotten his animosity.

DEN-JOHNSON CLYDE BROTHERS CIRCUS

Tigers can jump up to seventeen feet. Here is one of William Golden's beautiful Bengali animals hurtling with the greatest of ease over the head of its impassive trainer.

Then one day the tamer's favorite lion quietly bit off his master's head when he placed it in the animal's mouth. An accident everyone said, but they began to wonder. Then a member of the circus remembered seeing the tamer's rival pass behind the animal man shortly before the performance and pass his hand lightly over his head. They searched the other's room and came across a large container of pepper. Then the full horror of what had happened dawned on them – the lion had sneezed!

Lions and tigers are always associated together in the minds of the zoo or circus goer, yet in temperament and appearance the two could hardly be more different. The lion is a naturally lazy, and a ponderous beast; the tiger, with its broad, powerful shoulders and immensely strong hind limbs, is like a huge and impressively powerful spring and has a seventeen-foot leap. It is a very nervous, highly strung animal, and hates shouting or sharp words of command. Blaring bands disturb it, but quiet music can soothe. Its hearing is sharp, and its sense of smell far more acute than the lion's – and it can attack from the crouching position or even

OPPOSITE: *Different in size, different in temperament, different in habit, a mixed act is a performance of opposites; the successful presentation of such an act is one of the most difficult, and rewarding achievements for an animal trainer. Here a mixed act of tigers and a lion at the capable hands of Tajana, one of America's foremost wild animal trainers.*

when lying down, so quick are its reactions. Unlike the lion, which fights with one front paw at a time (the other it uses to keep its balance) the tiger fights, almost boxes, with both paws at a tremendous speed, using its hindquarters to propel it forward. In the wild, the tiger is a natural climber and will often lie along a branch or sit on a rock. This habit means that it learns to climb onto its tub far more quickly than the lion. More cunning and more daring than the lion, the tiger is generally quicker to learn. It is also a more cynical creature, cannot be bluffed as easily as the lion and requires different handling – the simile of the heavy powerful car and the light racer has been used more than once. The conduct of a mixed act of lions, tigers and leopards is in some ways a performance of opposites, and once one understands this, then the true genius of the animal trainer with his mixed act becomes apparent, especially as lions do not like tigers, and vice versa, and both dislike leopards, which they consider inferior beasts.

A tiger's moods differ from those of the lion. In spring they too are restless, but they also have long periods of tranquillity, although these are preceded and followed by other periods of great restlessness. They will not put up with injustice – the whip is rarely used. Should the trainer be attacked by a tiger, the others will merely watch and not join in, for they are individualists to a far greater extent than lions, but still as unpredictable as any other cat. As cubs, they are delightful and playful, but after the age of one year, they may attack without warning.

Panthers, leopards and pumas are the slyest of all the cat family, quickest to learn and quickest to revolt. None more so than the black leopard, the most savage of all. Domestic cats are little different in temperament to their larger brothers, but they are considered the hardest animals of all to train and if anything are even more unpredictable.

It was Barnum who said that elephants are the hook on which the circus hangs, and glamorous and frightening as the cats are, there would be few who would disagree that the circus is elephants or that elephants make the circus. There is something appealing about the great beasts, appealing and somehow rather pathetic. It would not be difficult to hate a mean-eyed lion or tiger or panther, but one could never hate an elephant. They resemble an animal of fiction. Everything about them is peculiar: the waving, immensely muscular trunk, with its highly sensitive fingertip end which can undo knots or turn keys in locks; the vast bulk of the beast; the little pig eyes which, despite their size, can exhibit an amazing range of emotion, the enormous feet and that ridiculous tail stuck on like an afterthought.

Old Bet, like her predecessor the "Ponderous Pachyderm," had people flocking to see her, for elephants have

ANNEFORD CIRCUS

FRED D. PFENING COLLECTION

always proved great crowd attractors – and not necessarily live elephants. On one occasion two of the earliest, and largest, British menageries were bound for London. One arrived safely, but the other reached London with a dead elephant on its hands. Their rival rejoiced and advertised with all the pomp he could muster: "Atkins' Circus, the Only Live Elephant in Town," but the other, not to be outdone, advertised his show as exhibiting the "Only Dead Elephant in Town," and the crowds deserted the live elephant for the novelty of seeing the dead one.

OPPOSITE: *Jumbo. The greatest elephant celebrity of all time.*

The most famous elephant certainly in circus history, and, arguably, in all history, was Jumbo, an African elephant. This massive beast, when he reached his greatest fame was 10 feet 10 inches tall, and weighed 8 tons; the circumference of his tusks was 27·5 inches. He had first come to the London Zoo in 1865 as part of an exchange with the Jardin des Plantes in Paris. He was then estimated to be four years old and was only a little over five feet high. He was put in the charge of a keeper called Matthew Scott, and over the years the two became inseparable.

Jumbo grew and grew and grew. Soon he was easily the largest elephant in the zoo and was patience itself as he took children on his back around the Royal Zoological Gardens led by the faithful Scott who reaped a handsome sum in tips. Then, after a number of years had elapsed, the great elephant started to become moody and intractable; worse, he was inclined to fits of temper and when these were upon him he seemed to lose all reason – a characteristic of elephant rages. The zoo officials were scared stiff of what might happen should one of these tantrums take place when Jumbo was outside his quarters. Thus, when Barnum saw Jumbo and made an offer for the elephant, it was with considerable relief that the zoo authorities accepted.

Little did they realize what this purely commercial transaction had started. Before they knew where they were, they found themselves, the running of their zoo, even their personal integrity called to question. Outcry swept the country. "Jumbo to be sold to America," rang the headlines and all Londoners protested at the loss of their pet. Then someone pointed out that Jumbo was being torn from his mate, Alice – which wasn't quite true as the two elephants rarely met and certainly never got on together. Instantly animal lovers were up in arms against the sale. Questions were asked in the House of Commons and Queen Victoria was said to be "very sad." The outcry was long and furious and Barnum was delighted. Never had any of his purchases received such publicity – and free publicity at that. In all, he spent about $30,000 on Jumbo, to buy him and take him across the Atlantic, and never was money better spent.

Jumbo was now American property, although one stockholder of the zoo tried to prove the contrary. The trouble was that Jumbo was singularly reluctant to leave. As far as he would deign to go was the street outside the zoo, where he lay down in the middle of the road and refused to move. Barnum's agent, now thoroughly distraught, telegraphed his master, "Jumbo has laid down in the street and won't get up. What shall we do?" The reply came the next day. "Let him lie there a week if he wants to. It is the best advertisement in the world."

The zoo authorities were not particularly distressed either, for the zoo attracted crowds such as never before, everyone determined to see the great Jumbo for the last time. On the day of departure it was estimated that no less than 18,500 had come to say farewell to "Dear old Jumbo." For London had Jumbo-fever. Jumbo relics popped up in many guises. There were Jumbos made of India rubber, ivory and porcelain. There were cups and teapots shaped to represent Jumbo, and any portrait or picture or model of an elephant in store or souvenir shop – irrespective of whether it was African or Indian – was immediately tagged as being an exact portrayal of the one and only Jumbo.

At length, a special cage was made for Jumbo, and Scott, who was now included in the bargain and was to accompany the great elephant on his trip to America, persuaded his charge to enter. Early one morning, when, so the Zoo authorities thought, all London would be asleep, Jumbo started on his journey to the docks. The word got round, however, that Jumbo was on his way, and the latter part of the journey and the final sailing resembled a tearful jamboree. But at last Jumbo was on his way to America.

Barnum had not been idle. When Jumbo reached New York City he was greeted by reception such as the place had never seen, Jumbo was drawn in state through the streets by some lesser animals of the elephant breed, and so began a career of unsullied distinction for Jumbo and his keeper and huge profit for his owner. Then on September 15, 1885, in the town of St. Thomas in western Ontario, disaster struck.

The show was over for the day. The animals were being loaded to move on to the next town. Most were carried to the station, but the elephants walked, including Jumbo and a smaller companion, Tom Thumb. As they were making their way up some railroad lines which were normally unused, to everyone's horror a freight train came racing down the line. The elephants at the back of the procession saw it in time and could escape, but Jumbo in the lead with Tom Thumb could not. The train hit Jumbo head on. Tom Thumb was thrown clear, but the big elephant collapsed on the line while the engine and its following cars were derailed. It was clear the animal was mortally wounded and he died within a few minutes, with his trunk holding Matthew Scott's hand.

Then began the macabre part of the incident. For years Barnum had made arrangements that should Jumbo die,

Barnum's white elephant, Toung Taloung, the famous sacred white elephant from Burma. "Well, ma'am," his keeper was heard to explain to a perplexed admirer, "he's not very white, perhaps, but then you see he's very sacred."

then he was to be skinned and stuffed, and his skeleton reconstructed. Within hours the grisly operation was in hand and, in time, the stuffed Jumbo and his skeleton appeared on exhibition with The Greatest Show on Earth. Scott, who had nursed and looked after Jumbo for over twenty years, went into a steady decline. From time to time he had periods of lucidity and for long he nursed the idea that a great box which traveled with the circus contained a fortune which Barnum was to leave him. When Barnum died the box was found to contain only copies of the Barnum autobiography. The shock was too much and Scott died some ten years after his beloved Jumbo.

Barnum had other elephant sagas during his long career as a showman, including a lifelong search for a white elephant. Eventually a white Burmese elephant was purchased in 1883 and Toung Taloung, as the beast was called, made its stately way toward America. A stop in London was included in the schedule and there, before an admiring audience, the white elephant proved a major attraction. The only trouble was that the elephant was not as white as had been expected. "Well, Ma'am," his keeper was heard to explain to a perplexed admirer of Toung Taloung, "he's not very white,

BARNUM IMITATES 4-PAW

FOREPAUGH HAS BEEN IMITATING BARNUM for years. For once BARNUM will imitate FOREPAUGH.

BARNUM has had an elephant artificially colored and will show in his parade

FREE

AT EASTON THURS., MAY 15

A WHITE ELEPHANT JUST LIKE FOREPAUGH'S WHITE-WASHED ONE

WAIT FOR BARNUM AND JUMBO!

FRED D. PFENING COLLECTION

The Battle of the White Elephants. Forepaugh exposed.

perhaps, but then you see he's very sacred." *The Spectator* put it differently, "Toung is neither big nor beautiful, nor anything else, except possibly 'sacred' among a people who are less known in England than any race in Asia. Mr. Barnum should give some sharp Yankee chemist a few thousand dollars to invent a new bleaching process, and then show his elephant in the colours which the populace expect."

The suggestion was not taken up by Barnum, but by his arch rival, Adam Forepaugh. And, lo and behold, a few weeks after Toung arrived in America an elephant of a dazzling white was on show. While the great and amazing beast was being shown to reporters, one more nosy than his fellows took a wet sponge which he tied to the end of a stick and scrubbed the side of the Forepaugh elephant. To his considerable interest the whitewash with which the animal had been daubed promptly came off to reveal an elephant of quite a different hue. He rushed off to tell Barnum who, characteristically, kept the knowledge to himself, but redoubled his shouts of "imposter" – excellent publicity for all concerned. Eventually, a heavy rainstorm in Philadelphia revealed beyond doubt what Barnum had been shouting about his rival, and Forepaugh's stratagem was discovered. Equally characteristically, Barnum had the last word. When challenged by a reporter at a banquet that his elephant was not very white, he turned to the man. "My boy," he said, "in my youth I was fond of attending sociables. At one such party I expressed an opinion that a young lady's complexion was not genuine. Unfortunately she overheard my tactless remark. As she passed me she said, 'God made these cheeks.'" Then turning toward his whole audience he continued, "Now, gentlemen, God made that white elephant, but I assure you that had it been made by Mr. Bailey or myself he would be as white as the driven snow."

Elephants can live for a very long time, the longest known circus elephant was ninety-five when she died, and of course they often outlive their circus. Thus elephants have a habit of being passed on. As some are more docile than others, a new purchaser may not know quite what he is getting when he purchases an elephant. The experience of two Baltimore circus owners, as related by Earl Chapin May, if not typical, certainly acted as a salutary lesson to other would-be elephant purchasers. One day, news arrived that the great "Lord" George Sanger was selling an elephant at the knockdown price of $500. Such a bargain was too good to miss, so the purchase was hurriedly made and soon Evangeline arrived in New York. Now whether it was the noise, or the new smells or that she was not used to walking on the right-hand side of the road, it very soon became clear that Evangeline did not care for her new home. She went wild, wrecking everything in her path, knocking over a fire hydrant on her mad journey – which gave the New York Fire Department and

CUS WORLD MUSEUM, BARABOO, WISCONSIN

A fine parade of elephants with the Hagenbeck–Wallace Circus in 1933.

countless children the time of their lives – and finally she was found holding court in an old folks' home. Eventually the recalcitrant Evangeline was corralled and sent by rail to Baltimore. Perhaps now the end of the new purchaser's problems was in sight. Not a bit, for the aged Evangeline, and aged she surely was, turned out to be the most disreputable, flea-bitten, ear-chewed elephant in all America. Her buyers withdrew to ponder on the truism that bargain elephants do not grow on trees.

This custom of passing on elephants from circus to circus had its comical moments, but it could have graver ones. For a killer or an habitual escaper could be passed on only too easily, and not until the beast had killed again did it show its true character. The big circus owners were for the most part sticklers about destroying an elephant which became unreliable or unmanageable, but some of the owners of smaller circuses were less responsible. Much money was invested in the beast, so a quiet change of name and a bargain price offered to another small circus owner only too happy to get an elephant cheaply, would set the rogue off on its travels again.

Though the elephant has a special place in the hearts of all circus goers, it is nothing to the reverence the elephant keeper pays to his huge charges. Those massive knobbly hunks of gray meat appear incapable of anything except moving as fast as their great bulk allows and of eating and drinking vast quantities each day. Yet the keeper will tell you different. The animal is a natural joker – those pig eyes bear a perpetual twinkle. There was one, which was inflicted with an unpleasant keeper who took delight in adding stones and grit to the elephant's food, and who was less than delighted when the elephant took its revenge and added sand to his plate which he unwisely left within range. When the Committee of Public Safety in the early days of the French Revolution banned feeding of the animals in the Jardin des Plantes and placed a guard on their cages to see their wishes carried out, a soldier was foolish enough to leave his rifle leaning against the cage and the nearest elephant seized it in its trunk, and, with deliberate malice, quietly broke the thing in two and cast the bits at the feet of the sentry.

Elephants are quite intelligent enough to know just what is wanted, but out of sheer good-natured devilment will obstruct and annoy. They never trot or gallop, they walk, at speeds of up to twenty-five miles per hour. They are no fools either, they know their weight, and if they feel that something might collapse under them, they will test it with as much delicacy as a ballet dancer. The elephant's voice has its distinctive tone, the wailing childlike cry of pain is unmistakable, and the soft whining grumbling, when the great beast is sick, would move the hardest of hearts. When ill, though, they take a fiendish delight in enjoying their illness and in being perverse – in many ways the elephant is like an oversized child; vulnerable, but also prone to fits of temper. When an elephant gets angry it loses all power of reason, and will crush anyone and anything in its path. Only when the attack dies down can be seen the pathetic remorse at its action and bewilderment in its expression at its short-lived manic behavior. Musth, the sexual excitement produced in the male by a hormone discharge from a depression in the skull at the side of the head, is just as dangerous as the short bursts of temper. Then there is no recourse but to chain the animal down until the musth has passed.

The animal almost always seen in the circus is the Indian elephant, either the ordinary Indian elephant or the smaller version which hails from Indo-China. The African elephant is a more angular beast, taller and more streamlined, but it is less tractable and more prone to attack than the Asian species. Most circus elephants are females – although referred to as bulls. They are more gentle and predictable than males, especially during the mating season, but when deprived of male company can become inordinately attached to their keeper or to some smaller animal such as a pony.

Elephant acts in the circus are fun, though one wonders if it is the general amazement and affection which the elephant always attracts, rather than the skill of the perform-

HUBERT CASTLE INTERNATIONAL CIRCUS

The elephant repertoire is somewhat limited but the great beasts still have an endearing, gentle quality about them as they display loyalty, obedience and a spark of mischief in their eyes. Here Pinson's Fabulous Pachyderms perform at The Hubert Castle International Circus.

ance itself. For when all is said and done, the elephant repertoire is somewhat limited. Their acts can be rendered down to variations of the four basic elephant tricks: sitting up and begging; lying down; standing on their heads; or hopping from leg to leg in a sort of dance, often accompanied by a form of ponderous pirouette performed with the dignity of outsize policemen. They can be taught to "dance" by dragging wet sacks across their broad backs, this causes them to twitch, and this twitching can give the impression that they are tapping time to the music. But they are quick to learn and take a huge pride in their performance, they will even practice by themselves. Lying down to command is one of the easiest tricks to teach, and one famous elephant was responsible for perhaps the largest traffic jam in the history of the early days of New York when its owner, in order to advertise his circus, instructed the keeper to get his charge to lie down in the middle of the thoroughfare and then pretend that he could not get the animal to move again. The puny efforts of the police and the fire department provided the onlookers with more free laughs than they had had for many a year.

The elephant is blessed with an insatiable curiosity. Anything left in its reach will be examined with great

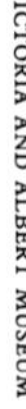

Elephantine Performances. One enthusiastic artist having seen an elephant performing at Astley's reckoned there was no end to their accomplishments!

thoroughness with the astonishingly sensitive end to its trunk, and more often than not conveyed to its mouth and swallowed. When Jumbo was finally cut up it was found that his stomach contained a small mint of currency of all sorts, as well as nails, screws, an assortment of stones, a bunch of keys and a police whistle.

Is it true that an elephant never forgets? Some say they do, others that they don't. Stories are legion from both quarters, but the classic tale concerns an elephant in a small tenting show in England. One summer the circus was touring in the county of Devon and in a village through which they passed a local joker with an overdeveloped sense of fun gave the elephant a bun filled with mustard. Not for three years did that circus come again, but when they reached the village the elephant took a drink in a nearby pond, and as they passed the cottage where the former tormentor was leaning on his gate watching the show go by, he received a trunk-full of muddy water!

All wild animals are unpredictable to some extent, but none so unpredictable, and thus dangerous, as the bear family. They are great characters and personalities with a well-developed sense of humor and they appear deceptively gentle. But there is always an air of uncertainty about a bear.

Its eyes are small and shifty. It is the bear, of all the animal kingdom, which must be treated firmly. The slightest sign of withdrawal or hesitation, and it will press home its advantage, yet it will waver if firmly opposed and can even, sometimes, be made to withdraw itself.

That great white wooly creature, the polar bear, is the most unpredictable of all bears. It has an interesting way of attacking, which it will do without warning. It lunges forward snapping at its victim's stomach and legs; then it hugs the victim's body crushing his head in its enormous jaws. There is no point belaboring its nose, as one could do with a lion or tiger – it is immune to such treatment, its hide is too thick to feel heavy blows, and its tenacity is remarkable – it will *not* let go. When faced with something unfamiliar some animals display a streak of cowardice, but not so the polar bear; when it lunges at an interloping object it seeks to destroy it. The story is told of a polar bear trainer who adored his charges, as apparently they did him. There was nothing his bears would not do, they were like members of a large wooly family. Yet one day the trainer, while cleaning the cage, slipped and fell to the floor, perhaps kicking a bear as he did so. Before he could recover, his bear had killed him. No ceremony, no fuss, a single blow from a front paw was enough. For something unusual, something not trained for, had happened and the animal's primitive instincts took over.

The bear is highly intelligent, frighteningly so at times. It cannot be deceived or duped like some animals and seems able to sum up its trainer in an instant. And you cannot strike it with a stick, for it will turn on you. Even more patience than usual is needed to train bears, but so intelligent are they, such natural actors, acrobats and comics that many animal trainers consider they are the most satisfying of all animals to train. Bears sit watching every movement, their small eyes never leaving the trainer for an instant, as though waiting for him to drop his guard.

Adult bears are at their most savage soon after a cub is born, and it is a very brave man who approaches them then. They are also apt to turn tricky in the autumn when self-respecting bears in the wild are turning their thoughts to hibernation. They do eat meat, but raw meat makes them dangerous and lots of cabbage and green stuff finds its way into their food, mixed with stew or soup. Some bears can live to an age of fifty years or so, but as they get older, they increasingly become less tolerant of man. They are greedy, and the trainer plays on this while teaching them their tricks. For there are a great many things a bear can do, it is a natural comedian. In the wild it will stand on its hind legs to reach for fruit, or, when a cub, will box with its brothers and sisters. These two aptitudes can be turned to good account in making it a bicycling bear – on a specially made bicycle with a low frame and saddle and high handlebars, for the bear's back

RINGLING BROTHERS AND BARNUM & BAILEY CIRCUS

NOVOSTI PRESS AGENCY

NOVOSTI PRESS AGENCY

OPPOSITE: *Hot Lips. The biggest hypocrite of them all, the unpredictable polar bear with Ursula Boettcher. All sweetness and kindness here, but do not trust him.*
ABOVE: *Critics of the circus say that animals do not enjoy performing. What about these bears of Vladimir Filatov's Bear Circus shown here in the Moscow State Circus?*
LEFT: *Don't argue with the ref!*

OPPOSITE, ABOVE: *Monkey business! The Rudi Lenz musical chimps at the Bicentennial Edition of Ringling Bros. and Barnum & Bailey Circus.* BELOW: *Gargantua the Great. Billed as the world's most terrifying creature, he must also have been one of the ugliest.*

legs are short. A while ago motorcycling bears proved a great attraction, but such an act had its problems for so enthusiastic were the cyclists that they were reluctant to leave the ring at the end of the act, and motorcycles can be lethal vehicles, especially when handled by bears.

Fun loving and mischievous as bears are, it is nothing to what can happen with monkey acts. Monkey business in the circus can become riotous. The chimpanzee is a favorite, but little does the audience really know how destructive these creatures can be – they have a vicious temper and a nasty bite. First brought into Europe in the early years of the seventeenth century, chimpanzees are heavily built creatures, the male considerably larger than the female, and they characteristically walk on the knuckles of the hand. They do eat meat but also love fruit and nuts. A bowl of warm milk with sugar is very popular, as are onions, which seem to help the chimp's digestion.

With such accomplished actors, their training has always involved watching their natural aptitudes and capitalizing on them. Monkeys are born acrobats, possessing a wonderful sense of balance, and are as at home on their hands as on their feet. They are wonderful mimics and positively revel in dressing up.

The most famous ape of all was the enormous gorilla, Gargantua the Great, which Ringlings acquired in 1937. Then seven years old with a height of five feet six inches, an arm spread of nine feet, and, supposedly, with the strength of twenty men, he weighed close to a quarter of a ton and was carried about in a huge air-conditioned wagon with bars of high tensile steel and bullet-proof glass. Billed as "The World's Most Terrifying Creature, the Mightiest Monster Ever Captured by Man," – in reality he had been brought back as a baby by a kindly sea captain – Gargantua proved a tremendous draw. He had a scowl of the utmost ferocity, he looked a mean, child-devouring monster while in fact he ate only fruit and vegetables. His favorite plaything was an immense truck tire, which he twisted and mangled and crumpled as though it were made of paper.

The sea lion act provokes more delight than any other animal performance in the circus for sea lions are the true animal clowns. Their talent seems endless, and so improbable in an animal of that shape and size. They can lift latches and open doors, balance balls on the ends of their noses, and are natural acrobats. They have few vices once trained, but that process can be a very painful one for the trainer as they have a very sharp nip indeed.

At first, they must become accustomed to captivity, and particularly to eating from human hands. Trainers feel they must get to know their charges for at least a month before

RINGLING BROS. AND BARNUM & BAILEY CIRCUS

CIRCUS WORLD MUSEUM, BARABOO, WISCONSIN

NOVOSTI PRESS AGENCY

The sea-lion is a natural performer.

OPPOSITE ABOVE: *Concentration!* BELOW: *A trained racoon – washing day.*

attempting anything at all with them. They need to be named very early on and they respond to soothing talk. Each is given its own pedestal and this is its domain, woe betide any other sea lion who might happen to trespass, for they are very jealous. Their acts which seem so unnatural, are all adaptations of natural movements. The tossing of the ball in the air and catching it on the point of the nose is the same movement they do when they throw up fish so that they fall head first down the throat – otherwise the fish fins would stick in their gullets. Many observers have noticed how in the wild the sea lion will balance bits of driftwood on its nose, keeping them up with sensuous movements of their long, flexible necks which can stretch to twice their apparent length. Sea lion "singing" is an adaptation of their barking; their ladder-climbing is nothing more than a demonstration of how they wriggle up onto rocks.

They adore applause and love showing off, and if things are not quite as they would like they can be as temperamental as film stars. They are always greedy and usually get most of their food in the ring as rewards for their tricks. They are immensely fast movers, but travel tires them and any sharp change of temperature will upset them. They are devoted beasts and become immensely attached to their masters or whomever feeds them. Should that person go away they have been known to pine, literally to death.

NOVOSTI PRESS AGENCY (MOS FILM) AND NATIONAL FILM ARCHIVE, LONDON

NOVOSTI PRESS AGENCY

KELVIN HALL CIRCUS

A unique animal act has recently been introduced by the Moscow State Circus using yaks, the great, shaggy, wild oxen of Tibet. With elaborate ceremony, the amazing, the remarkable, the first-ever act of performing yaks is announced to the audience. The ringmaster explains that hitherto these great members of the bison family had been thought untameable, creatures of the wild which would never bow to man's hand, but now the impossible has been achieved, in a truly incredible feat of animal mastery, performing yaks are about to be shown before an audience. With a flourish, the ringmaster snaps his fingers and two of the huge beasts come snorting into the ring. Already those in the front seats are beginning to fidget nervously, and their fears are little allayed when they see that there is a small army of attendants waiting in the wings. Waiting for what? For trouble? Without warning the two great creatures suddenly face each other, and with a thunder of hooves, which can be heard all over the circus, rush together in a headlong charge and meet with a crash which makes the whole arena shake. Then one of the yaks dashes off into the recesses of the hall, leaving the other, by far the larger of the two, looking round menacingly with lowered head as it contemplatively paws the ground. By now

OPPOSITE: *Contemplation! Old Regnas and Friend, at the Kelvin Hall International Circus, Glasgow, one of Britain's permanent winter circuses.*
ABOVE: *Willful, headstrong and the very devil to teach. A zebra training session.*

those in the front rows are already beginning to clamber unobtrusively over the backs of their seats, as though afraid that any sudden movement might attract the great yak in their direction, for it is clear beyond doubt that this animal is quite out of control. But the yak never moves, instead it lowers its head still further, it seems to those nearest it that its eyes mist over with a red film. This is a signal for a wholesale evacuation of the front seats, and others farther back start looking longingly toward the nearest exit. The ringmaster cracks his whip in vain, attendants rush forward bearing stout ropes to tether the clearly maddened animal. And then it charges. Some scream hysterically, others, those farthest away, impotent bystanders of what is about to become a terrible disaster, hide their eyes. Then, in a cloud of dust and with a noise like rending cloth, the huge yak comes to a halt within inches of the side of the ring. Someone blows a whistle and, as meek as the smallest calf, the huge yak trots amiably out of the ring looking to neither right nor left. For a stunned moment or two there is only silence in the huge auditorium, then a thunderous outburst of applause breaks out from the body of the hall, while those who had so hurriedly vacated their seats return to them more than a little sheepishly. Humbug, but what wonderful humbug; how old Barnum would have loved it.

Pigs too have long been popular animals to train, for despite their looks, they are intelligent and learn quickly. "The Pig of Knowledge" was a popular side-show feature in many a fair such as the one which was billed as being able to "Spell, read, tell points of Sun rising and setting, kneel at command, tell the hour to the minute by a watch, tell a card and age of any party. In color the most beautiful of his race, in symmetry the most perfect, in temper the most docile." Sanger reckoned on being a master at training pigs. He would select a pig, a fat and comfortable-looking one, a contented pig, one from which the best bacon is made. He would tether the animal so it could only go round in a circle and then start it moving. At a click of the fingers, the pig, which has highly acute hearing, could be made to stop, at another click it would go on. And with these basic tricks firmly in the animal's mind the scope for an ingenious trainer was almost unlimited.

No survey of circus animals can be complete without mention of some of the fictitious beasts which have appeared from time to time and billed as something unique. In the early days these were often called a "Non Descript," such as the one which appeared in pantomimes in the early nineteenth century in London. A strange beast this, with the skin of a lion, the head of an ass, eagles' wings, cats' feet and a fish's tail. Another "Non Descript" was a true fish, or so they said, in the belly of which no fewer than 1,700 mackerel were found. This monster was twenty-five feet long and eighteen inches in circumference with five rows of teeth. It must have been a conger eel. It took the combined efforts of seven horses and one hundred men to draw it up the beach where it remained a colossal attraction, until smell overcame curiosity. Yet another "Non Descript" proved fascinating to a credulous London public. This one was called:

THAT SINGULAR NONDESCRIPT

Which since its arrival in England occupied the attention of the naturalist, the historian and the whole of the cognoscenti and literati.

A short description of it cannot fail to create a lively desire to observe it. The Head is like that of a Pig, the Ears like those of a Wolf whilst the Body and Legs resemble the Human Being, the Breast, Arms, Elbows, Wrists and Arm-Pits, being as perfect as the finest human form ever seen. Every BEAST of the FOREST have a Hock behind, but this Singular Prodigy has the Cap of the Knee before. The CLAWS resemble those of the FEROCIOUS TIGER. It may be truly said - "Taking her for all in all - We ne'er may look upon her like again!"

Religious scruples are laid aside, and all sex and all sorts of People, join in admiration of the noble and interesting Beast which at once paints a striking and rare instance of

ANIMAL BEAUTY
and
NATURAL CURIOSITY

This Singular Phenomenon was brought from the rolling Sands of

ARABIA

and so lately discovered that Naturalists have not been able to furnish any description.

Other strange and wonderful creatures would appear from time to time. There was the "Noble Casheware . . . one of the strangest creatures in the Universe, being Half Bird and Half a Beast." This peculiar animal would apparently eat iron, steel or stones and was shown in conjunction with such fellow creatures as a Leopard from Lebanon, an Eagle from Russia and a "little black hairy monster bred in the Deserts of Arabia, a natural ruff of hair about his face, walks upright, takes a glass of ale in his hand and drinks it off, and doth several other things to admiration." This was at Bartholomews Fair where there was also an elephant which fired a gun.

So have I seen at Smithfield's Wondrous Fair,
When all his brother Monsters flourished there
A lubber'd Elephant divert the town
With making legs and shooting off a gun.

LIBRARY OF CONGRESS

SAN ANTONIO PUBLIC LIBRARY

A bizarre animal called the Bonassus appeared once at Wombwell's menagerie. It resembled, so one paper said, nothing so much as a mangy goat. A Vedo, or Peruvian God Horse, was another to fascinate the crowds. And in 1761 a peculiar beast which was called a Gormagunt made its appearance in New York. It was of an "uncommon shape with three heads and eight legs." Another, which was washed up on the beach of Staten Island in 1825, was described as "very like a whale" some twenty feet long, with a whale's tail and black, bony and sunken eyes. It was made of shoe leather and the tail was used as a wardrobe by the troupe who showed it! Some beasts called Mocos made a brief appearance at Boston in the 1830s. They were described, truthfully for once, as "animals not treated in natural history, nor ever before seen in this country." Fittingly, though, pride of place in the menagerie of humbugs belongs to Barnum.

It was St. Patrick's Day in New York. Barnum's Great American Museum was in its heyday and people were flocking in their thousands to see his wonderful exhibits. Barnum had heard that on St. Patrick's Day, the entire Irish population of New York were going to make a gala visit to the museum and he was delighted. Beaming all over his face he watched the Irish with their families crowding into the building. Then his smile froze as it became clear that though huge numbers were going in, very few were coming out. He went to investigate and discovered that indeed they were not, for everyone had brought their lunches with them and looked like taking up permanent occupation for the rest of the day. He decided to try to get them to depart another way, and had a workman paint a large sign which said, 'To the Egress." "To the Aigress," the visitors muttered, "now, that's an animal we haven't seen," and bedazzled by the glories of the Great American Museum, they dutifully followed the signs through a labyrinth of passages until quite suddenly they found themselves in the street again. Only then did they realize that "egress" is another word for exit.

OPPOSITE ABOVE: *The Snake Wagon, a never-failing attraction in the old circus parades.*
BELOW: *Menagerie of Humbugs. The giant, man-devouring Bovalapus! A fine action poster of this magnificent beast.*

CLOWN

The liberty horses have left the ring. The last of the carpet clowns with a couple of flip-flaps and a final caper have followed them. The music changes tempo and a single light illuminates a shuffling figure as he makes his way with some pretense of dignity to the center of the sawdust. He wears a long top coat of an outrageous tweed which is far too big for him and all but sweeps the ground. Around his neck is an open white collar and a wisp of a black bow tie. His face is white and he has on a floppy shapeless hat over his bald pate. On his feet is a pair of outsize shoes and on his back he carries an enormous trunk.

This strange figure walks into the middle of the ring, seemingly unconscious of the total concentration of five thousand pairs of eyes watching his every movement, or of the ripple of excited anticipation which followed his entrance. He seems uncertain about where to put down his great trunk and he wanders disconsolately round the ring with puzzlement and concern written all over him. At last he seems satisfied. With deliberate and exaggerated care he places the trunk on the ground and, with equal deliberation, opens it. He reaches in and brings out a tiny fiddle. As though pleased with his performance, his face, which had not so much as moved a muscle, breaks into a broad smile of greeting, and the audience roar. Grock the incomparable, King of Clowns, has arrived.

The smile is replaced with a frown of intense concentration. The maestro raises a hand, bidding silence. The huge audience stills. With the air of an accomplished performer, Grock places one foot on a chair. The ridiculous and diminutive violin is put to his cheek. With rapt attention he strums a string or two to tune it. He looks up to indicate that he is ready. With a flourish he throws his bow in the air intending to catch it, but misses as it falls to the ground. A gesture of

OPPOSITE: *Grock, King of Clowns.*

annoyance, a frown creases the serene white face. He tries again and once more fails to catch the bow. With an imperious gesture, he summons a screen behind which he can practice. The audience, somewhat mystified by now, watches the bow rise above the screen and sees it fall again. Time and again Grock tries the trick. Small boys in the front rows can be seen biting their nails as they will him to succeed. The audience is hushed as though witness to a great event and all want the poor man to perform the feat which clearly means so much to him. At length, satisfied that now he can do it, Grock returns to the ring. He bows again to his audience as though thanking them for their consideration. He takes up his position by the chair again and with a beatific smile throws his bow in the air once more. It falls to the ground. Perplexed, his face strained with the effort, he studies it intently. He throws it up again. Once more it falls to the ground. In apparently sheer exasperation he hurls it toward the roof, twice as high as he has thrown it before, and as it falls he deftly catches it. His face lights up from ear to ear in a smile of the sheerest delight and the audience erupt. Such was the great Grock, who those enjoying the good fortune to see him in his great days

Clown acts of 1872.

consider the greatest circus clown that ever lived.

The scene shifts. There is a change of character. We are looking at the celluloid screen in the early days of the silent movies. It is winter in New York. There is a riotous party in full swing at the hotel. The scene is gay and despite the cold the windows are open. Enter, along the snow-covered sidewalk, a shuffling figure. His shoulders are bowed, he walks in a curious splay-footed fashion. His trousers are too long and almost collapse over his shoes. His coat is too small and shows bare his wrists. He has a small moustache and on his head a bowler hat. Over his arm hangs a cane.

The figure stops outside the hotel to look at the scene within. His shoulders droop, his whole attitude suggests sadness and longing. A car is drawn up in the street, a huge opulent car all silver and glitter. A ravishing beauty, muffled to the ears in fur comes out of the hotel with her escort who wears immaculate evening dress, a shiny top hat and has an ebony cane held in a hand on which a ring sparkles brilliantly in the night. The little man watches them pass. He raises his hat – raises it, does not hold it out for alms, the lovely creature looks at him and smiles. She would linger, but her escort hurries her along, sparing only a fleeting glance at the man on the sidewalk. The car door is opened by the chauffeur. They enter and it closes on them. The car is driven off into the night, leaving the little man outside the hotel. But his look of sadness has been succeeded by one of extreme coyness and appeal, his head is tilted to one side like that of a puppy. For by that one glance the lovely creature has transformed the little man's world. He shuffles off into the night – faster this time, and swinging his cane. Not a word has been spoken, none were needed. Brilliant mime and brilliant artistry by the immortal Charlie Chaplin were enough.

In action more eloquent than words, Grock and Charlie Chaplin were able to convey their thoughts. In these simple scenes they managed to run the gamut of human emotions and, what is more, they were able to convey these to their audience. Their genius was to associate their audience with their emotions. It is a gift given to very few.

The story is told of Volkerson, a clown adored by several generations of the Danish public, who, when he was too old and frail to be allowed to fall, would be gently lowered to the ground by the others in his act. The crowd loved it, as they loved him. This intimacy with the audience is unique to a clown in the circus. It would be hard to imagine a troupe of trapeze artistes winning the adoration accorded a well-known entrée clown – they are too far away and their act, although a wonderful spectacle and a tremendous thrill, appears impossible and the average person cannot associate himself with it. The animal trainer and the equestrian both appear remote, gaudy, unapproachable figures. But in the clown it is possible to see and recognize another mortal. The character portrayal is comprehensible, the audience see him every day of the week, here he is in a comical, eccentric, but still recognizable guise. This is the character artistry of the clown.

The origins of this remarkable creature, the circus clown, can be traced back to the great Joseph Grimaldi – although he was always a pantomime clown and never worked in the circus in his life. But as the diverse strands of what we have come to call the circus came together for the first time at the hands of Philip Astley, so the diverse strands of clowns and clowning were married by the genius of Joseph Grimaldi.

It would seem that the Grimaldis were of a long line of traveling showmen and artistes – with their distant origins in Italy – who traversed Europe in the fifteenth and sixteenth centuries. Certainly Joseph Grimaldi's father had been born in Europe and spent the first forty years of his life on the Continent. There seems fairly strong evidence to show that Grimaldi senior was in fact a dentist, but it was as ballet master at Drury Lane Theater in London that he first became known to the public. For thirty years he was the most noted artiste of his day, founder of a new style of pantomime, dancer and clown, acrobat and tragedian. "Old Grim," as

Joseph Grimaldi and his celebrated oyster act.

he was universally known, was a short-set, saturnine fellow. A curious, cruel man, a practical joker and humorist, but with an overwhelming obsession with the morbid. For hours he would walk in cemeteries and graveyards musing on the nature of the deaths of the inmates and particularly how many of the assembled company had been buried while in a fit or a trance. His fear of being buried alive was pathological, so much so that in his will he stipulated that before burial his head was to be cut off – a deed which was in fact done. His eccentricity and suspicious nature went to the lengths of faking his own death to see what would be the reaction of his sons. His younger, Joseph, suspecting a ruse, was all sorrow and compassion, but the elder one was so overjoyed at the event that he could not forebear dancing around the death chamber rejoicing to such an extent that the "corpse" could bear it no longer and rose in wrath from his "death-bed."

"Old Grim" had a presentiment that the fourteenth of each month held the key of his continuing span on earth – he was in fact born, christened, married and indeed died on the fourteenth. Each month as the fateful day passed, he would announce in his broken English, "Ah! Now I am safe for anoder month." This was the atmosphere of superstition and rigid discipline in which the young Joseph Grimaldi was brought up.

The future clown had been born to a young dancer of the Corps de Ballet a week before the Christmas season of 1778 was due to open at the Drury Lane Theater. Joseph's mother was a Londoner, born and bred. All her life she had been associated with the theater, sometimes on loan to the great Garrick as an occasional fairy, at other times as a dancer. It was through her that young Joe inherited his love of Cockney London and his instinctive knowledge of what his audience wanted to see and how to make them laugh. From his father, he inherited his circus skills as juggler, tumbler and brilliant mime. But the interpretation was all his own for Grimaldi was the first professional clown.

Almost before he could walk, the young Grimaldi had appeared on the stage at the Royal Circus and Equestrian Philharmonic Academy which was Charles Hughes's answer to Astley's amphitheater then enjoying great success. Old Grim was both partner and ballet master to the new venture and in his latter role he had charge of some sixty children whom he trained to perform "exercises in music, dancing, oratory, etc." His regime was strict. Whenever a child became particularly unruly it was placed in a basket and hoisted to the top of the flies by a rope; here the victim languished until Old Grim relented or had need of the basket for another miscreant. Whether the young Grimaldi suffered such treatment is not known, but certainly when he was still very small he was introduced to what was known as "skinwork." Dressed as a monkey he cavorted about his father on the end of a chain and the climax of his act was to be swung by the chain into the side scenery, where one must suppose he was intended to sit and gibber. On one memorable occasion, the chain snapped and young Grimaldi winged his involuntary way into the pit, fortunately landing in the lap of an old gentleman who was considerably surprised.

Through the years, Joe Grimaldi persevered in his clowning. Old Grim died in 1788 and soon the Great Grimaldi referred to Joseph and not his father. We must delve into the remarks of his contemporaries to get any sort of impression of Grimaldi – although even so great a critic as Charles Dickens declared such a thing as impossible. The clown had a large, fat face, as "plump as a Dutch cheese," and a short, stumpy, well-muscled body, the embodiment of the patriotic figure of John Bull – the British equivalent to Uncle Sam. His "winking, reeling, *drunken*" eyes, "large, globular and sparkling, which rolled in a riot of joy," expressed one commentator. His nose was a "vivacious excrescence capable of exhibiting disdain, fear, anger and even joy. We think we see him now," the author of the article continued, "screwing it on one side; his eyes nearly closed, but twinkling forth his rapture; and his tongue a little extended in the fullness of his enjoyment; his chin he had a power of lowering, we will not say to what button of his waistcoat, but certainly the drop was an alarming one. Speech would have been thrown away in his performance of Clown; every limb of him had a language."

And when he did speak, his voice, described another, was either "richly thick and chuckling, like the utterance of a boy laughing, talking and eating custard all at once; or a gin voice, heaved from the very bottom of his chest; or, most notoriously, a tone composed of laugh, scream and speech." When he opened his "oven-mouth" his laugh, an odd descending of merry notes, was a comedy of itself, infectious, the whole house laughed with him.

What was the Grimaldi magic? That he was versatile is undeniable; a noted swordsman, juggler, tumbler and small-animal trainer. He would analyze a scene, a setting, a situation and through his own instinct of the correct balance within his performance and his innate feeling for what his audience wanted, he would transform the commonplace into something memorable. It is an art which Charlie Chaplin showed in his earlier films; in another medium it is that of Alfred Hitchcock; it is the art of the greatest clowns. Grimaldi's jokes and situations live on and are the foundation for many acts even today. In his time he was called the "Michael Angelo of Buffoonery," and few great clowns would not cheerfully and gratefully acknowledge their unrepayable debt to Joseph Grimaldi, whose name is perpetuated in the circus in the "Joey."

His humor was irresistible, and he injected a degree of practical satire into his clowning – a development from the court jester's wit of former years and a forerunner of that of Vladimir Durov who poked unmerciful and highly popular fun at authority in the days of the czars of Russia. He was a character actor and could squeeze the last chuckle of comedy from the most everyday occurrence.

He was renowned for his powers of construction. At Grimaldi's hands, another clown would become a wheelbarrow; coal scuttles became boots; barrels became soldiers; and vegetables became human beings. Crowds would roar with laughter at his misfortunes and the greater his humiliation and embarrassment the more they loved it. Pretending to steal was a favorite skit – and this in the days when such a crime meant death or deportation – yet through it all he managed to appear a lovable villain, exalting in his own folly and wrapping the whole act in irresistible humor.

In private life Grimaldi was earnest, sincere, very hard working and modest to a degree. He was loved on the stage and, to the surprise of many, revered off it. But when away

OPPOSITE: *"Tonight I assumed the motley for the last time – it clung to my skin as I took it off, and the old cap and bells rang mournfully as I quitted them forever." Grimaldi's last song, June 27, 1828 (after Cruikshank).*

from the theater he was unlucky, for everything he turned his hand to went wrong. His investments failed, his wife died soon after their marriage, his son – who was said by some to have possessed a talent as great as that of his father – became ruined by vanity and debauchery. On June 27, in the year 1828, at Drury Lane Theatre, the scene of so many of his triumphs, the great clown clowned for the last time. He was prematurely old and stage weary by now, unable to stand for long, so a chair was brought for him, and from there he sang the old and much-loved songs which had so delighted Georgian and Victorian London.

There is a poignancy about the clown who is too old to be a clown. But nothing has been written to match the exquisite sadness of the speech Joe Grimaldi made as he bade farewell to his beloved audience after giving them a lifetime of enjoyment. A formal speech had been prepared for him by a friend, but the emotion of the moment was too much for him. He cast his paper aside and spoke from the heart:

> It is four years since I jumped my last jump – filched my last oyster – boiled my last sausage – and set in for retirement. Not quite so well provided for, I must acknowledge, as in the days of my clownship, for then, I dare say, some of you remember, I used to have a fowl in one pocket and sauce for it in the other. To-night has seen me assume the motley for a short time – it clung to my skin as I took it off, and the old cap and bells rang mournfully as I quitted them for ever.

Although Joey Grimaldi was the first true clown, as we know the term, his clowning ancestry goes back into the dim mists of the past, for throughout history and on many continents, there have been clowns – or certainly comedy makers. The ancient Egyptians had the *Danga*, a black pigmy from central Africa, a comical fellow who, by his mime and wit, diverted Pharaoh and his court. Jesters – the *parasites* – who sang for their supper, were a feature of life in ancient Greece. In Rome, clowning became more sophisticated; clowns were given names and wore distinctive dress. Many were dwarves who were supposed to bring good luck. *Stupidus* muddled along, getting in everyone's way and usually ended up soundly beaten for his pains by the number one clown – an early example of comic opposition, the Abbott and Costello, the Laurel and Hardy of the ancient world. *Stupidus* was an amusing, harmless oaf who wore a long pointed cap over a shaven pate and was dressed in a tunic covered with patches. *Mimus* was another clown type who appeared at funerals and mimicked the old ways of the dead; while *Cicirrus* was the smart clown. He wore a coxcomb and by his wit and repartee clowned his way through life, making fun of the serious, deflating the pompous and ridiculing the preposterous.

The East too had its clowns. Ancient China had the

NATIONAL PORTRAIT GALLERY, LONDON

F'seng who would burst into the middle of a serious play to wake up the audience. The Chinese also had their buffoon – the *T'cheou* – who was a rough country yokel. The *P'rang* were the Malayan clowns with huge masks and mighty turbans, while in old India, *Vita* was the wandering wit and musician and *Vidusaka*, with his mask and gigantic wooden ears, a greedy simpleton, shouted abuse at the audience.

By the Middle Ages in Europe the clowns of old were becoming stylized. The court jester was an accepted member of society, a part of the establishment of king, noble or petty prince. His dress too was becoming distinctive. In England he wore the coxcomb – a form of hooded cap with bells – these showed that he was little more than a child at heart, a deceit which was intended to take the sting from his patter – although on many occasions his wit and effrontery offended rather than entertained and his failed drollery often enough must have cost him his liberty or his head.

There can have been few court jesters as fortunate as Rahere, jester to King Henry I of England, who from the wealth he earned was able to create the foundation of St. Bartholomews as a monastery and hospital.

Rahere was permitted to hold an annual fair on the site to help defray the costs of caring for the sick. This was the famed Bartholomew Fair.

Here acrobats and jugglers, and of course clowns and fools, were to be seen, many with performing animals. Mountebanks, the quack doctors, were often accompanied by clowns to help attract customers to buy their magic potions. Here also were the Merry Andrews, Jack Puddings or Zanies – each a distinctive type of merrymaker. Nor was England alone in this; in Germany were the Merry Councillors, while France possessed her own minstrels and *jongleurs*.

Elsewhere, Jews in the Middle Ages had their *Marshallik*, who provided merriment at weddings and poked fun at guests and at the bride and groom. In many communities there were Lords of Misrule who, to quote one authority, ensured that "the revelry ran high and the fun grew fast and furious." Even the Church was not immune and the Feast of Fools was license to untrammeled mockery at the expense of the clergy who they supplanted on the chosen day with their own "Bishops" and "Archbishops of Fools," whose spectacles had lenses of orange peel and who played dice on the altar – in Scotland they were known as the Abbots of Unreason.

A parallel stream of influence on the clown of today was provided by the pantomime performers, and none more so than the *commedia dell'arte*. The precise origins of the *commedia dell'arte* are obscure, but their evolution can be likened to the spontaneous development of a popular cult – although their ancestry, rooted in the plays and mimes of ancient Greece and Rome, is not hard to detect. By the

VICTORIA AND ALBERT MUSEUM

John Ducrow, son of Andrew the great horseman, with his animal tea-party.

latter half of the sixteenth century, however, certain companies of Italian players had become renowned for their distinctive type of acting. In essence it was improvisation, brilliant improvisation - only the scenario was known beforehand, the rest they made up as they went along. Soon stock jokes and situations began to develop, soon each actor came to be identified with a specific role. From each town or province came the principal actors – Harlequin from Bergamo, Pantaloon from Venice, the Doctor from Bologna, Punchinello from Naples. Their characters also evolved and it was not long before Harlequin, who had always been the tumbler of the troupe, began to turn into a creature of wit and humor, with a spiteful twist to his nature, a sort of fiendish tumbler. There too were the *Zanni*, the comic servants of the *commedia*, one a cunning character, the other a blundering oaf.

The *commedia dell'arte* visited, and quite enraptured, Paris in the late sixteenth century. Their art was fantasy at its best. Instantly, the audience was transported into a land of monster and make-believe, where the actors might create shivers of fear and apprehension but where the whole was so fantastic as to be more entertaining than frightening. The *Comedie Italienne* became the rage of Paris and it was not long before the resulting plays began to assume a French hue. The Italian Piero had become Pierrot, Colombina was now Columbine and a new character Gilles or Gros-Guillaume, emerged – a French clown. Soon the puppet shows and tightrope dancers were being rivaled by mime shows at the great fairs of Saint-Germain and Saint-Laurent. Pantomime – as the term was first used – was becoming an art form, with Harlequin playing the lead role.

The Harlequinade found its way to England in the sixteenth century and gained an immediate popularity. It was in high demand and even rivaled the native Punchinello – the puppet Punch. The masques of the Stuart era were indeed often begun by a character wearing bright and fantastic dress – a role performed by the carpet-clown of today. By 1800 Harlequin was a stereotype creature of sparkling silk and symmetrical patches which had succeeded the motley uniform with which he had started life. He also possessed magical powers and the mask, which at one time had hidden all his face, now covered only his upper features: when it was up he could be seen, but when down he was supposed to be invisible. He was supported by a butt – Pantaloon – an old man who invariably did the wrong thing, and a simple rustic "clown," the *stupidus* or buffoon, known variously as Blunder, Dulman, Simon, Clodpate or Clodpoll, a sort of country idiot who sported a red wig. Old Grim was this sort of clown, while Joey Grimaldi used to work in a trio of harlequin, pantaloon and himself as clown.

So the clown gradually evolved. When Astley and Hughes opened their amphitheaters a Mr. Merryman was to be found in the cast. It was he who got in the way, annoyed the ringmaster, and amused people between acts. His true title was "Clown to the Horsemanship," for he assisted the equestrian riders, or hindered them. One of Astley's Mr. Merrymen was Charles Hughes himself, before he broke away to found his Royal Circus. Another, who worked for Hughes, was called Ricketts, the same Bill Ricketts who in 1792 set up a circus in Philadelphia and can be said to have created the first circus in the United States – he in turn had his Mr. Merrymen.

The best known of Astley's clowns was Dicky Usher. He employed the boys from nearby Westminster School to write his jokes and sketches – the best he performed in the ring – an interesting and early use of the scriptwriter, unpaid. Dicky Usher possessed a keen sense of publicity and one day, to attract people to his act, he entered the Thames in a barrel apparently pulled by four geese – which he named Gabble, Gibble, Gobble and Garble. To all intents and purposes the geese were towing him downstream, but in reality a boat was pulling him forward by a sunken towrope. The publicity stunt was repeated several times by different clowns in later years, and it was always received with acclaim.

As the first half of the nineteenth century passed, Mr. Merrymen gave way to the white-faced clown we know today. His mask is said by some to derive from that of Pierrot in the Harlequinade; others attribute it to Gros-Guillaume, the French clown of the *Comedie Italienne*, who dipped his face in flour – and whose final flourish to his act was to blow it all

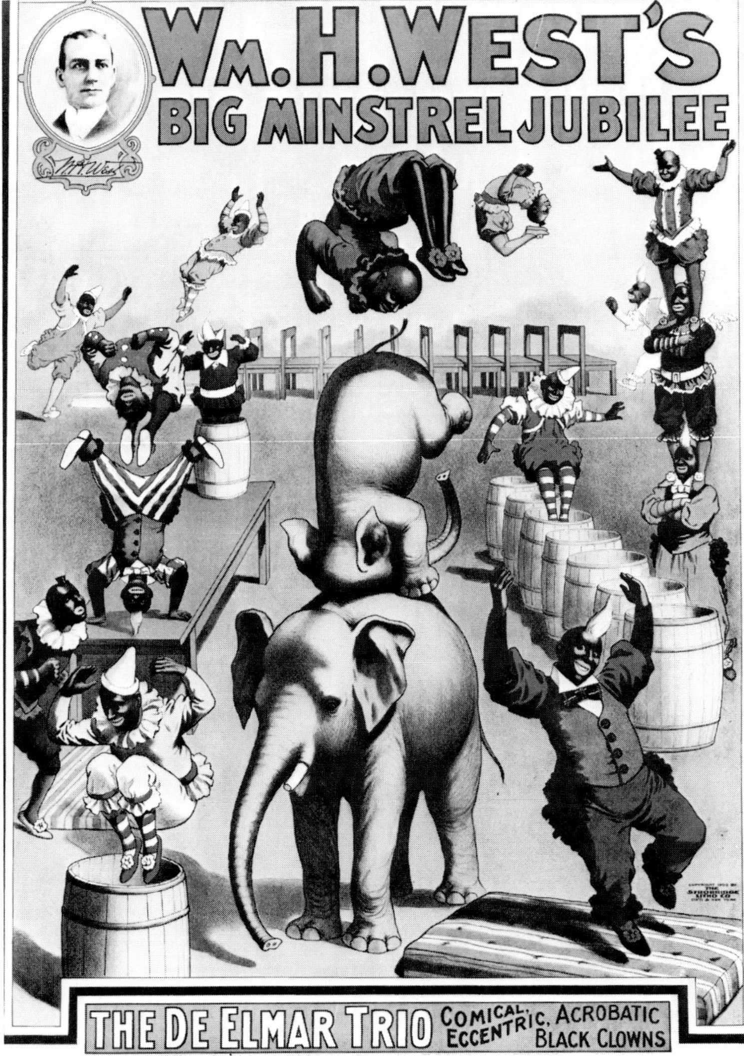

Minstrel Clowns, a popular act on both sides of the Atlantic in the last century.

off again, to the immense delight of the audience. Others still associate it with the age-old habit of comic characters to disguise their faces – the Romans used soot on theirs, "devils" in the Middle Ages sported red noses and their more earthly counterparts used the lees of wine. More recently, minstrels, who were the rage on both sides of the Atlantic for decades from the 1840s, and who had succeeded the dusky-faced gentlemen who were collectively known as Ethiopian Serenaders, used burnt cork. The appearance and the music of the minstrels was another milestone in the evolution of the circus clown.

Talking clowns and Shakespearean clowns, who would regale their audience with witty prattle, subtle jest, quotes and parodies, were soon lost in the huge circuses in the golden days of the circus. From then on, and to the present day, it is basically a mime show which we see at the circus. Mime, usually with a heavy and distinctive make-up.

NATIONAL FILM ARCHIVE, LONDON

NOVOSTI PRESS AGENCY

CIRCUS WORLD MUSEUM, BARABOO, WISCONSIN

But it is useless smearing on grease-paint – the result will look a mess. Every trace of make-up must be applied with exquisite care, although later the experienced clown can don his disguise in a matter of a few minutes, and in the dark if he has to. The design of the face make-up must conform to the contours and lines of the face, otherwise the friendly smile may turn into a fearsome grimace, enough to send any child screaming to its mother. Eventually, after much trial and error, the winning face emerges, one too which conforms to the personality of the wearer. In England the chosen design is then painted on an egg – the clown's "face" is now his own, in effect he has patented it. But what of his dress?

Grotesqueness is the key – a theme adopted by clowns through the centuries, because human beings laugh at grotesqueness as they do at deformity. Too-large shoes, a coat which could fit a giant, trousers which would barely fit a dwarf, disproportion and lumpishness characterize the dress of most clowns. Coco, a famous British clown, had two styles of dress; one was an old cap with peak at the side, a big baggy coat, a too-large dress shirt, collar and black tie askew, steel-rimmed spectacles and a walrus mustache. His other costume was a floppy, baggy check suit, huge round nose with raised eyebrows, vast, flapping boots twenty-five inches long and lank red hair which he could make stand on end – the fright wig. Gradually, as he perfected his act, he increasingly assumed his second dress, and it was as a red-haired clown that he came to be known and loved.

Grimaldi adopted a number of costumes but they were all designed to create something apart from his fellow men. Sometimes he would caricature a dandy in all his finery; at other times he would wear a fancy-dress version of a servant's livery. The blue crest he sometimes adopted was a take-off of that on a horseguard's helmet. The red cheeks, were an aping of a bucolic rustic or perhaps a mocking of the fashionable beauty-spot. Chaplin concentrated on ill-fitting clothes and an absurd appearance which was heightened by his flat-footed, shuffling walk.

To the average member of the audience, a clown is a clown, a clever fellow, a very funny guy, but his seems an easy job and one soon mastered. They could hardly be more wrong. As Coco, (Nicolai Petrovich Poliakoff), who was a favorite with European audiences for many years, described in his book *Coco the Clown*, when he was setting out on his illustrious career he was told that he must first become an acrobat, then a trapeze artist, a rider and a tumbler before he could think of becoming a clown – he was also a brilliant juggler, as it happens. Whimsical Walker, who bestrode the clown stage in England for much of the first half of this century, was in turn a tightrope walker, a trapeze artist and an equestrian before, in old age, he turned to clowning. Indeed many clowns do not take on their new profession until well into their

LIBRARY OF CONGRESS

ABOVE: *Clown Cavalcade with Barnum & Bailey at the turn of the century.* OPPOSITE, ABOVE LEFT: *Clown Face. The immortal Grock.* RIGHT: *Clown Faces. Gary Henry and Tom Sink of the Hoxie Bros. Circus in 1976.* CENTER LEFT: *Clown Face. Oleg Popov, the little genius of the Russian circus, who uses hardly any makeup.* RIGHT: *Otto Griebling.* BELOW LEFT: *Emmett Kelly as the immortal Weary Willie, the hobo clown.* RIGHT: *Emmett Kelly Jr., carrying on the family tradition.*

HUBERT CASTLE INTERNATIONAL CIRCUS

ABOVE: *Clown Costume. Lee Marx. One of the clowns with the Hubert Castle International Circus.* OPPOSITE, ABOVE LEFT: *But sometimes animal acts go wrong. Popov and the lion.* RIGHT: *Coco. Bertram Mills' great clown in the costume known and loved by thousands.* BELOW LEFT: *The much-loved Felix Adler.* RIGHT: *Clown Act. Lou Jacobs the master clown and a favorite of American audiences for years. Here seen at the Ringling Bros. and Barnum & Bailey Bicentennial Edition.*

sixties, when age and infirmity have barred them from further active life in the circus which they have probably served all their days. And some clowns have lived to an immense age, one famous American clown was still amusing children when he was over a hundred. For the clown is probably the most versatile performer in the circus. It is difficult enough to walk a slack wire, it is incomparably more so to pretend to fall off and at the same time wrap the performance in high comedy. There is nothing easy about the art of clowning.

The great Grock once said that his acts were conceived by what some call luck and poets called inspiration. Inspiration it may well have been, but no amount of inspiration will suffice unless the clown also has that sixth sense of knowing what an audience likes and how he can make them laugh. The tale is told of how Grock, who amongst his other accomplishments was the musical clown supreme – he could play no less than seventeen musical instruments – was clowning at a piano in the ring. The piano was on boards but the rest of the ring was covered in deep sand. So deep that his chair stuck firmly in it. Such a consummate artist as Grock would never be seen struggling to get the chair out, so rather than push the chair to the piano, he pushed the piano to the chair and the crowd loved it. Another twist, another touch of clowning magic was added to Grock's repertoire. Coco's famous water acts would bring the house down at Olympia in London. But they all started when a bucket of water became dislodged and fell on Coco's head during a performance, stunning the clown and sending him reeling about the ring as though drunk, to the utter delight of the audience. From there it was a simple matter to find a less solid bucket. Inspiration came to the aid of Billy Hayden, a British clown who worked on the Continent. He was at first a minstrel, but when performing in Germany one day he had the brilliant idea of wearing a white face rather than a dusky one. By that one change he escaped from the grind of mediocre clowndom to become an instant success.

The creator of the burlesque, the knock-about clown in the circus – the Auguste (he is called the Toni in Italy, the Red-Haired Clown in Russia) is commonly believed to have been a man by the name of Tom Belling. Belling was a colorful character, a brilliant acrobat, juggler, tightrope walker and horseman, who had led the life of a gypsy for many years and walked across Russia and much of Siberia with a small traveling circus. Then he had taken to running the stables of a Russian prince, at a fabulous salary. His fortune was soon dissipated and for all his life Belling lurched from great riches to extreme poverty. During one of the latter spells, in 1864, he found his way to Berlin where he performed as acrobat, juggler and musical clown with the famed Renz Circus. Father Renz was a stickler for discipline and, for falling during a performance, Belling had been banished to his

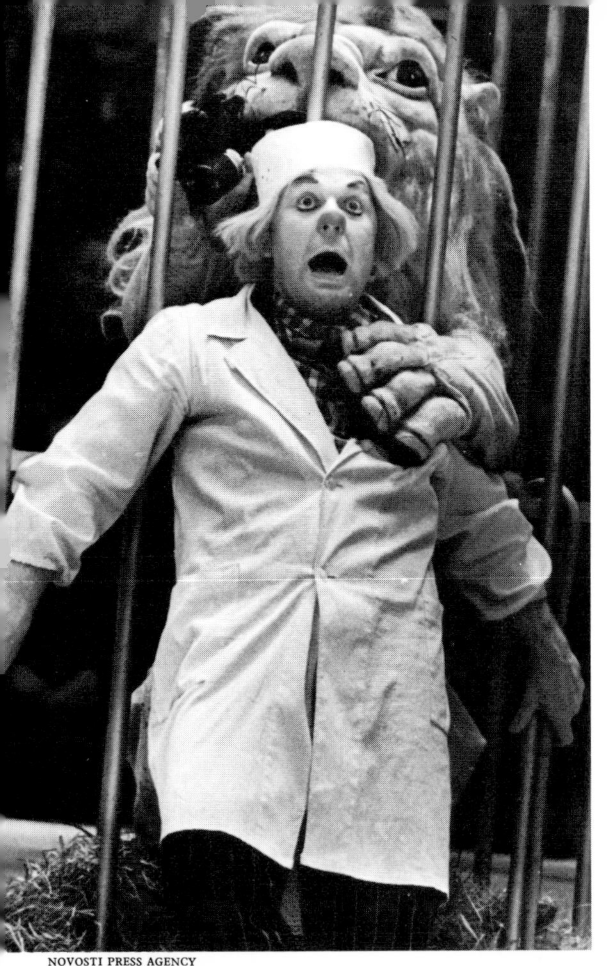

NOVOSTI PRESS AGENCY

VICTORIA AND ALBERT MUSEUM

CIRCUS WORLD MUSEUM, BARABOO, WISCONSIN

RINGLING BROS. AND BARNUM & BAILEY CIRCUS

OPPOSITE, ABOVE: *Clown Act. Water "slosh" acts are always popular. These are the Brizio clowns from Italy.*
BELOW: *Good old-fashioned slapstick at the Blackpool Tower Circus with Charlie Cairoli and Jimmy Buchanan.*

room for four weeks – a very serious matter for a clown with no money saved. Wearying of his incarceration, the prisoner tried on a wig back-to-front, put his coat on inside-out and made his way stealthily to watch the performance hoping to remain unrecognized. To his horror, he came face to face with old Renz. Staggering away from the dreaded presence, Tom Belling fell backward into the ring itself. He tried to pull himself upright on one of the ropes but missed his hold and fell again. The crowd, at first stupified by the sudden appearance of this remarkable creature were mesmerized into silence, but at his second fall and imagining he was part of a new act, they roared with delight and someone in the back shouted "Auguste, Auguste" ("Stupid" in the Berlin dialect). Belling recovered himself and fled from the scene only to be confronted by Renz beaming with delight, who said "You are good. You are good," and gave him another push back into the ring. So the Auguste was born.

There are four types of clown act; reprise clowns are those who interrupt serious turns and make amusing nuisances of themselves; musical clowns, who can usually play a bewildering selection of instruments; entrée clowns, or gag clowns – the clowns supreme of the circus; and carpet-clowns, also called run-in clowns who are those who come in to fill in an interval between acts while scenery or props are being shifted, and who often mix with the audience. In small circuses they may be the tentmen, grooms and other "extras" of the show. Occasionally they are old performers, those whom it would be cruel to fire from the only world they have known and loved, and who have turned to clowning as age and infirmity have taken their toll.

Clown types have now narrowed down to three; the white-faced Joey – in spangled suit and white dunce's hat; the knock-about fall-guy clown, the Auguste; and the Charlie, the successor of the tramp act of Charlie Chaplin. To the average audience a clown act is one of high comedy, any fool, they say, can be a clown. But it is not enough to paint your face and wear funny clothes. The art of the great clowns through the ages is that they have been able to portray their feelings by a change of expression or a simple gesture. Emmet Kelly, the hobo clown, is a case in point.

He started in the circus as a trapeze artiste in the 1920s and from time to time he doubled as a white-faced clown. For twelve years he worked this routine in circuses across America. Then gradually a Hobo act, using as character a migrant worker he had seen many years before, began to evolve; and so the immortal Weary Willie, the sad-faced clown, arrived on the scene. Weary Willie would mournfully and lackadaisically work his way through an audience, never talking, never laughing, never changing his expression, but, through superb mime, convulsing audiences throughout the United States and Europe.

BBC COPYRIGHT

BLACKPOOL TOWER COMPANY. PHOTOGRAPH BY BARNET SAIDMAN

He would come up to a woman in the audience and level a soulful stare at her, quietly munching an enormous cabbage or a loaf of bread, and never taking his eyes off his chosen victim. Soon he found the knack of spotting those women who found his act irresistibly funny, or better still, the escort of a lady who did not. At other times he would join the audience as they shuffled forward to take their seats, and place himself next to an unsuspecting person, never uttering a word.

While Kelly was the sad-faced guy out on his luck and doing nothing about it, another hobo clown had a different technique. This was Otto Griebling who performed last at the centenary of The Greatest Show on Earth at Madison Square Gardens in 1970, on his 74th birthday – he died two years later. He had been born in Coblenz near the turn of the century. His father, a grocer, died when the boy was thirteen. His mother then emigrated to America leaving the young Griebling apprenticed to a bareback rider and clown rider. In 1930 he had a bad fall and broke both his legs. Never again could he do his riding acts so instead he determined to turn full-time clown.

While still on his back he taught himself juggling. He read every book he could lay his hands on about the art of mime. He studied all he could find on clowns and the theater. For twenty years he worked up his routine until in 1951 he joined Ringlings and for years worked alongside Emmet Kelly. When Kelly left, Griebling took over the limelight and immediately made a tremendous impact.

His dress was that of a tramp, but with heavier makeup; his clothes, if that were possible, were even more disreputable and appeared to be held together only by the matted dirt with which they were covered. He never spoke – in fact, his voice box had been removed when he had cancer of the throat – but every gesture was calculated, although it appeared spontaneous. His timing, or tempo, was exact and the result of long years of careful study. Some think he was the supreme clown – but certainly, as with Grimaldi, they could say of Otto Griebling "every limb of him had a language."

Griebling would stride into the ring banging two tin plates together to attract attention. A little bit of plate juggling caught the audience's eye, and then, with his head on one side, he would listen intently to the applause. He would cross to the other side of the ring, repeat the performance and listen again. Thus he would play one side of the ring off against the other until merely by walking over, putting his head to one side and pretending to listen, he would have his audience applauding wildly. But when one side did not come up to his expectation, the expression of disgust and disappointment which he adopted caused the applause to redouble – he was a master of audience arousal.

A play in which he was supposed to deliver a thirty-

OPPOSITE: *Clown Costume. Whimsical Walker the great English clown.*

pound block of ice to a mythical Mrs. Schultz was another routine certain to have the audience in convulsions as the ice gradually melted away. He was a true clowning genius.

Another of the great clowns is Oleg Popov, star of the Moscow State Circus – known to his many admirers as the Sunny Clown. He started his career as a juggler and slack-wire artiste and later became a traditional clown with the usual heavy makeup, but found that this hindered the style of clowning which came most naturally to him. He now uses practically no makeup and his preparation for a performance consists of darkening his eyelids and mouth, and giving a touch of shadow to accentuate his already turned-up nose. A baggy jacket, enormous shoes and a distinctive floppy check cap – and he is ready. He is another master of mime, a little genius who can switch his character and mood by a simple change of expression and with a few props. He can give quite ordinary actions a humor of their own, for he, like other masters of his profession, can extract mirth out of nothing and less than nothing. It may be the current range of Russian washing-machine which breaks down when first used, it may be something else which is topical and he can transform the petty everyday annoyances into something enjoyable and amusing. Some of his work is on the lines of the satire of his great Russian forebear, Vladimir Durov, but it is a more pointed satire that combines the gentle fun poked at society with the irrepressible slapstick and repartee of, say, the Marx Brothers. But it is irresistibly funny.

Popov prides himself on being a clown of the people – a "simple little fellow in love with life" – and so have been the great clowns in history. Emmet Kelly, in his book *Clown*, said, "I am a sad, ragged little guy who is very serious about everything he attempts – no matter how futile or how foolish it appears to be. I am the hobo who found out the hard way that the deck is stacked, the dice 'frozen,' the race fixed and the wheel crooked, but there is always present that one, tiny, forlorn spark of hope still glimmering in his soul which makes him keep on trying. . . ."

Charlie Chaplin once described the philosophy behind his own dress: "The costume helps me to express my conception of the average man, of myself. The derby, too small, is striving for dignity. The mustache is vanity. The tightly-buttoned coat and the stick and his whole manner are a gesture towards gallantry and dash. . . ."

Deburau, the greatest mime of all time, who held all Paris in thrall at his genius in the 1830s and 1840s, put his portrayal of Gilles, the Pierrot, slightly differently, "Gilles is of the people. Gilles is at times happy, sad, sick, well, beating people or being beaten, musician, poet of comedy, always poor, always of the people. He knows what makes people laugh, what amuses them, what makes them angry . . . he possesses them, to their very souls."

Five Celebrated Clowns. A magnificent poster showing some of the clowns with the Sands, Nathans Co.'s Circus in 1856.

A reporter, on seeing Grimaldi, once said, "The face of Grimaldi is a source of laughter, night after night, to many hundreds of people, it is a living jest-book, in which may be read all the whimsical notions which owe their birth to his prolific fancy. There is not, perhaps, a more perfect *figure of fun* to be found in existence . . . his buffoonery is inimitable and in the pit there immediately appears a sea of pleasure; and the people roll backwards and forwards like waves." For a clown can transform a circus by his presence and personality and the infectious gaiety of which he is master, the pegs on which the circus stands.

Through it all we see the touch of Grimaldi. Grimaldi was topical, he was master of the many facets of his art, above all he could transform the ordinary into something comical – and he was first to do so on the stage. As have clowns since then, he gave great pleasure to his audience, but he also gave more, for he could give happiness. And that is a gift bestowed on very few.

Be jolly, be alive, be light,
Twitch, flirt, caper, tumble, fall and throw,
Grow up right ugly in thy father's sight,
And be an "absolute old Joseph," like Old Joe.

ON THE GROUND

With the sinking of the paddle steamer, the year 1885 started disastrously for Buffalo Bill's Wild West. This mishap, together with bad weather which led to poor attendances, dampened all their spirits.

Therefore it was a chastened troupe which arrived at last in New Orleans; and they were to remain chastened for forty days as torrential rain poured down. The only bright spot had been the performance, with a gun, of a young lady touring in New Orleans with her husband in the Sells Circus and whom Cody had seen and promptly signed up – although no written contract was drawn, nor indeed did she ever have one with Buffalo Bill. She had been born in Woodland, Ohio on August 13, 1860, and christened Phoebe Ann Moses, Sitting Bull called her Little Sure Shot, but to the world she was known as Annie Oakley.

In those days game abounded in the woods around the Moses family homestead and Annie would often borrow her brother's musket and shoot for food. Her prowess and reputation increased. By the age of twelve she was almost a professional hunter, shooting game for the market and to keep the family, for her father had died when she was only six. She also entered, and for the most part won, shooting contests. On one of these, she was pitted against the famed Frank Butler and beat him fair and square. Soon afterward they married and, as a husband-and-wife team, toured the country giving exhibition shoots and displays of marksmanship of a very fine order.

Shotgun, rifle or pistol, they were all the same to Little Sure Shot. She was also an excellent trick rider – one of her favorite tricks was to untie a handkerchief tied to the pastern of her horse while at full gallop. On one occasion she shot a dime piece held by some hapless attendant between his forefinger and thumb. The pips of playing cards were

ANNIE OAKLEY
To Miss Annie Oakley From Her Old Home Friends Greenville Ohio July 25th 1900
A FEATURE OF NUTLEY N. J. AMATEUR CIRCUS MARCH.94.
SHOOTING DOUBLES FROM A WHEEL
Annie Oakley
LONDON 1887
A SPECIAL FEATURE WITH
A FLYING DOUBLE SHOT
COMPETING IN GRAND AMERICAN HANDICAP INTERSTATE PARK, L.I.
BUFFALO BILL'S WILD WEST.
THE WILD WEST IN A BLIZZARD TRINIDAD, COL. SEPT. 10 1898.
IN THE AIR AT ONE TIME
A NEW WAY OF SPLITTING A CARD WITH A REVOLVER
THE PEERLESS WING AND RIFLE SHOT

fair game and many a pack must have been ruined by Annie Oakley in her day. However, her greatest feats were reserved for glass balls which were flung into the air: on one memorable occasion, using three 16-bore hammer guns which she loaded herself, she shot 4,772 out of 5,000, and on her second thousand only missed sixteen.

As well as thrilling the crowds with her incredible feats with a gun, Annie Oakley's act served to prepare the audience for the noise and bangs which were to follow, for Cody was very conscious of the fact that nicely brought up gentlefolk were not used to the rip-roaring excitement and shooting which was the hallmark of the Wild West. If they could see this slip of a girl shooting like a man he reckoned that the audience would gain confidence. One of Annie Oakley's most popular tricks was to fire twenty-five rapid shots into separate playing cards and distribute them to the audience. Thus it came about that complimentary tickets, for many years after Little Sure Shot's death, were known as Annie Oakleys – for they had a hole punched in them.

Johnnie Baker, who was usually billed as The Cowboy Kid, was another outstanding marksman in the Wild West Show. To the average audience he was the epitome of "these brave, generous, free-hearted, self-sacrificing rough riders of the plain," as the cowboy was then romanticized, who literally "lived in the saddle, enduring exposure, hunger, risk of health and life" and "directed his aspirations to an emulation of the manly qualities necessary to be ranked a true American Cowboy." Such was an example of the ballyhoo which surrounded Johnnie Baker. Cody virtually adopted young Johnnie who stayed with the show as marksman and ultimately as "arenic director" to the very end. A principal attraction was the simulated rivalry between Annie Oakley, who coached the young cowboy, and Johnnie Baker. But it was never a fair match as Annie always won.

Cody himself was no mean man with a gun, but always billed himself as "A Practical All-round Shot" and he filled his show with other marksmen, the most noted of which was Captain A. H. Bogardus.

Bogardus had first been a wildfowler who shot ducks for the market, but so phenomenal was his prowess that he soon took to competition shooting. This was a time when shooting clubs were sprouting all over the United States and Bogardus with his trick and stamina shooting was a popular attraction. His favorite game was to run up a high score of hits and then promptly to beat it next time out. Passenger pigeons were the popular target and on one occasion he accounted for five hundred in 528 minutes, and using a muzzle-loader which he loaded himself. When pigeons became scarce the competition shooter turned to domestic pigeons, meadowlarks, even to quail and sparrows, but soon the outcry from the humane societies became deafening and

Bogardus invented a machine which threw hollow glass balls $2\frac{1}{8}$ inches in diameter – a forerunner of the clay pigeon, which he was also to invent. The early editions were made of baked red clay which sometimes were as hard as stone and needed to be hit square before they shattered. But it was with glass balls that Bogardus made his reputation.

He was an imposing man, just under six feet in height, who dressed impeccably, and sported a goatee beard and fine mustache. His greatest performance was to shatter 5,000 glass balls in just under 500 minutes, a feat which he achieved in New York City in 1877. For this he used a double-barreled shotgun with interchangeable barrels and had two traps operating. As the shoot continued, the barrels started to sweat, despite being dipped in water to keep them cool; so did Bogardus and by the time 2,000 had been broken, the great shot was in shirt sleeves. By 3,000 he was suffering from acute cramp. By 4,700 he was sitting down to shoot but with the 5,156th glass ball he had scored his 5,000. It had taken 480 minutes and 45 seconds. No wonder he was called the "Master Manipulator of the Shot-Gun and Champion Wing-Shot of the World," and no one disputed that he had surely earned the title.

The whole shooting world was to be taken aback some months later, though, when a complete unknown said that he could better anything Bogardus did – that was brash enough, in all conscience; but the interloper even proposed to do it using a rifle! The feat was clearly impossible and the challenger Dr. W. F. Carver was written off as a cheapster and poseur. But Carver persisted in his challenge and even sent the newspaper editors half-dollar pieces with holes neatly drilled through the centers. On June 1, 1878, Carver arrived in New York City. He was a magnificent figure of a man, six feet two inches in height with long waving hair and a vivid red mustache. He wore a costume of black velvet shirt, light gray trousers and deerskin gloves and a fawn-colored sombrero completed the outfit.

Carver's history was as amazing as the man. Born in New York State in 1844, he had been taken out West at the age of four and fallen into the hands of the Sioux Indians who had massacred his mother and sisters. He had been brought up as a Sioux brave until a white trader spotted the boy and, struck by his appearance, enquired about his history and then brought him back East. After a brief and scanty education, Carver added the letters D.D.S. to his name and returned to the West as a dentist. Thus "Doctor" W. F. Carver became a professional hunter and a quite remarkable competition shot. Bogardus and he never actually met in a make-or-break contest, but his performances were nonetheless startling enough on their own. On one memorable occasion, using six Winchester rifles he broke 5,500 glass balls in seven hours dead and used only 6,212 shots.

Tumbling is one of the oldest of athletic arts. These are ancient Egyptian tumblers.

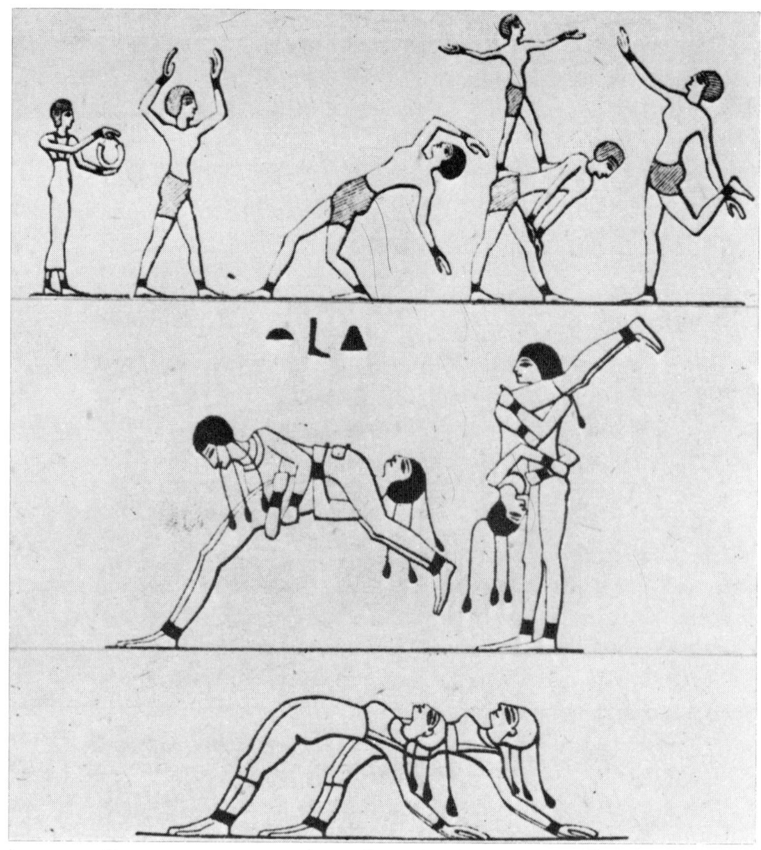

Carver too, was signed up by Buffalo Bill, and the followers of Annie Oakley and the magnificent doctor had a rare time cheering on their own champions. There were other challengers too; another doctor, Dr. A. H. Ruth shot 984 out of 1,000, Annie Oakley dropped only 37 out of her 1,000, while Carver continued his amazing career and staggering feats of not only shooting skill but sheer athletic stamina. At New Haven he performed the incredible feat of shooting for six consecutive days at 64,888 targets, breaking 60,016 of them, a drop of something over 4,000. Not satisfied by this, he tried again on a later date. This time out of 60,000 he demolished all but 650.

According to one authority, the style of the old ground acrobatic feats reflected the nature of their national characteristics – deeply thought out and methodical by the Germans; graceful and bold by the French; full of vigor and endurance by the Anglo-Saxons; impetuous by the Italians; light and delicate by the Spaniards; while the Japanese performed their act as though it were part of a solemn religious rite.

Japanese acts started to make their appearance during the 1870s in Europe and elsewhere and created a sensation with their skill and versatility. Their dress of silken kimonos added an extra dimension to the circus scene. It would appear to have been the Japanese who first introduced western artistes to what is known as the perch-pole act. One man would balance a long and very flexible bamboo on his shoulder and another would shin up and secure his wrist or his ankle to a loop at the top, from which insecure perch he would perform every kind of gymnastic feat while his compatriot kept the whole device aloft. A variation is to use a ladder instead of a pole.

Nothing, though, compares with the whirlwind of the Arab tumblers who sparkle and scintillate in India-rubber jumps across the floor, performing flip-flaps in what appears to be almost perpetual motion, who throw each other about like a juggler with his balls. Early Arab troupes were often thirty or even forty strong and of all ages. They literally filled the ring with astonishing feats – twists, triple pirouettes, scintillating flip-flaps – all conducted with a fury which was almost frightening, according to reports of the time. From afar, an Arab act looked like a turbulent pond of white. And they were no mean exponents of the juggling art.

Juggling is another of the traditional fairground arts which the circus has adapted to its use over the years. The word is derived from the Latin *joculator* and associated with the bards and jesters of old. It is still an integral part of the art of the clown and many of the great names of the clown world were accomplished jugglers. Patience and perseverance are the watchwords in juggling and, of course, an infinity of practice. Of all circus arts, juggling is the one which owes less to artificial aids and more to natural aptitude than any other. That is to become an ordinary juggler, but to become a master of the art requires an extra piece of indefinable magic, an instinct faster than rational thought which makes the hand act almost by itself.

"Nothing compares with the whirlwind of the Arab tumblers who sparkle and scintillate in Indian-rubber jumps across the floor." Bedouin Arabs were a popular attraction in circuses during the last century.

VICTORIA AND ALBERT MUSEUM

OPPOSITE, ABOVE: *Jugglers at the Moscow State Circus.* BELOW: *The Drouguettes, a juggling quintet.*

One who had this magic in full measure was the immortal Paul Cinquevalli. Many of the best jugglers are also skilled in other circus talents. Cinquevalli was no exception and it was as a trapeze artist that he first made his reputation. He was born in Prussia and had spent his early performing career with a band of traveling acrobats. His own specialities then were leaping and acrobatics, but he had long wished to turn juggler. His wish came true when one day he had a crashing fall from his trapeze and so injured his ankle that he could never perform on the swings again.

In one of his most famous tricks he placed a stemmed wine glass in his mouth, in this rested a billiard ball and on top of the ball was balanced a regular-sized billiard cue, point downward! This was difficult enough, but at the end of the cue on the heel end which was some ten feet up in the air by this time, rested not one billiard ball but two. In fact all was not quite as it seemed as the two uppermost billiard balls were slightly "doctored," the one on the cue heel was very slightly flattened and between the two was a slim rubber washer. Nevertheless, the achievement of getting the whole contraption up and balancing a billiard cue, point down on the rounded surface of a billiard ball – which was a normal one – is still astonishing.

One trick, which had no trickery, was even more astonishing. In his mouth he placed a deep dish and on its upper edge balanced the curved part of a very flexible coachman's whip. At the handle end he placed an ordinary plate and then set the whole revolving. A trick which had the crowd gasping was the catching of a forty-pound cannonball on his neck. The deviation of an inch would have killed him instantly.

Another of the greatest jugglers of all times was Rastelli, who died in 1931 of blood poisoning at the age of thirty-four – though some say it was of overwork for he never left off practicing. He could juggle nineteen objects at the same time – nine balls and ten plates. But his greatest feat was with footballs, ten of them. As he sat on a stool he held a soccer ball on each instep and another one on each knee. Two more were balanced on a mouth-stick, and a couple on a forehead stick as well, while he had one spinning on the top of the forefinger of each hand.

Juggling with humans is always an impressive and popular feature in any circus performance. This is called the Risley act. Someone lies on his back in the form of a cradle which supports the lower spine and enables him to keep his legs in the air for a phenomenal length of time while he juggles with his feet. This was the antipodean act, as it was called, of the old fairground, a popular attraction in the eighteenth century. In those days they would juggle with balls, barrels and particularly a wooden contraption shaped like a Maltese cross. Then in the early years of the nineteenth cen-

NOVOSTI PRESS AGENCY

HAMID-MORTON CIRCUS

NOVOSTI PRESS AGENCY

BLACKPOOL TOWER COMPANY. PHOTOGRAPH BY BARNET SAIDMAN

ABOVE: *Sensation at Astley's. The great Dutch Equilibrist's bottle feat. Herr Amidi Neuporte in 1846.*
OPPOSITE, ABOVE: *A modern Risley Act.*
BELOW: *Ball work at the feet of the Diors Sisters.*

tury a gentleman by the name of Risley had the brilliant idea that it would be more spectacular to juggle with a human being. So the Risley boys came into being and a sordid chapter in the history of the circus began. For these waifs were, according to legend, kept like animals – the Risley boys in circus history were the lowest of the low and when being tossed up in the air and turned by the feet of the Risley artiste, they had to be as stiff as boards, yet as bouncy as rubber balls – no easy combination. A circus rhyme of the day went:

Risley kids and slanging buffers, [performing dogs]
Lord only knows how they suffers.

For their training was said to have been even more brutal than that meted out to wild animals. When one of

Leonardo, Wizard of the spinning plates.

these unfortunates fell during a performance it was even said that his master hurriedly burned the body.

Despite these gruesome origins, the Risley acts, or what the French called *Les Jeux Icariens* – because the person being tossed about at the end of the legs was supposed to emulate the flight of Icarus who flew toward the sun until the heat melted the wax holding his wings together; but with a normally safer ending – live on and are a regular feature of circus programs today. Human pyramids are often formed on the outstretched feet, juggling with tables, chairs, balls and small animals are all part of a modern Risley turn.

Around the time Mr. Risley invented his act, leaping was almost as popular with the circus audience as the equestrian feats. This too was a common fairground act, a development from ground tumbling. At first the leaper would take off from a springless but slightly inclined platform – the jump-up board – to give him sufficient elevation to perform his feats in the air. From this primitive ramp the early circus leapers made their jumps and soared over horses, men and elephants (when they came in vogue). The highlight of Ricketts's performance was his leap from this primitive launching pad over ten horses. The younger Astley took such leaps in his stride, as did all the early names in the history of the circus, Ducrow, Levi J. North, the Franconi and many others.

BRARY OF CONGRESS

Equilibrists of 1898. The Livingstone, Davenne and de Mora troupe performing with the Forepaugh and Sells circus.

It was not long, however, before the primitive springboard appeared to many to be inadequate both as a spectacle and as a drawer of the crowds. Someone, who is lost to history, had the idea that instead of running along the ring floor to the incline and thus over what ever obstacle lay ahead, a better momentum could be attained by running down a long incline and then up a long springy board to an even more springy pole placed across their path and from there up and over the elephants or whatever was in the way. This was the springboard in use in the heyday of the great leapers when the relative merits of performers would be argued with as much vigor as the worth of today's football teams. On this type of springboard, the enthusiast felt, there seemed almost nothing that man could not do, and enthusiasm for leaping feats lasted until the advent of the three-ring circus when such personal performances as these would have been lost in the vastness of the arena.

The single somersault – either the ball-up, when the leaper tucks in his legs as soon as he takes off, or the lay-out, when instead he executes a swallow dive and then tucks just before landing at the farther end – was easy meat. So too became the double, which demanded a prodigious leap to perform well. Competition was hot between leapers and a form of contest would be gone through at each circus performance as to which of the team could leap furthest over what obstacle. The winners were the folk heroes of the hour. But if a man could do a double, what was to stop him doing the triple? So started the long history of the triple somersault from a springboard, a quest which has been the cause of more deaths in the circus than any other single feat.

The sheer mechanics of the triple are awe-inspiring. It has been calculated that the average man must leave a springboard and do a single somersault at an angle of around thirty degrees from the horizontal. The same angle is necessary for a double, but the leaper must of course leave the springboard with a vastly increased velocity to stay in the air long enough to turn twice before he falls into the hands of the catchers waiting on the far side. Momentum, angle of flight and sufficient height are the three factors involved. Too high and he will fall short; too low and he will run out of impetus before clearing the obstacle and fall short again; too slow and he will run out of momentum at the wrong time. To do a triple it was necessary to rise a third higher than with the double, and that involved a prodigious leap.

The triple nagged the conscience of any respectable leaper. The double was now commonplace, various trick acrobatics were incorporated in the act – the number, size and sort of beast over which they jumped was varied. But still the triple shone as a tempting jade. Many tried and many died. A number performed it in practice once or twice, and then failed the next time. One leaper overstepped the mark when doing a double, found he was still turning, held his tuck, as the expression goes, and landed safely. The lure of the dangerous and seemingly impossible proved irresistible. Yet surely if it could be done in practice it must be possible to do it in public and to announce it beforehand.

It seemed, as those lucky ones who had survived the experience avowed, that the human brain could not keep control after two quick turns in the air, that it lost all sense of direction and worse, of timing. An aerialist attempting the triple has the faintly comforting knowledge that if he does not succeed, at least some fifty or so feet below him lies the safety net and that he will have recovered his full consciousness by the time he is due to hit it. The leaper has no such consolation. At the height of his leap he may be little more than fifteen feet up in the air, by the time his turn is complete he may be less than the height of an average door above the ground or his catching blanket – there is simply no time to adjust. Either it is a perfect leap and he can land exactly as he should or his friends can call the undertaker.

The leapers knew this, they knew of the steadily

lengthening list of fatalities, yet still they persisted. Hardly a year passed when somewhere a leaper did not either kill himself or was so seriously injured, and mercifully perhaps so frightened, that he never tried again. Then, in 1874, came the breakthrough when a leaper called John Worland performed the triple at St. Louis. His first two attempts all but succeeded, at his third try he landed on his feet. The impossible had been done, and before a paying audience. He tried again a couple of years later, but ended up sitting down. The failure nagged him. Skeptics reckoned it was a fluke, that it had happened by mistake and could not be done deliberately. Worland seethed and finally could take the sneers no more. He announced in New Haven, Connecticut, that before the assembled dignitaries of the town, and a bevy of newspaper men, he would perform the triple. As the great circus writer Earl Chapin May describes in his classic *From Rome to Ringling* which was published in 1932:

> At the appointed hour the big band stopped. James Melville, of a famous old circus family, acted as master of ceremonies and orator. Runway, springboard and landing tick were carefully placed and meticulously inspected. Gentlemen gymnasts lined up on the runway. One of them ran gracefully down, hit the spring-board and turned a single. Another followed and turned a double.
>
> There was a brief pause noted by life insurance agents. John Worland flicked imaginary flecks of dust from his spangled trunks and leotard, ran lightly to the waiting spring-board, sprang from it with a modest effort and, balling up, actually turned thrice before he straightened out and hit the tick, all standing and in perfect order. The triple somersault – from a circus springboard, as per announcement and before a paying audience – had become undeniable circus history.
>
> John Worland established his unequalled record because he had mastered the double somersault; would never allow himself to turn a single; knew from long experience that he finished his double without exhausting his energy and ability; believed he could make a third revolution in full control of his mental and physical faculties.

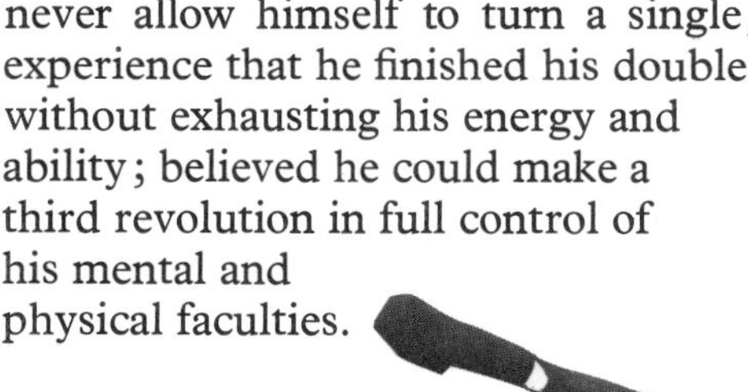

The climax of the act of the Putzai troupe with the Blackpool Tower Circus. All eyes on the last man.

BLACKPOOL TOWER COMPANY. PHOTOGRAPH BY BARNET SAIDMAN

ABOVE: *The Deblars. A famous unicycle troupe of the 1930s in a street parade of their own.*
OPPOSITE: *Rudy Horn, master of the unicycle in one of his most difficult tricks.*

Worland lived to tell the tale but the leapers passed into history. Attempts were made at various times to bring them back into circus vogue, but these never lasted very long. Somehow the breathtaking magic of the true leaper seems to fall flat on a modern audience. But one day, who knows, when the big three rings lose their appeal and circus performers demand the chance to be able to show off their prowess in a more intimate atmosphere, then the leapers may return, and competition once again become fierce between giants of the springboard in the circus ring.

The first of the cycling enthusiasts appeared on the circus scene during the 1840s. Invented in 1816 by a certain Jean de Drais as an apparatus for recreational exercise, it consisted of two wooden wheels placed one in front of the

BLACKPOOL TOWER COMPANY. PHOTOGRAPH BY BARNET SAIDMAN

other some three feet apart and connected to a plank. The person seeking exercise placed one leg on either side of this and proceeded to walk. At the front end was a sort of handlebar which merely helped to keep the contraption upright rather than steering it. The discomfort of the machine and the belief that it could give rise to diseases of the legs soon placed it in the realms of passing fads. The idea remained forgotten until something known as a velocipede was designed by another Frenchman called Michaud. This device had a proper handlebar and pedals on the front wheels, and with these, the way was open for circus acts using the cycle in its general forms. So the acrobatic velocipedes found their way into the circus repertoire.

The first man to master the unicycle, which had been invented in 1869 by a Mr. Hemming who called it the Flying Yankee Velocipede, was an Italian called Scuri who realized the dream of many a circus performer and created a completely new act. He could do everything that his two-wheeled brethren could describe and a lot more, he was even known to have jumped over a table on his single wheel. Another cycle artiste of the time was Harry French whose specialty was to play a mandolin on a unicycle, ride down stairs carrying his brother on his shoulders and finally to skate around the arena with each foot on the axle of unconnected wheels.

The invention of the penny-farthing bicycle, with one enormous wheel and a tiny one in the rear, gave further scope to the cycling artiste. Now with greater stability, acrobats would leap from one bicycle to the other performing remarkable gyrations on the way. As the bicycle became more sophisticated so the circus repertoire of cycling tricks expanded. In the years before the turn of the century we had bicycle polo. Others dived into tanks and tubs of water still on their precious bicycles, a form of bicycle wall of death in a cylinder some twenty feet across was another attraction, but all these were eclipsed by the greater thrill of the motorcycle and later the car in death-defying feats.

The ingenuity of these cycling circus performers was extraordinary. Mademoiselle Ella Zuella – billed as the "Aerial Queen, the Female Blondin" – would ride backward and forward on her velocipede along a thin wire one hundred feet up in the air, maintaining a perfectly easy and graceful position as she defied the laws of gravitation. A penny-farthing-type machine was the one chosen by the Great Leonati, the inimitable Spiral Ascencionist, as he rode his "writhing bicycle" up and then down the dizzy, curving course of a spiral roadway some fifty feet in height. No wonder he was known as the Gymnastic Autocrat of the Aerial Art. His act was only bettered by that of a young Australian, Minting, who in 1902 rode a unicycle up and down a similar incline. Starr, The Shooting Star, would dash down his "Ladder of Fame" from a platform some fifty feet up with such speed that he shot all the way round the circus ring before he came to a stop. Prodigious Porthos elected to hurtle across a fifty-foot gap on his bike; while the Great Diavolo, dressed as Lucifer himself, would descend from the King Pole on a ramp and at ground level turn a complete loop the loop. Bills acclaiming his performance announced:

OVERLEAF: *The Great Diavolo. A thrill act which had the audience gasping – and no wonder.*
FRED D. PFENING COLLECTION

> The Above Incredibly Difficult, Dexterous and far more than outdaring Devil-Dare Achievement. It depopulated other places of amusement. The Metropolitan Press devoted whole pages to Picturing and Praising it. It was the chief topic on every tongue, from the Battery to far beyond the Bronx. Its well-nigh awful audacity fairly stunned the hundreds of thousands who managed to get in ahead of the countless throngs vainly clamoring to see it, and everywhere it was the same. What more is there to say than that we alone exhibit it?

Variations of the cycling theme were provided by, amongst others, the Lady Alphonsine, who walked her way up a shorter but similar spiral roadway to that used by Leonati and others, on a large ball. The way up to the top was unremarkable, but on the way down "It is necessary to restrain the enormous wooden ball, always on the verge of escaping, and the feet patter frantically, vibrating like the sounding-board of a mandoline," reported one contemporary account. Not a pursuit to be encouraged, however, as it spoils the shape of the leg by undue development of the calf.

The invention of the motorcar was the signal for a fresh rash of thrill acts. Of these, the most remarkable was probably L'Auto Bolide, as it was known in France where it was invented, or The Daring Dip of Death as it was billed in the Ringling show when it first appeared in the early 1900s. The poster writers had a field day in describing the act, and for once one imagines they did not overstate the case:

> You see the handsome girl, who is to make the daring attempt to loop the gap in an automobile, ascend to the elevated platform and your heart goes out in sympathy for her. There are a few moments of intense silence while the automobilist takes her position in the car. Suddenly you are conscious that the car is moving. You want to turn your head away, but a fascination stronger than your will holds your eyes rooted upon the automobile and its daring occupant.
>
> As the car descends the incline it gathers speed. You are dimly conscious that its speed is so terrific as to be beyond comparison with anything you have ever seen. An express train is seemingly slow beside it. You think of a pistol shot, a speeding arrow, a meteor. It is all there in one. Before you can realise it, the car has descended

FOREPAUGH & SELLS
THE VERITABLE CAP-S
THE EXTREME AND ABSOLUTE LIMIT OF SENSATIO
TERRIBLE TEMERITY AND ILLIMITABLE, INIMI

BROTHERS ENORMOUS SHOWS UNITED
1902-S-Nº 90
NGER DERIDING,
DEATH DEFYING
ATE DARE DEVIL
DIAVOLO
LOOPING THE LOOP
OF ALL HAZARDOUS EXPLOITS
COPYRIGHT 1902 BY THE STROBRIDGE LITHO CO CIN'TI & NEW YORK
M REACHED AT LAST. BEYOND THE TREMENDOUSLY
INTREPIDITY OF DIAVOLO, NO MAN MAY GO.

THE BARNUM & BAILEY GREATE[ST]
SHOW ON EAR[TH]

[B]ARNUM & BAILEY'S BEWILDERING, TERRIFIC NEW SENSATION
AUTOS THAT PASS IN THE AIR

SISTERS LA RAGUE IN THEIR MAD AUTO RACE, PASSING EACH OTHER IN SEPARATE CARS WHILE FLYING AND SOMERSAULTING THROUGH T[HE AIR]

the incline, turned upside down and still inverted, has shot into space. Twenty feet away, across a veritable chasm of death, is a moon-shaped incline. Your breath comes fast. You gasp. Your heart seems to stop pulsating.

"Will the auto strike the incline?"

"Will it be upright?"

"Will the daring occupant come through the 'Dip of Death' unscathed?"

These and a thousand other thoughts rush through your brain in so brief a time as to defy computation.

With tooth-shaking violence the auto lands at the far end and apparently uninjured, graceful, and smiling, the driver springs to the ground to receive the applause of the crowd. That applause surges around her in waves of thunder. Under the influence of the reaction, men, women and children, become deliriously enthusiastic. You want to spring to your feet and throw your hat in the air and cheer. And why shouldn't you? At the risk of her life she has given you an experience you have never had before. She has accomplished the limit of modern arenic sensations.

OPPOSITE, ABOVE: *A typical dare-devil act. The Sisters La Rague in their Mad Auto Race.* BELOW: *A modern thrill act. Eddy Ventura loops the loop.*

IN THE AIR

She was petite, under five feet tall, with an unbelievably narrow waist and tiny feet. But her shoulders and upper arms were as well developed as a middle-weight boxer, and she had a fierce temper. Yet this small person bewitched all who saw her perform. She was the Pavlova of the circus and the treasured memory of Lillian Leitzel still lingers with those who had the privilege of seeing her in action.

Her act was divided into two parts. In the first she floated in easy rolls up the rope to the Roman Rings where her effortless and seemingly weightless performance has never been equaled. But it was to see the second part of her performance for which people would have been prepared to pay a small fortune, if they had been asked. To stunning applause Leitzel would descend to the ground, take her bow and blow kisses to her rapturous and utterly captivated audience, then, as though by magic, she would grasp another rope and be flown to the top of the big top. There a single spotlight would focus on her glittering person. She would slip a loop of padded rope over her right wrist. The loop was attached to a swivel. And with an effortless movement of her graceful body she would begin to turn in what is known as a full-arm plange when the body swings round using the arm as a pivot.

Each time she completed a full gyration her right shoulder was temporarily dislocated, but her tremendous muscles forced it back into the socket. Up to now the crowd had been totally silent, even the popcorn and peanut sellers were told at their peril not to utter a word, then the audience began to count and as the diminutive figure revolved at the top of the tent the cry came up "fifteen . . . sixteen"; "Thirty-seven . . . thirty-eight"; "seventy-four . . . seventy-five"; "ninety" – a sigh would go up, but the amazing little aerialist would continue. On a number of occasions she performed

OPPOSITE: *Lillian Leitzel. "She was petite, under five feet tall, with a narrow waist and tiny feet. But her shoulders and upper arms were as well developed as those of a middle-weight boxer, and she had a fierce temper. She bewitched all who saw her perform; she was the Pavlova of the Big Top."*

CIRCUS WORLD MUSEUM, BARABOO, WISCONSIN

Alfredo Codona and Lillian Leitzel.

FRED D. PFENING COLLECTION

over one hundred complete turns. The performance became an athletic event, a development decried by those who loved Leitzel and understood the true beauty of her art. The strain and endurance were incredible. Cold day or hot – and the temperature in the roof of a Big Top on a hot day can be twenty or thirty degrees hotter than on the ground - Lillian Leitzel, their Lillian Leitzel - for her audience began almost to assume a proprietary responsibility for the little artiste – would regularly do her hundred turns. A consummate artiste, she would mount to the roof with her hair held back, as turn succeeded turn, her beautiful golden hair would float further and further out until it followed her like a shower of gold. She was a wonderful performer of exquisite grace, beloved of all who knew her – especially the circus children to whom she was always Auntie Leitzel.

She was born near the turn of the century in Bohemia and came to the United States with a family bicycle act when she was only ten. She soon eclipsed the other members of her family and when they decided to return to their native country, Lillian Leitzel elected to remain. A few seasons in small acts, another couple in vaudeville where she soon became a star, and then, in 1915, she joined Ringlings and became a sensation.

Though a superb artiste she had a temper to match her

FREE LIBRARY OF PHILADELPHIA

A beautiful Ringling Bros. and Barnum & Bailey poster showing the incomparable Leitzel.

exquisite brilliance. Her rages and tantrums were legendary. She was married three times; her first husband's name, she always said, she could not remember; the second departed, so they said, after losing a finger in a kitchen affray with his tempestuous wife – she chopped it off with a butcher's knife; the third was Alfredo Codona.

Their marriage lasted for three years. Then in February 1931, while Codona was performing in Berlin, and his wife was appearing with a circus in Copenhagen, it happened. The date was February 13, a Friday. Her rigging man, who accompanied her everywhere, was standing below her rope where she performed her Roman Ring act, as he always did, for he worshipped her and felt that if ever something should go wrong he would be quick enough to rush forward and break her fall. Something distracted his attention for a moment, and in that moment a swivel supporting the ring on her wrist snapped. Lillian Leitzel fell head first to the ground. She stood up and appeared to be all right. She wanted to go on, but they took her to hospital. Her husband saw her the next day, and she seemed as unmoved and gay as ever. He was persuaded to go back to Berlin, but the next day Lillian Leitzel died.

Alfredo Codona vanished for several months after the death of his wife, and then he returned to his flying act, but with a brittleness, a fierceness and recklessness that had been lacking before. It was almost as though he were willing, and half hoping, that the Gods would take him too. He

Zoeanna Henry on the Spanish Web.

HOXIE BROS. CIRCUS

remarried, but then tore his shoulder muscle so badly during a performance that he had to quit the ring. The downward descent to his self-appointed doom gathered pace. His money soon ran out, and his wife found she could no longer tolerate living with him and sued for divorce. Together they went to the lawyer's office and Codona asked to be alone with his wife for a few minutes. The lawyer left and when he had done so Alfredo Codona pulled a pistol from his pocket and shot his wife and then himself. The legend of Lillian Leitzel had come to an end.

In his own line as an aerialist Alfredo Codona was as supreme an artiste as had been the diminutive Leitzel. Some considered he was the greatest flier there has ever been and he was the first to perform consistently the dreaded triple somersault which has caused the death of so many performers.

A swing, a leap and a catch, it all sounds so simple when broken down into essentials, but who knows what heartache, has gone into the training of an aerialist before he can gain the skill and confidence to perform in public? The argument has gone on for decades as to whether an aerial performer is born to the job or whether he can be made into one, the argument will doubtless continue for very much longer, but an unassailable fact is that fliers must not only have a degree of fearlessness, they must also have an innate longing to perform in the air. Then and only then will the magic confidence begin to grow and the timing, the synchronization, of their swing on which their life depends start to develop. "Time, time, time! It pounds through the life of the circus like a blood flow and by its beat everything is gauged," wrote Alfredo Codona many years ago, and it is this sense of time on which an aerial performance is based.

Codona had been almost brought up on the stage. At the age of one year he was in an act with his father who brought him on in a carpetbag and would then balance the baby on his head. Soon he was an accomplished tumbler and it was here that he learned the all-important lesson of timing. Progressing from simple bends to handstands, roll-overs and flip-flaps, through it all Codona was learning about coordination until the clockwork regularity of his routine became second nature and he began slowly to acquire, through bitter and painful experience, the sixth sense of his art.

For when the body is turning in the air, when the lights and illumination throw strange shadows, it is not sight, but timing and instinct on which an aerial performer depends. Many years ago an acrobat had a highly impressive act in which he swung from a trapeze feet first through a blazing hoop and turned another somersault to catch another bar on the far side. He could not see the bar, he merely knew it was waiting for him on the other side of the hoop. One day it was not there and he woke up in hospital.

HAMID-MORTON CIRCUS

By the hair of her head – The incredible Ming Wong at the Hamid-Morton Circus.

Many have tried to determine what goes on in the mind during the treble somersault. Codona worked out that his body was traveling at more than sixty miles per hour at the start of his triple. By the time the second somersault was accomplished he had virtually blacked out and only in the split second at the end of the third somersault, when the body straightened out in time to be received by the catcher's hands did the brain recover enough for him to be conscious of what was happening. At such speed of revolution it is impossible to see and grasp at those seeking hands or to adjust consciously the momentum or arc in order to find them, they must be there and at the right point in the swing, otherwise the catcher can never take the extra weight and strain of a swinging body. To old circus hands there is no sound more reassuring than the healthy smack of hand upon wrist at the moment of a successful catch. The catcher's is the less glamorous job, but the success of the whole act depends upon his strength, reliability and, above all, his experience.

In the air it is possible to regulate the speed of the turn. To turn faster the aerialist tucks up his knees and bends his head so that his chin almost touches his breast; to turn slower the legs must be stretched and the head straightened – but these movements can only last for a split second. They cannot be done consciously, they must be done by instinct as a result of experience. Curiously, too, the slope of the ground has a direct bearing on the swing of the trapeze artist. Although the bars and supports are perfectly level, if the ground slopes downward the acrobat will swing faster, if it is upward then his swing will be slowed. Should the ground tilt on one side or the other, the slope will draw the trapeze down to such an extent that it may be necessary to fix the rigging higher on the downward side.

The flier's is a strange world, a special world. It is true to say that there is no other circus act where psychology plays a greater part. Aerial work takes more than just blatant courage, it requires training and needle-sharp concentration. It takes a positive act of will to hurl the body through the air, and superstition sometimes plays a part in the aerialist act – for death is never far away. This is not so much because of the inherent difficulty of what the aerialist is trying to achieve. Accidents are usually either due to the mechanical failure of some piece of apparatus or they happen because the performer has changed his mind in midair. There are many stories of premonition in the aerialist world and even more about "casting," the circus expression for the unexplainable phenomenon of letting go. There was an occasion in Berlin many years ago when a troupe of girls performed not very difficult aerial feats above the ring. Their principal role was to look decorative and daring whenever the spotlight came their way. On the second day of the act, for no known reason, one of the girls fell into the net but she was quite unhurt. The next day the same thing happened to another, until by the end of the week no less than six of the girls had fallen like flies after a squirt of an aerosol insecticide. There seemed no logical reason for their fall and when asked they just said, "I felt I had to let go," and let go they had.

The reassuring net below looks a safe and sure haven if things go wrong up there, but to land wrongly on the net can be as fatal as if the unfortunate victim had landed uncompromisingly on the floor of the ring. Many performers have broken their necks because they did not ball up before impact. Rope and knot burns are common enough in practice, and broken bones and dislocated joints frequently occur when the aerialist does not land correctly or hits the outer cords of the safety net.

The trapeze artiste is a comparative newcomer to the circus hierarchy. Leapers and tumblers, either on the flat or

The inventor of the Flying Trapeze, the Frenchman, Léotard.

from suspended planks or springboards were common phenomena for centuries and in many lands. On August 1, 1838, in the French town of Toulouse, was born a man who was to create the flying trapeze - the celebrated Léotard. A gymnast almost from birth - his father ran a gymnasium in the town - Léotard rapidly acquired a reputation for skill, daring and, above all, athletic grace. When he came on the scene the fixed trapeze was still something of a novelty and had caused the death of more than one aerialist who had been rash enough to display his skill beneath the basket of a balloon. But Léotard was not content with the static bar, for the first time he tried to perform on a moving one. He wisely chose to place his rigging across a swimming pool and after a lot of hard, wet work he discovered that by letting go of a swinging bar at the right moment, his momentum would carry him to another, especially if his father, who accompanied his famous son wherever he went, was to swing it forward at the right time. Thus the flying trapeze was devised.

Toulouse was a comparative backwater; not until a traveling troupe from Franconi's circus in Paris visited the town did Léotard achieve recognition. He was engaged for the Cirque d'Eté in Paris and, with his father in attendance, arrived in the city in the summer of 1859, to be immediately stricken with typhoid. Not until November 12 did he make his début, and what a début! According to one account, he came on like a "gladiator," then, to the music of the most popular waltz of the time, he began his series of leaps from one trapeze to another "like a tropical bird jumping from

THE NEW YORK HISTORICAL SOCIETY, NEW YORK CITY

Aerial feats. How Adam Forepaugh titillated his customers' appetites.

branch to branch." Despite professional jealousy, which was fierce in those days, Léotard was guest of honor at a great dinner given by his fellow artistes who presented him with a commemorative medal. All Paris took him to their hearts. Léotard ties, Léotard walking sticks, Léotard medallions were on sale everywhere, overnight Léotard had become a national hero, bakers even created a Léotard pastry.

Yet his act, by modern standards was simplicity itself. At either end of a long line of planks covered with thick mattresses stood a platform some six feet high. On one of these stood Léotard's ever-watchful father. Hanging from the roof were two swings and a pair of handgrips and his repertoire on these consisted of basic swings, somersaults and turns. But Léotard flew, and no one had done that before. He was engaged in Paris at the then astronomic fee of 500 francs a day and this was the level of his charges as he performed all over Europe from St. Petersburg to London to Madrid. It was while he was in Spain that he contracted smallpox and shortly afterward died – he was only thirty-two. Imitators appeared in their hordes, but the great Léotard holds a treasured place in circus history and his name is remembered in the costume which athletes, gymnasts and others still wear.

The summer after Léotard took Paris by storm, an-

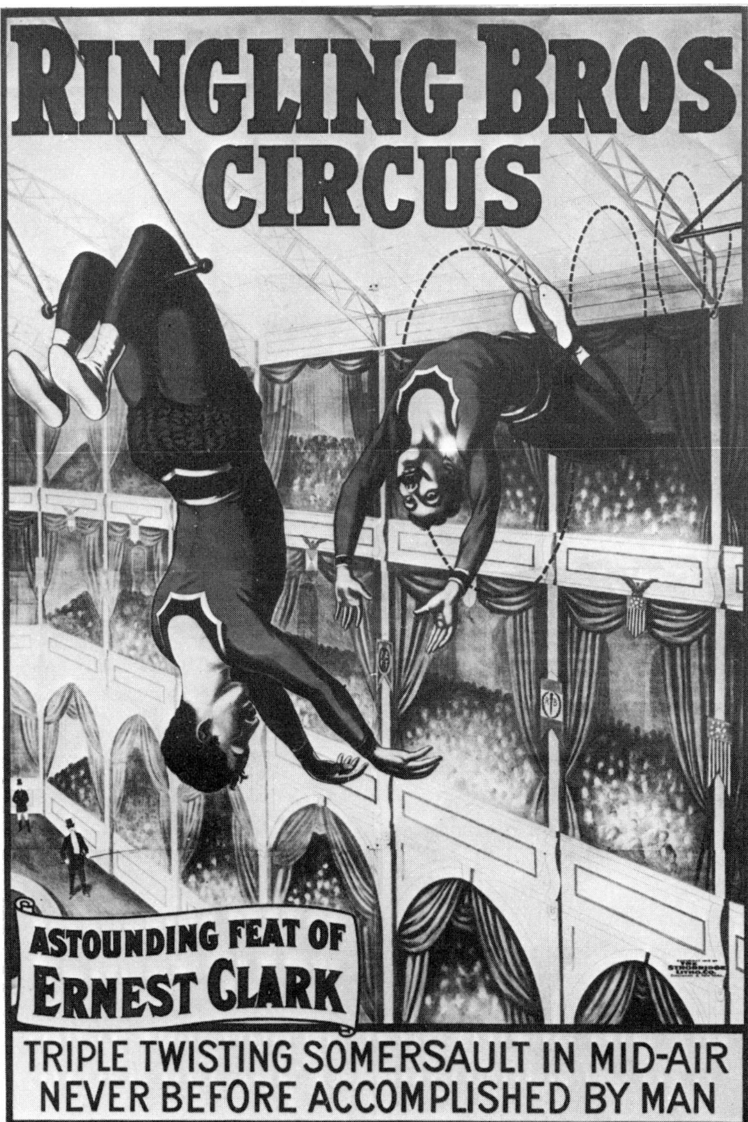

FRED D. PFENING COLLECTION

Ernest Clark, Trapeze Artist.

other intrepid Frenchman was to accomplish a feat which was to make his name reverberate around the world for, on June 30, 1859, Jean François Gravelet, better known as Blondin walked (strolled would be a more appropriate word) across the Niagara Falls.

For centuries tightrope walking has been a popular feat at fairs and private performances. Across rivers, gorges, streets and thoroughfares, from one church tower to another, from one ship's mast to another, all have been the scene for great tightrope-walking acts. Not content with a simple crossing, others would undertake the perilous feat with every conceivable type of burden or handicap, carrying a chair, or a companion, with their feet in baskets or even blindfold. And they would perform on the wire, handstands, headstands, somersaults and all the arts of the posture master, but several

An early tightrope walker. For centuries tightrope walking was a popular feat at fairs and private performances. Rivers, gorges, streets, from one church to another – all have been the scene of great tightrope walking acts.

dozen feet above the ground and with no safety net.

Jacob Hall, the Rope Dancer, was one of the most celebrated of wirewalkers in the days of Samuel Pepys and he drew huge crowds to witness his remarkable feats on the rope which he set up in Charing Cross or sometimes in Lincoln's Inn Fields and he was a frequent performer at Bartholomews Fair. He had a rival, though, a Dutchwoman, who delighted her audience because, according to a report at the time, "she seemed every moment in danger of breaking her neck." An early Philadelphia paper mentions in 1724, "Roap Dancing" by a "little boy of seven years old, who Dances and Capers upon the Strait Roap, to the Wonder of all Spectators." Thirty years later, one Anthony Joseph Dugee, after an apprenticeship to "The Grand Turk Mahomet Caratha," thrilled New York with his slack-wire work which included juggling and standing on his head, during which he ate his supper. He married into the profes-

HUBERT CASTLE INTERNATIONAL CIRCUS

A sensational picture of the Rock-Smith Flyers, one of the greatest flying troupes and winners of the recent circus championship in London.

sion too; his wife was the "Female Samson" who thought nothing of resting an anvil weighing three hundred pounds on her breast and allowing a couple of men to pound away at it with sledge hammers. So popular was the art of wirewalking that a Boston paper expressed grave concern over the health of New England children who tried to emulate their professional betters by sliding down fences risking "wounding themselves in every quarter."

Signor Spinacuta was another popular entertainer in the early days of the American circus. He was a noted "roap-dancer." He used to perform with baskets tied to his feet and also had a troupe of trained monkeys. Around this time, a Madame Saqui was the talk of France. Her most celebrated performance was to walk across a rope strung between the towers of the cathedral of Notre Dame in Paris and she appears to have become a camp follower *extraordinaire* and followed the all-conquering army of Napoleon, giving her performances in the open air before the admiring troops. She danced until she reached the age of seventy and died penniless in 1866 having pawned all her jewelry.

However, when the word wirewalker is mentioned it is invariably of Blondin that one thinks, for though he had many imitators, not only was Blondin the best and the most original, but he was also the first to attempt really death-defying feats. He was born in 1821 in St. Omer in France. His father, a veteran and hero of many of Napoleon's campaigns, first took the young Blondin (he became known as Blondin after his first professional engagement) to see some ropewalkers at the age of five, and from that tender age the great artiste knew that there was no other career for him.

As soon as he reached home after seeing the wire-walkers who had made such an impression on his young mind, Blondin set to work to build his own tightrope. First he tied a rope to the backs of two chairs, but these collapsed under him. Next he tried to tie a cord to two trees, but the cord broke. Then a kindly sailor showed him how to tie knots and found a boat's cable for the youngster to try with. It worked, and from that moment the young Blondin was never so happy as when he was practicing his tightrope walking. His parents smiled indulgently at their son's efforts and in due time sent him to the Ecole de Gymnase at Lyons where he could study his art under professional guidance.

Six months after entering the gymnasium, Blondin performed for the first time in public. He was a sensation and soon his fame spread. In 1851 he was asked by the celebrated Ravels, who could trace their ancestry to the early 1600s, to join their family troupe on a tour of America. From that moment Blondin was made. He arrived a hero, having rescued a fellow passenger who had fallen overboard, and soon the talent of the great artiste found a wider audience, for Blondin was an accomplished performer in all branches of the circus except equestrianism.

The tour was a great success, but somehow Blondin was not content. He was not sure why, after all, he was now a star performer whose skill was hailed wherever he went, nevertheless he felt restless. He wanted to do a feat beyond even the extraordinary, but he did not know what. Then, so the story goes, inspiration came to him in a dream after a heavy banquet. He now knew what it was that he must do to convince the world of his quite remarkable talent.

As soon as he could he traveled to the Niagara Falls to see if it were possible in the first instance to rig a rope across the huge chasm. He found it was, but also came to the conclusion that to do so during the winter months was to risk an unnecessary death as the spray would freeze on the rope and make it impossible to walk on.

When the spring of 1859 came, Blondin moved into a village near the falls and announced his project. A hemp cord was stretched across the Niagara River, 160 feet above the raging torrent on one side and 170 feet on the other. In all it was 1,100 feet long. There could have been no more awesome place for Blondin to choose. The papers spoke of the elemental majesty of nature, and the continual stunning noise was enough to numb the senses of those who lingered too long. But the project caught on. When the great day arrived there was an audience of no less than twenty-five thousand people sitting on the scaffold seating which had been erected for the occasion or lining the banks on both sides of the chasm.

The only person not nervous on that great day appeared to be Blondin who unhurriedly inspected the fastenings of the rope on the American side and with an equal lack of urgency picked up his pole, stepped nimbly on to the rope and started walking toward Canada. In the center, above the wildest of the raging water, he sat down unconcernedly and looked at the scene about him. Then he lay on his back, turned a back somersault and walked rapidly to the other side, where he was greeted with a spirited rendering of the *Marseillaise* from a Canadian band. The crossing had taken a bare eight minutes in all.

After a short break, Blondin appeared on the rope again, this time bearing a huge tripod camera on his back. Some two hundred feet from the shore he unhitched it and, apparently with all the time in the world, proceeded to take pictures of the crowds on both banks. Then he shouldered his equipment again and proceeded to walk backward to the Canadian side again. This time he picked up a chair, and, in the middle of the rope, placed the chair on it and sat down, crossing his legs in the calmest way imaginable, as the papers described. Nearing the American side he once more stopped, put his chair on the rope and stood on it. By now some of his audience were nervous wrecks. Many had fainted, a number were physically sick, never had they dreamed that a man could do, or would be even willing to try to do what they had just seen performed by the little Frenchman. When Blondin finally returned to America it was to a roar of acclaim such as had seldom been heard. The Canadian audience joined in and the only person not emotionally moved was Blondin himself. The whole performance had taken a little less than one hour.

Headlines in newspapers across the world exploded with the news that a Frenchman named Blondin had achieved the impossible and walked across the Niagara Falls on a tightrope. Even so, many disbelieved what they read. Some said Blondin never existed, others that the whole thing was newspaper fiction. To quell all skeptics, Blondin took to the rope again. On July 4, he walked across blindfolded in a heavy sack. On the 16th of the same month he took a wheelbarrow with him. On August 5, and again on the 19th he carried a man on his back and the story is told that when the man started to fidget on one of the crossings Blondin turned to him and said, "I must request you to sit quiet or I shall have to put you down!" On August 27 he tried a new variation and crossed as a slave in heavy shackles. On September 2 the following year, he gave a gala performance before the Prince of Wales, who graciously declined an offer to carry him across.

Fame and honors poured upon him and the Frenchman sought other places to try his feat. His next choice was at Jones Wood on the Hudson River. Here he had to contend not only with considerable sag, which made the return more like a climb than a walk, but also a strong wind which swung the rope a full twenty feet. Blondin remained as unmoved as ever, and next time crossed with his feet in bushel baskets.

In April 1861, he came to England, preceded by his manager who, when asked by a nervous sponsor what would happen if Blondin fell replied, "Why, he can't." Perhaps on the strength of this assurance Blondin was promised £1,200 for twelve performances, a phenomenal amount of money in

OPPOSITE: *Beauties of the air. The incomparable Mademoiselles Ellsler with their celebrated double tightrope act.*

those days for a performer of his type. The colossal Crystal Palace was chosen as the venue. A rope was wound round the great spiral staircases at each end of the huge enclosure. Weights held the rope steady. Crowds thronged the galleries, and an even larger audience stood below. A narrow passage of bare boards showed where Blondin would fall if the impossible should happen, for he frowned on the use of a net.

Wearing an Indian headdress, with gold medals clanking on his chest, Blondin went through the full range of his repertoire. He crossed blindfold, he turned somersaults, he did headstands and at the end he was greeted with rapturous applause.

Challenges to test Blondin came from all sides. Some wanted him to cross rivers or valleys, others to walk from one spire to another, someone with a twisted imagination wanted him to walk over a succession of blast furnaces. With the challenges came the requests: one offered £100 to "carry his wife across"; another, no less than £500 if Blondin did the same with his wife, only this time he was to "let her slip when about halfway." One of his most celebrated tricks was to carry a stove on the rope - one of Mr. Walker's Patent Self-Feeding Stoves - and to cook an omelet in mid-rope.

He toured many of the main British cities. In Liverpool he walked across a cage full of lions with a wheelbarrow, and in a very high wind, which all but blew him off. The crowd gasped, the lions' comments were not recorded. There seemed nothing the remarkable Frenchman could not do and England went Blondin-mad. The occasional doggerel verse was also produced:

Of all the sights in England now,
And I've looked everywhere,
There is not one of any sort,
With Blondin can compare;
He is the marvel of his age –
That everyone admits –
So *fit* it is that he should beat
All others into *fits*:

The world counts seven Wonders up
An eighth I will install,
The Hero of Niagara,
And greatest of them all.

Though small in stature, slight in build,
With truth it may be said,
He's never *undersized* but when
You see him *over*head,
A tripping of his own ac*cord*
Like some fantastic elf
To whom is given *rope* enough
But not to *hang* himself.

ROYAL AMPHITHEATRE,

Proprietor and Manager, Mr. WILLIAM BATTY, Amphitheatre House, Bridge Road, Lambeth, Surrey.
Licensed by the Lord High Chamberlain, and under the Patronage of Her Most Gracious
MAJESTY THE QUEEN, & H. R. H. PRINCE ALBERT

The Immense Applause bestowed, is a convincing proof of the daily increasing popularity of this Favourite Place of Amusement; the BROTHERS

SIEGRIST,

Will introduce their New Performance of Feats of Strength in the Air—It is impossible to describe their Incredible Evolutions; in addition to which, Mr. BATTY has engaged the **MADEMOISELLES**

ELLSLER,

WHO WILL MAKE THEIR FIRST APPEARANCE ON

THE DOUBLE TIGHT ROPE,

Likewise will be displayed, the GLOBE ASCENSION; VAULTING; the Exercises of the NICOLO FAMILY; and the most pleasing Scenes in the Arena; embracing the Principal Artistes of the Establishment.

On MONDAY, October 11th, 1852, (and during the Week,)

Commencing with **Miss EMILY COOKE** and **EUGENE GODOLPHIN,** who will perform their truly Laughable Petite Ballet, entitled

JEANNETTE & JEANNOT

Or the Enlistment for the Great Wars of France.

Mr. HEMMING, the most Daring Horseman of the Day, in his admired Leaping Act, in the course of which, he will

THROW SUMMERSAULTS

From Feet to Feet, during the Rapid Evolutions of the Steed.

Miss FROST will appear on a Swift Courser, in a pleasing Act, as the

FISHWIFE OF NEWHAVEN,

Mr. POWELL, the popular British Horseman, will have the honour of appearing on Two Horses, in his Wondrous

LEAPING ACT

As the Bounding Springer of the Alps.

To be succeeded by the Extraordinary and Unparalleled Performances of **M. M. SIEGRIST,** on

LA PERCHE

VICTORIA AND ALBERT MUSEUM

BBC COPYRIGHT

FRED D. PFENING COLLECTION

ABOVE LEFT: *The Australian-born Con Colleano, the Wizard of the Wire.* RIGHT: *Skill on the wire. Daviso Martini from Italy.*

Blondin is usually associated with his remarkable high-wire feats, but he was also an accomplished, not to say phenomenal performer on the low rope. With the ends of pitchforks tied to his feet, he would run up and down the rope, dance, turn somersaults and display other amazing feats. The climax of his act was when he placed a chair on the rope, climbed over it to sit down and then jerked the chair along the cord while he still sat in it.

Imitators followed Blondin, but none, it seemed, with the panache of the great Frenchman. Niagara proved a tremendous attraction and the Blondin feat was repeated on several occasions. Female Blondins popped up all over the place. One who called herself Madame Genevieve (her real name was Young), seems to have led a charmed life. On one occasion she attempted to cross the Thames on a rope, but unwisely chose a time late on a winter's afternoon for the feat. Before she was halfway across it was almost too dark to see across the river. To add to her complications, the rope supports started to give way and she had to plunge ignominiously into the icy river. She tried a similar act in Manchester, but the platform to which one end of the rope was tied caught fire. On a third occasion she was just crossing nicely when a dense fog descended like a blanket and all she could see were two pinpricks of light to show where she was going.

Of more modern wirewalkers the most distinguished was Con Colleano, who brought a new and incredibly graceful dimension into the art of wirewalking. A natural athlete, Con

NOVOSTI PRESS AGENCY

NOVOSTI PRESS AGENCY

ABOVE LEFT: *The Tsovkra Tightrope Walkers of Daghestan.* RIGHT: *The Volshanskys. Russian geniuses of the high wire.*

Colleano was born of Spanish-Irish ancestry in Australia around 1910, into a distinguished circus family. He was performing with the Ringling Brothers and Barnum & Bailey Circus with Alfredo Codona; in fact, some called him the Codona of the wire – and no higher praise could there be, except that it was a comparison of equals. Colleano was the first man to perform the forward somersault on the wire – a trick in a different league to the often-performed backward somersault, for in the forward, the leaper cannot see the wire where his feet are to land.

Of more recent memory are the fabulous Wallendas whose three-tier performance on the high wire has left audiences across the world stupefied and sweating at the sheer bravado of the feats. Since their debut in 1928, theirs has been a triumphant progress, the epitome of balance, skill and daring. On a wire forty feet above the ground and bearing long, flexible steel poles, they cross the abyss on bicycles, with another member of the troupe perched on a chair on another pole strung between the bicycles, or, the highlight of the act, on foot in three tiers, with the upper one, a girl, standing on a chair precariously balanced on yet another pole. An astonishing feat at any time, yet more so when one considers that conditions at that height – the light, the temperature, the air currents – make any aerial performance just that bit more difficult to do.

For sheer nerve, lunacy some called it, pride of place must go to those aerial acts which are described as thrill acts,

The Wallendas, probably the greatest high-wire act ever. Here performing in the open air.
OPPOSITE: *Geronimo the Intrepid. The Dive of Death into an Apache war drum.*
FRED D. PFENING COLLECTION

the death-defying stunts which had our ancestors gasping. A gentleman who billed himself as Desperado – his real name was Ernest Gadbin – a German-born acrobat – mastered what was perhaps the crowning achievement in the "Death Defying" world. This nerveless performer cast himself from a platform eighty feet above ground in an incredible swallow dive onto a highly polished wooden slide which was sprinkled with cornmeal to make it even more slippery. The farther end of the slide was upturned so that Desperado – and there can have been no performer who more properly earned his name – shot off again into space to land in a net at the far side of the ring.

Another who would regularly cast himself off into space was Aloys Peters – the man with the Iron Neck – who, in the 1930s, featured in a number of circuses. The official description of his act read:

> Having climbed to the top of the Agricultural Hall, he walks upside down through a series of inverted croquet hoops. Then he fixes a noose round his remarkable neck, hangs by his toes and a trapeze, and pushes off. For a sickening second you see him whirling through 75 feet of space and he lands quite at his ease with not so much

Zazel the Beautiful Human Cannonball.

as a welt on his Adams' Apple! His safety depends upon the perfection of his gear – one flaw in the rope might plunge him to death.

A variation of the act which, not unnaturally, caused palpitations in the audience was that of Cubanos, "The Flying Dutchman." His speciality was to take a running jump off a platform near the top of the arena at a trapeze some thirty feet away and somewhat below. As his hands gripped the trapeze the bar of the trapeze broke and Cubanos hurtled toward the ground seventy feet below, only to have his fall arrested a matter of inches from the ground by some elastic ropes, up to then invisible, attached to his ankles.

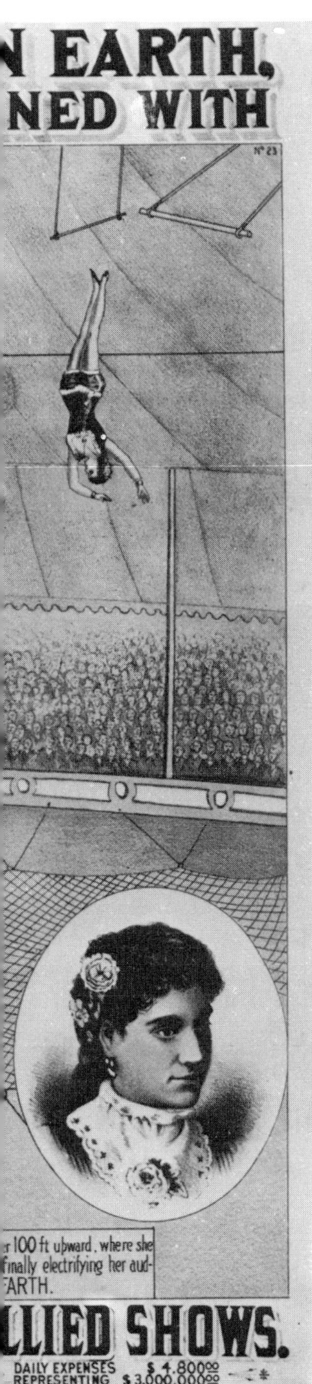

FRED D. PFENING COLLECTION

The human cannonball has long excited circus audiences. Always a ripple of excitement seems to go through the house when a cannonball act is announced. High drama as an enormous gaping cannon is brought into the ring, the performer, the intrepid performer with a cheerful wave of the hand slips into the muzzle of the gun. Only the head and torso stick out, with a last smile at the crowd and a nod of the head, an explosion occurs somewhere in the inner recesses of the cannon and, in a cloud of smoke, the human projectile is shot across the arena to land in a net on the far side. They are not of course actually shot; the explosion of a small charge triggers off a powerful spring and it is this that sends the intrepid one on his way.

Zazel is the name most often associated with the act, and many a Zazel has appeared in the circuses of Europe and America. The original Zazel was an English girl who, clad in pink tights, was "fired bodily from a cannon with violent velocity." Her act ended when she fell short of the net and spent the next twelve months in a plaster cast. Zachini is another name associated with the Human Cannonball, or the Man-Bombshell, as it was sometimes billed. Ildebrano Zachini designed a new form of cannon which worked on compressed air and could throw his brother, Hugo, 70 feet upward and a maximum of 135 feet into a net at the far side of the Big Top.

However, for sheer devilry and courage, Aerial, The Flying Man, who had huge adjustable wings attached to his shoulders, must take the prize. Apparently effortlessly Aerial, "the only Living Human Being who utilizes wings as do the birds," would soar around the tent as free as an eagle and, more particularly, land in one piece.

SIDE SHOW

"Ladies and Gentlemen. You are about to witness the most amazing, the most stupendous act ever performed by man. The gentleman you see before you will now walk into a common quart bottle, such as this very one I have here. You cannot believe it? But you will. Come inside and see this astonishing, this unique, this incre . . . dible phenomenon. Admission only tuppence." So one could imagine went the spiel for an act starring a man who was to gain notoriety in 1748 as the Bottle Conjuror.

For days the papers had been full of advertisements saying that at the New Theatre in the Haymarket in London this remarkable act would be performed, on the stage and before the very eyes of the audience. That night the New Theatre was packed. The time for the great event arrived, and passed. The audience started to become restless, but their anxiety was a little set at ease by the arrival on the stage of the manager who promised them their money back if the performer did not show up. Then a wag shouted from the gallery that for double their money the feat would be performed into a pint pot, and the awful realization struck all those who had been so credulous that they had been duped. It was the signal for a riot such as London had not seen for many a day. The genteel among the audience forced their way to the street, with the loss of wigs, swords, coats and much self-respect. The commoner folk fought their way to the stage and tore down scenery, props and curtains, while others ripped up the seats and made a huge bonfire in the street outside. The "Bottle Conjuror," or William Nicholls, as he had given his name to the theater management, seems to have vanished from the scene and was not seen again after this brief excursion into notoriety. The incident, though, was a supreme example of how gullible people can be, a gullibility exploited at fairgrounds across the world.

A famous fair. Southwark Fair through the eyes of William Hogarth.

For the side show really belongs to the carnival and fair and not to the circus at all. Astley, and the showmen who succeeded him, were always ready to exploit the extra attraction. The guillotine, "as used in France," brought the curious flocking to his amphitheater, while the wax heads which he had brought back from his Paris excursions proved an even greater draw and his Men in Miniature fascinated all who saw them. Strange and interesting animals appeared from time to time – forerunners of the occupants of the great menageries which by the middle of the nineteenth century had become an integral part of the larger circuses. Although the credulity of even Astley's early audiences must have been stretched when they heard the great man announce with due solemnity that this was the "Krokudile wat stopped Halexander's harmy, and when cut hopen had a man in harmour in its hintellects." Establishments such as Rackstraw's Museum in London – which displayed a "large collection of curiosities finely preserved in spirits" and a Musical Child "no more than four years old" – were typical of the amusements enjoyed by people on both sides of the Atlantic. While

The Ringling Bros. and Barnum & Bailey collection of strange people. Madison Square Garden, 1938.

representations of the latest "'orrible murder," were certain to fill a stall. Apart from anything else, there was little enough other entertainment for people to amuse themselves with. But it was Barnum, with the exhibits that he used to show in his Great American Museum, who really developed the side show into a circus rather than purely a fairground art.

Indeed it was at Barnum's American Museum of Living Curiosities, which accompanied the Greatest Show on Earth where the art of the circus side show was to reach its zenith. His "Marvellous Assemblage of Strangest Human Beings, a Wondrous Study of Nature's Wildest Vagaries, a World of Oddest, most Amazing Physical Exceptions" packed the place. Man's morbid curiosity about the strange, the deformed and the bizarre, found its outlet in gazing on Barnum's incredible collections of "monsters": the tallest and bulkiest of giants; the tiniest and prettiest of dwarves; phantom-like living skeletons; most enormous fat folk; living galleries of tattooing art; the only full-bearded lady, and so on. These were all the curiosities which nature can devise, on exhibition before the public: they were sometimes referred to as the Very Special People.

Barnum had first tasted the pleasures of showmanship when he exhibited Joice Heth and he evidently had a passion for the "curious" – more than one would believe mere showmanship warranted. He packed his museum with the odd and the weird and although the outcry over the Feejee Mermaid made him more than a little cautious, he was nevertheless always on the lookout for more exhibits to fascinate his public. So when the first Siamese Twins, Chang and Eng, appeared on the scene it was inevitable that sooner or later Barnum would sign them up.

In the early years of the nineteenth century, two boys were born to a poor Chinese fisherman who had moved some years before to a village sixty miles from Bangkok. The boys had a normal birth and were handsome specimens. The amazing thing, though, was that they were joined together at the lower part of the chest by a thick strip of flesh in the middle of which was a navel. This peculiar attachment, however, seemed no real handicap to their lives. To ignorant villagers such an event portended dire events, but of more immediate consequence it brought travelers from far and wide to look at the strange little beings. It was suggested that they be split by surgery, but wisely their mother decided that they must stay as they were. So the boys grew up together. The children had been born face to face and at first the band joining them was short; but, by constantly pulling it, soon the twins were able to stand up together and, more importantly, side by side. They learned to play and above all, swim and it was while swimming that they came to the attention of a Scottish merchant called Robert Hunter who spotted what he took to be a strange creature with two heads and numerous limbs, only to discover that this was Chang and Eng. At first the Siamese government refused to allow the twins to leave the country, but Hunter returned some years later with an American sea captain and the two managed to prevail upon the mother to let the twins come to the West – and this time the Siamese made no objection.

In August 1829, the twins, billed as "The Siamese Double Boys," made their debut in Boston. Successful tours in Philadelphia, New York City and other places followed and then a trip to Britain and the Continent. In the mid-1830s, by now fully established on the entertainment scene, they came under Barnum's wing; but not for long – they thought him mean – and they then went touring on their own. Their act had now developed. They would show the crowds how they could do flips and somersaults; they had always liked animals and soon added small animal acts to their repertoire; and their feats of strength always had the crowds gasping. At length, wearying of the life of itinerant performers the twins decided to settle down. All thoughts of returning to Siam had now gone and in 1839 they became American citizens, and adopted the surname of Bunker. Some time before the twins had married two sisters, Sarah Ann and Adelaide Yates, and so began one of the most curious of relationships.

But it did not seem to hamper the remarkable twins who had overcome many problems in their time, and the

SCIENTIFIC AMERICAN, 1874

Chang and Eng, the original Siamese twins.

two fathered twenty-two children between them. In time one roof could no longer harbor the increasing families so they moved to two houses a mile apart. For three nights the twins and their wives stayed in Chang's house, then they moved for the next three to Eng's house. Then came disaster as they lost their land during the Civil War. At their wits' end, the twins returned to Barnum and to the showman's life which they had given up so thankfully many years before.

The twins, now in their fifties, were not the success they had once been and after a number of years on the road they returned to their farm. It was in January 1874, when they were sixty-three years of age, that Eng woke up one night with a terrible presentiment. He listened for his brother's breathing, but could hear nothing. He called for help and then it was discovered that Chang was dead. Eng then started to feel terrible cramp; and massage seemed to do no good. He grew progressively worse and then he too died.

All their lives the twins had been plagued by medical men anxious to examine the extraordinary natural phenomenon; sometimes examinations had been necessary

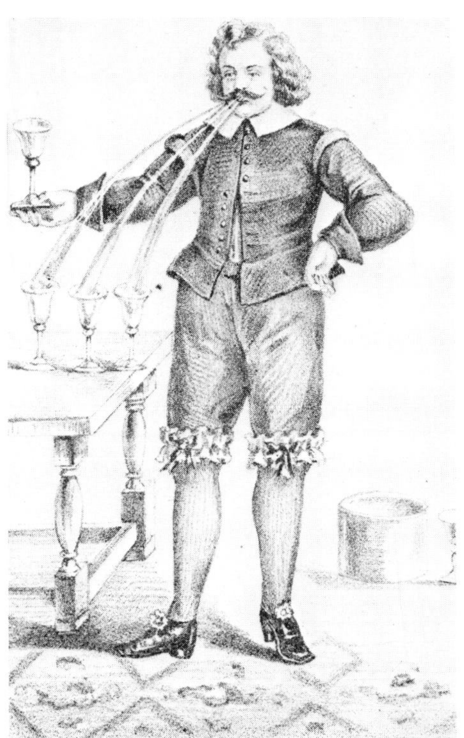

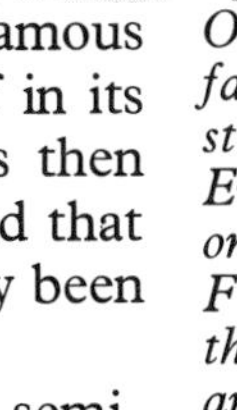

Our ancestors found a fascination for the strange and peculiar. Eve Fliegen who lived on the smell of flowers, Floram Marchand the Water Spouter, and Joseph Clark, Posture Master.

to prove that they were indeed no hoax. Now that the famous twins were dead, the medical fraternity fell over itself in its efforts to be allowed to carry out an autopsy. It was then found that the two were linked by an artery system and that Eng's body was almost empty of blood. He had literally been drained of blood by his dead brother.

Folklore and legend are full of human, or semi-human monsters; misshapen creatures whom Nature seems to have forgotten. Nowadays sociologists preach of exploitation, and pity has taken the place of revulsion. But no discrimination by society can equal that to which these people have been subjected by Nature. Nor must it be forgotten that it is by exhibiting themselves that these "Very Special People" can best make a living. They find no shame in this. They accept their physical shape and its problems as challenges to be overcome, and they do it with an equanimity and good humor which puts many other people to shame. When reading of some of these people whom our ancestors without exception classed as "monsters," it is astonishing to read of the dedication and application with which they tackle their peculiar handicaps.

Barnum looked on his freaks as money-makers, yet he also treated them as friends to whom he had given an opportunity which they would not otherwise be offered. They were exploited, surely, but exploited by mutual consent. Tom Thumb is the crowning example of this, and the showman's relationship with the little man is a peculiarly touching chapter in circus history.

Some of Sanger's contortionists at Balmoral, Scotland.

In former days, monsters, or more delicately, *miraculae naturae*, were ready attractions at fairs in any country, that is, if they were not murdered at birth as being manifestations of the devil's works, or even the devil himself in disguise. The fate of many must have been like that of the legendary Northumberland monster, a creature with the head, mane and feet of the horse but the rest of its ghastly body that of a man. This horror was scalded to death at the hands of the local schoolmaster.

Our ancestors found a continuing fascination for the twisted and the deformed. In 1566 it is recorded that no less than thirty-four dwarves served at a banquet in Rome given by a high churchman. In many courts in Europe dwarves and freaks did duty as jesters and when the supply of natural dwarves ran out, artificial dwarfing was practiced. The ancient Romans were among the first to create the artificial dwarf – the *pumilo* – who reached high prices in a thriving market. A concoction of the grease of dormice, bats and moles smeared on the backbone was said to produce stunting; this was a less reprehensible practice than some adopted in other societies where infants were kept in boxes to restrict their growth, or immature bones were bent and twisted to produce the most horrible of deformities.

Bartholomews Fair was a favorite haunt of the peculiar. Some were just giants of "Prodigious Height and

BLACKPOOL TOWER COMPANY. PHOTOGRAPH BY BARNET SAIDMAN

The three Merkys at the Blackpool Tower Circus.

Bigness," others were more extraordinary – like the lady who gave rise to the following advertisement in 1667:

WONDERS OF NATURE

A Girl, above sixteen Years of Age, born in Cheshire and not above eighteen inches long, having shed the Teeth seven several Times, and not a perfect Bone in any part of her, only the Head; yet she hath all her Senses to Admiration and Discourses, Reades very well, Sings, Whistles and all very pleasant to hear.

GOD SAVE THE KING

Two-headed creatures have always been a source of mystery, and also some confusion from time to time. "The wonderful Two-Headed Girl is still on Exhibition in New England," declared one Boston paper, "She sings duets by herself and she has a great advantage over the rest of her sex, for she never has to stop talking to eat, and when she is not eating she keeps both tongues going at once. She has a lover and the lover is in a quandary, because at one and the same moment she accepted him with one mouth and rejected him with the other." And then the writer goes on, "Now is she her own sister? Is she twins? Or having but one body (and consquently one heart) is she strictly but one person? Does she expect to have one vote or two? Has she the same opinion

CIRCUS WORLD MUSEUM, BARABOO, WISCONSIN

RINGLING BROS. AND BARNUM & BAILEY CIRCUS

OPPOSITE: *Millie-Christine, the two-headed Nightingale.*
LEFT: *Modern mites. Michu and Juliana at their circus wedding with ringmaster Harold Ronk presiding.*

as herself on all subjects, or does she differ sometimes? Would she feel insulted if she came to spit in her own face?"

Another pair of Siamese twins, Millie-Christine, was or were, often billed as the two-headed girl, or, more graciously, as the Two-Headed Nightingale. Born as slaves in North Carolina in 1851, theirs was a story of real exploitation. From the age of four they were displayed under various managements until they came again into the care of the man who had originally owned them, J. P. Smith, a kindly Southern gentleman. On Smith's death, the twins became their own managers and for many years they appeared on stages across America and Europe. Their chief act was a duet – one sang soprano, the other contralto, accompanying themselves on the guitar as they sang.

Although Tom Thumb is always thought of as Barnum's chief midget, the showman found a number of other miniature people to captivate his audiences. "Commodore" George Washington Morrison Nutt was one of those who came into his orbit. He weighed only twenty-four pounds and stood a bare twenty-nine inches; but every one of those inches was full of fire.

Another was Lavinia Warren, a truly petite and very lovely little lady some thirty-two inches tall who had been born in Massachusetts. Tom Thumb fell in love with Lavinia, to the fury of the little Commodore and it seemed that a battle royal was imminent. But Tom Thumb was accepted

Captain Bates and his redoubtable wife Anna Swan the Nova Scotia giantess – the most formidable Lady Macbeth in drama history.

CIRCUS WORLD MUSEUM, BARABOO, WISCONSIN

and, before an immense congregation estimated at over 2,000 and from the highest echelons of society, the two were married in New York. Exerting all his charm, Barnum had persuaded the grudging Commodore to act as best man, and Minnie Warren, the bride's sister, who was even smaller, was maid of honor. In due time Barnum announced that the rapturously happy midgets had produced a child, but the baby which was shown before an admiring public and subsequently "christened" was not theirs and it mysteriously and conveniently "died" soon afterward.

On Tom Thumb's death, Lavinia set off to tour on her own and met an Italian midget, Count Primo Magri, who was just under four feet in height. The two appeared before the public on many occasions. They also ran an opera company of midgets, featured in a number of films and ran a side show on Coney Island. Soon the days of fascination for the curious en masse were over and Lavinia retired, to die eventually in 1919.

From the small to the huge; the giants, of which the most widely celebrated was Anna Swan, seven feet five-and-a-half inches tall in her stockinged feet and attractive as well. Barnum had heard of Anna through some Quaker connections and sent an agent to try to persuade her to join his museum. He succeeded and Anna, the Nova Scotia Giantess, became a feature of the Great American Museum. Anna later married another Barnum giant, Captain Martin Bates. The couple had a baby – the largest baby on record, some thirty inches long and weighing nearly twenty-four pounds – but it survived only a few days. Anna Swan was nearly burnt to death on the two occasions when the Great American Museum caught fire. The second time she was involved in a dramatic rescue; for she was too large to go through any of the windows and the staircase, by then engulfed by flames and smoke, was considered too unsafe for anyone of her weight – which was reported as being close on four hundredweight at the time. Her best friend, the living skeleton, stood by as long as he dared, but he had to go when the smoke and the heat became unbearable. Eventually a hole was made in a wall and the giantess was hitched to the cable of a nearby derrick and gently lowered to the ground. Anna was quite a versatile lady despite her colossal size, and no mean actress. After the first museum fire she appeared on the New York stage as what must have been the most formidable Lady Macbeth in drama history.

Chang the Chinese Giant was another attraction in the late 1860s in London and on the Continent. He was seven feet four inches high, although some of his advertisements give him several more inches. An immensely imposing figure in his thick-soled Chinese shoes and mandarin cap, he was often photographed with his regular-sized wife and a Chinese dwarf. Chang was no performer, but held levées, usually four daily, during which he looked inscrutable and very large. He returned to Peking but reappeared again in time for the Paris Exhibition of 1880. The giant eventually died, aged only forty-eight, in Bournemouth, England in 1893.

Some giants and giantesses were not quite what they seemed. The story is told of a black giantess who left the small rolling show, where she had worked for a number of years, to get married. She had proved a great attraction and the showman, loth to pass over such a lucrative side show, dressed up a strapping tentman in the giantess's dress and got him to black his face. The deception worked perfectly. They held a spirited "conversation" in no known language and which the showman "translated" in the most realistic way. All went well for several months until a drunk staggered up to the stage and forced a kiss on the reluctant woman. He

Chang the Chinese Giant. Seven feet, four inches tall with his high-soled shoes and Mandarin cap.

VICTORIA AND ALBERT MUSEUM

departed with a black face and the act had then to vanish.

There were other subtleties which were only too easy to practice. Anyone looks taller than they are when seen from below, but a well-known showman's trick was to envelope the giant in flowing robes, which hid high heels and cork raisers in the shoes. It also hid a step on which he or she stood.

The side shows of the day were full of fat women, human skeletons or those with rubber skins or other peculiarities. The bearded ladies, though, are always a popular attraction and have held a unique fascination for centuries. In the Middle Ages they were believed to have the power of an oracle; there was even a bewhiskered saint – St. Paula the Bearded – who was a clean-shaven maiden until one day, when pursued by a medieval mugger, she prayed for Divine protection and grew an instant beard. Her would-be assailant was so frightened by the apparition that he ran away screaming and St. Paula was saved.

Barbara Urslerin, the hairy-faced woman.

The most famous of nineteenth-century ladies was Madame Clofullia. Her maiden name was Josephine Boisdechines and she was born in Switzerland in 1831 with a light down all over her body, which soon, to her parents utter horror, became long dark hair. Some suggested that the hair on her face be shaved, for by the time the prodigy was seven or eight years old it was already several inches long, but wiser counsel prevailed and to the end of her days Clofullia's superabundant hair remained soft and not bristly.

The fame of this attractive young Swiss girl covered with hair soon spread. For years her strict father resisted the most tempting offers to show off his remarkable daughter, but finally such a sum was mentioned that he could only accept. In 1849 the hairy lady started a show career which was to bring her and her husband, Fortune Clofullia Jr., a small fortune. France soon fell to the charm of the First Bearded Lady. A tour of England was a huge success and in 1853 she was invited to appear in Philadelphia. It was then that Barnum engaged her together with her son, Little Albert, who was covered in short blond hair and christened by the press the "Infant Esau."

Madame Clofullia, like a good many Very Special

CIRCUS WORLD MUSEUM, BARABOO, WISCONSIN

Tripp and Bowen in their celebrated tandem act.

People, had no act in particular and merely stood to be admired. But some of Barnum's collection of Living Curiosities exhibited other skills, such as his Amazing Armless Writers, Carvers and Artistic Workmen or the most famous of all, Eli Bowen.

Born in 1844 in Ohio, Eli Bowen was one of a family of ten, the others were all normal. But at the age of thirteen he was spotted by a tenting circus and from then on he remained in show business all his life. "One of the handsomest of men," he was described by one paper, and from the waist upward Bowen was a veritable Apollo, but his feet were joined to his hip joints. Despite his deformity he refused to allow himself to be just stared at; by diligence and painfully hard work he taught himself to become a tumbler and from there he gravitated to the perch pole. Here his curious weight adjustment and the immense strength of his forearms stood him in good stead and soon he was billed as the "Legless Aerial Gymnast, the Perch Pole Marvel."

His greatest friend in the circus was Charles Tripp "The Armless Wonder," and their combined act which they performed for years – on a tandem bicycle – invariably brought the house down. Their wit and ready humor was legendary and made them one of the most popular pair in show business. "Bowen," Tripp would say to his legless friend, "watch your step," and quick as lightning would come back the rejoinder to his armless companion, "Keep your hands off me."

Strongmen have also proved a popular attraction in

FRED D. PFENING COLLECTION

Marvelous, Indescribable and Extraordinary EXHIBITIONS OF STRENGTH. *A vivid poster of the Barnum, Bailey and Hutchinson Show.*

circus, fair and showground alike. The most famous of them all was Eugen Sandow who was born in Konigsberg in 1867. The young Sandow's parents wanted him to become a doctor and he was sent to Brussels to study anatomy. While there he met a Professor Louis Attila who ran a gymnasium and it was he who persuaded Sandow to become a professional strong-man. They went into partnership and toured widely giving exhibitions of strength, but somehow Sandow could not get the break he needed. Then, sitting outside a cafe one day, he saw a Try-Your-Strength machine. He tried, and broke it. This he proceeded to do to many more of the machines in the town, he then sat back to await events. They were not long in coming. Within hours the police had called and remained skeptical until he demonstrated his remarkable strength on one of the few surviving machines. The press soon got hold of the remarkable story, and Sandow was launched.

He and a companion toured with a number of circuses as the Rijos Brothers, and as Samson and Cyclops they astounded the London public with their feats of strength. Large sums were offered by Sandow to whomever could emulate or better their efforts, but they always won. In 1893 Sandow went to America and on one occasion wrestled with a muzzled lion with its claws padded – he won in short time.

NEW YORK PUBLIC LIBRARY

NOVOSTI PRESS AGENCY

ABOVE LEFT: *Eugene Sandow, a Tower of Strength.* RIGHT: *A modern strongman act. Alexandre Brilliantov lifting 160 kilograms with his teeth and another 65 within his hands.*

While there he founded a number of schools for physical training and culture and even reintroduced Ducrow's Poses Plastiques, so perfect was his figure – but they proved an uncertain attraction. He died suddenly at the age of fifty-eight of a hemorrhage after lifting a car out of a ditch single-handed.

Most Very Special People were created by nature, but there was one brand which had been fashioned by man – the tattooed men or women, the Living Galleries of the Tattooing Art, as they were described. Such phenomena have been on the showman scene for centuries, but they still have a fascination of their own. One such was the Painted Prince or Prince Giolo who was a prime attraction in London at the beginning of the last century. In him, evidently, "the whole Mystery of Painting or Staining upon Human Bodies seems to be comprised in one stately piece." His foreparts were magnificent, depicting many special items, but his "more admirable Back Parts afford as lively a Representation of one Quarter Part of the World as we are ever likely to see," – or so ran the bill.

Another was Captain John Constantinos, described

CIRCUS WORLD MUSEUM, BARABOO, WISCONSIN

The Wild Men of Borneo.

as a "noble Greek Albanian." As the poster said, this man of curious nationality had been captured in Chinese Tartary and, as punishment for engaging in rebellion against the king, was tattooed from head to foot. "Every inch of his body is covered with 388 beautifully delineated figures in indigo and cornelian, of beasts, birds, fishes, reptiles and hieroglyphics," the advertisement declared, and then with the utmost relish added, "The prolonged and horrible agony of this combination of barbaric art and vengeance necessitated over seven million blood-producing punctures." It need hardly be added that the so-called Captain had never put foot out of England in his entire life.

Fascinating as were the indigenous "curiosities," ones from abroad seemed to hold a special place in public regard. Perhaps it was because they were seeing sights which accorded with what they believed such outlandish peoples should look like. They accepted as true Barnum's assertion that his Aztec people really were the last survivors of the Central American race, or that his Wild Men of Borneo actually hailed from that country – although they were in fact

A poster showing the giraffe-neck women of Burma, a Ringling Bros. and Barnum & Bailey sensation.

honest American citizens. Zip the What-is-it? – a name said to have been invented by Charles Dickens – was a man with a remarkably pointed head on which was perched an artificial top-knot. Dressed in a gorilla skin he looked like nothing on this earth. This was hardly fraud, but rather harmless humbug and people like to be deceived, or so Barnum always asserted.

People also like to believe the improbable and the citizens of London were only too eager to swallow the tale of the "Man with one Head and Two Bodies" who, with his brother, had come out of "the Great Mogul's Country." Perhaps too, their sense of propriety was satisfied and their conscience assuaged by the assertion that "both here since baptised in the Christian Faith and become Christian."

Foreign troupes have always been an attraction in the circus. One of the first was a party of Arabs which Franconi introduced to Paris in 1847, and the act was repeated by Sanger ten years later. Hagenbeck made his second fortune by importing and showing ethnological groups and in his time Singhalese, Hottentots, Zulus, Lapps and Ashantis, among others, passed through his hands and proved immensely popular wherever they were exhibited. Pawnee Bill's Great Far East, a show "never before granted to startled American eyes" aggregated all that was wonderful from foreign parts. Here "every trick which for centuries has puzzled Western Societies and laymen" was laid bare, "apparent miracles, passing all understanding and conception" were performed daily before astonished eyes. A mango tree grew, flowered and fruited within a matter of minutes. A girl vanished. Pigeons flew out of eggs. Damayanti, a nautch girl supreme, danced the egg dance of Sahmakin, "one of the most difficult feats ever essayed by modern terpsichoreans." The Singhalese performed a striking "stick and silver" dance and cannibals from Africa devoured "real" flesh.

Another ready draw in side-show and fairground booth alike was the Pig-Faced Lady or the Hog-faced Gentlewoman. Opinion is somewhat divided about whether there has ever been a real pig-faced lady but certainly there does seem to be considerable authentication that from time to time such phenomena did occur. One was fathered, and the tale is confirmed in a carving in a cathedral in Belgium, by an Englishman around the middle of the seventeenth century. This gentleman had pronounced religious views but had become somewhat confused by the many sects which arose in England during Cromwell's time. At length he ended his perplexity by embracing the Jewish faith so imagine his horror when the next child his wife bore him was a pig-faced girl. Later recanting his new religion he persuaded a friendly monk to apply copious quantities of holy water to the stricken child, and, miracle of miracles, her face became human again.

Another, called Tanakin Shrinker, was born early in the seventeenth century in a town on the River Rhine. A dowry was offered by her father of no less than 40,000 crowns to whomever would marry her. Swains came from far and wide but each and every one refused the proffered trotter. Apart from her looks, conversation was difficult as she could only say, "Ough, Ough."

In fact this seems to have been a handicap common to most pig-faced ladies. It certainly was to perhaps the most famous of all, Miss Atkinson, who was born in Ireland and who became quite celebrated in her day. "This prodigy of nature," one commentator wrote, "is the general topic of conversation in the metropolis. In almost every company you may join the Pig-Faced Lady is introduced and her existence is firmly believed by thousands. . . . Her person is most delicately modelled in the happiest mould of nature and in the carriage of her body, indicative of superior birth. Her manners are, in general, simple and unoffending; but when she is in want of food, she articulates, certainly something like the sound of pigs eating, and which, to those who are not acquainted with her, may perhaps be a little disagreeable!"

Most "Pig-faced Ladies" did not articulate at all, for the simple reason that they were bears with shaven heads and necks – which prompted one newspaper to fulminate against such bear-faced impositions! Wearing a shawl and flowing dress and covered with a wig, with their paws hidden inside gloves, the bears were remarkably like pig ladies. The long dress had further uses, for hidden under the chair would be a small boy who at the appropriate moment would prod the bear with a stick. A gentle poke and the animal would murmur politely, a more vigorous one and it would grumble mightily. A clever team of questioner and prodder, and a reasonably amenable bear, could all but carry on a lucid conversation. It was never a far cry from the freak to the fake.

"A Wizard Dream of Supernatural Sights . . ." "Matchless Works of Magic," thundered the Barnum bills. Tales of "Mirthful and Astounding Visions" or "Strange Spiritual Manifestations," whetted the appetites of all comers. Who could possibly resist such excitement as "The Birth of Aphrodite?" This magic triumph opened with a view of the ocean; the horizon illuminated by the prismatic, shooting rays of the northern lights – plausibility was never a bar to the showman. "The life-size *Apparition of Venus*, bathed in the rosy tints of the aurora borealis, rises from the waves, ascends into airy space, and after assuming a number of bewitching poses, disappears by diving head-long into the deep." Or there was the illusion effected by mirrors, of The Witch's Head, a box in which a "Living, Speaking Human Head" was exhibited. The box was then taken from the table and shown to the audience with the head still in it. And what of the Alaska Wonder, Neptune's Bridge, Grecian Metamorphoses, or the Gnome's Carnival and other spectacles which enthralled audiences at circus side shows, carnivals and fairs across many lands? Magic and sorcery have held a fascination for man since time immemorial, nor is religion so remote from superstition. Interest in the power of the supernatural, the white arts, and the black arts go back for hundreds of years. Magical and illusionist acts were first performed in private, or in tavern and saloon bars. They gravitated to the fair and the side show, from there to the stage, the circus and now to television. Man's fascination for the unexplainable has deep roots, our ancestors thought of fire as supernatural, more recently the electric light created consternation at first. But this is the fascination of curiosity for we like to be frightened and we like to be fooled.

The great age of magic corresponds almost exactly with the great age of the circus. When Barnum, Forepaugh, Sanger and others were packing them in to watch their great circuses, Robert-Houdin in France, Maskelyne in Great

NOVOSTI PRESS AGENCY

Magic. The water trick at the Moscow State Circus.

Britain, Alexander Hermann, Chung Ling Soo and later Kellar and Thurston and a great many others drew vast crowds to watch their magic and their illusions in halls and often in circus side shows across many lands. Many of these magicians, and myriad ones of lesser note, performed in circus side shows in the earlier days of their careers; many of their acts were blatantly copied and plagiarized for the enjoyment of circus audiences.

It was one of the earliest magicians, the Italian Cagliostro, who said – "The world is my oyster which I with fraud will open." He founded an order of Egyptian masons and as its "grand Cophtha" directed its affairs, and its finance – a sequence not altogether unknown today. He called his tricks miracles and announced that he had found the secrets of the age-old philosophers' stone and the elixir of life. Around the time Astley was performing in Paris, Cagliostro was casting his magic spell and bamboozling the nobility, until the Catholic Church stepped in and condemned him to perpetual imprisonment.

Cagliostro's were ancient tricks and sorcery, but now the age of science was beginning and one of the first to take advantage of the new phenomena was the Frenchman Robert-Houdin, a watchmaker by trade. His ingenious mechanical devices and automatons amazed and delighted French audiences, and others farther afield, for nearly forty years from the 1830s. This too was the age of another watch-maker magician, the great John Nevil Maskelyne. The Egyptian Hall in Piccadilly was the scene for many of Maskelyne's triumphs – here was a permanent menagerie, and for nearly thirty years Maskelyne astounded audiences with his illusions. This was at first with Thomas Taplin Cooke and then with the man with whom his name is forever coupled in the minds of British audiences, David Devant. A versatile man with many inventions credited to his fertile brain, Maskelyne is perhaps best known for his automatons which could play chess or cards, and perform on musical instruments.

"Trapped by Magic" – the first time in a levitation act that a hoop was passed over a body – was the *piéce de resistance* of the Maskelyne and Devant act from its first performance in 1898 until the secret was passed to the great American magician Kellar – it is now a standard trick on many bills. Bodiless heads and busts were the stock in trade of magical side shows; of equal delight were the spine-killing decapitation acts, with or without the added attraction of blood and gore. Disappearing elephants (a Houdini special), bicycles, motorcycles – and, when they were invented, cars – and pianos, complete with virtuosi who worked on their keyboards until finally vanishing into nothing, leaving only a few lingering notes behind them, soon became the stock in trade of the profession.

Invention of "Sawing the Lady in Half," another hardy standby to the side-show world, is credited to P. T. Selbit, a British journalist who turned to magic and became one of the great illusionists of all time. But this was a raw act until it came into the hands of one Horace Goldin, a Polish emigré who came to America in 1889 at the age of sixteen. An early showman's life with side shows was the forerunner of a spectacular and very profitable career, but it is for his popularizing of Selbit's "Sawn Lady" that he is best known. At one time, so popular had the act become that he hired half-a-dozen other theater companies to play the cities which he himself could not reach. A consummate showman, he would have nurses and ambulances ostentatiously standing by at the theater entrance "in case anything went wrong!" With an equal flourish he would insure his "victims" for vast sums with local insurance companies, and he would thrill his audiences and titillate their anticipation in a dozen different ways.

The king of all the great magicians of this era was the great Harry Houdini. Houdini, or rather, Erich Weiss, was born of Hungarian parents in Wisconsin - although some say he was born in Hungary - in 1874. From an early age he was fascinated by magic and magicians and soon after his professional career started he took the name Houdini in deference to his magician forebear Robert-Houdin. Nine years of near poverty and small town acts followed, gradually his showman genius came to be recognized in America.

A keen student of magic, he read all he could of the art. For hours he would pore over his rapidly accumulating library of magic, dissecting and developing the great feats of the old masters of deception – always conscious of the

The great Harry Houdini in chains and padlocks.

unpayable debt he owed his magician forebears. In later years, as he toured Europe and other areas, he would make a point of seeking out the graves of past magicians, and, if they were neglected – as more often than not they were – then he himself would pay to arrange that their resting places were properly looked after.

In 1900 he determined to stake all on a trip to Europe, and five years later he was able to return to New York, his reputation made. He was a show-business hero and, more important, would demand and get a four-figure fee for his performances.

Throughout this time he had been perfecting his technique. Genius and escapologist supreme, he may have been, but his act by no means came easy to him: the sheer physical and mental exhaustion of his performance left him completely drained of strength. Houdini was a remarkable performer, and a remarkable man. Hated by as many as loved him, he was in turn generous and jealous, kind and vitriolic. Through it all he was the complete professional, with a true genius for showmanship and an uncanny instinct for effect. He was also careful after having once been trapped in his early days in a pair of handcuffs the lock of which had been jammed with lead shot. Ever after he saw each and every padlock or fastening opened and shut before his eyes, for what could to the prankster have been a trick to hoax the master escaper might have ended fatally – especially during his more elaborate stunts.

To only one other person would he trust this literally vital task – one William (Jim) Collins, an Englishman who in 1910 swore never to reveal Houdini's secrets. Nor did he, and when Houdini died, the faithful Collins partnered the master's brother Hardeen, another magician. Collins was in his way as brilliant as his master. A superb engineer and metal craftsman, Collins was the mechanical brain behind the Houdini brilliance, and dreamed up many of the magician's tricks and turns.

Some of these are well known and have been emulated dozens of times but some are still unique to the great Houdini for no one has been able, or foolhardy enough to try them.

His proud boast was that "no manacle, restraint or prison can hold me . . ." and he wagered huge sums to support it, and always won. Being buried alive in coffins, chained, tied and roped into a wooden box and thrown into the river were some of the exploits in which Houdini reveled but probably the more simple means of restraining the man proved the hardest for him to overcome. Perhaps the most difficult of all was to struggle out of a swathe of damp sheets which clung and stuck to him like a thing possessed. His most prominent early trick was to escape from a straitjacket which had been put on him by attendants of a lunatic asylum – who assuredly knew their stuff – yet he was out of that and appeared

HUBERT CASTLE INTERNATIONAL CIRCUS

A modern escapologist and magician. The Canadian Dale Harney. Here he is wriggling out of a straitjacket while suspended in mid-air, upside down from the end of a rope which has been set on fire.

from his cabinet with the straitjacket over his arm in a matter of minutes.

How did he do it? Certainly his physical and mental training was such that he could hold his breath for three minutes – a prodigious time – his control over his muscles was incredible and he could untie simple knots or undo simple fastenings with his toes. He was master of the old ploys of puffing out the chest or flexing muscles when the bonds were being placed round him. Those were his physical skills, but when even his remarkable physical attributes were exhausted, trickery entered. It is said that a duplicate rope was one of his favorite devices; some avowed too, that he had a knife secreted in the cabinet with him. He also had a book, according to one authority, with which he whiled away his idle moments waiting for his audience to reach a proper state of excitement and the orchestra which accompanied his acts to climb to their chosen crescendo.

On frequent occasions, he was searched by medical men to ensure that there were no devices hidden about his person, but no one ever thought of looking at the soles of his feet where, some believed, he used to tape a piece of wire. Nor did they ever think of restricting the movements of the faithful Collins who would go unremarked and could report to his master on the exact type of lock to be used or the layout of the cell in which Houdini was to be secured. Perhaps his role was even to hide pieces of wire or a blade inside the place where Houdini was to be confined.

The breath-taking performances when Houdini was bound, shackled and placed in a wooden box, which itself was secured by rope and thrown into a river, were preceded by a visit the previous night when the box was gently prized open and the long nails securing the sides replaced with short ones which would yield on the slightest pressure from within. And so, miraculously, the great Houdini would escape.

Cheating? Perhaps. Many suspected it though none could prove it. But was the Feejee Mermaid a cheat or was it humbug? There is a subtle distinction which Barnum and others have found. However, when all is said and done, what Houdini managed to do required nerve, skill and immense courage and he risked death on innumerable occasions, but these alone were not enough, for the proper presentation of his act also required consummate showmanship and that the great Houdini had in plenty. After all, is that not what the circus is about?

Of all illusionist tricks to mystify the public and the one most surrounded by an aura of wonder, the Bullet Catch or the Great Gun Trick, is perhaps the most impressive. It is said that Philip Astley was the first to introduce it onto the public scene, using a simple sleight of hand transference he would catch the bullet on the point of a dagger. Soon imitators had developed the more spectacular catch between the teeth, soon, too, started the long list of fatalities which this trick has caused, not because of its inherent danger – most bullet catchers have died peacefully in their beds – but because usually some smart aleck with an overdose of cunning has switched bullets or weapons. Wax bullets, soap ones covered with powdered graphite – although once these caused a near fatality when the missile failed to disintegrate on impact – were the tricks of the trade. Sometimes a gun which had a blocked-up barrel was used. In the days of muzzle loaders the switch was easily effected, either when the bullet was bitten off, or when a "doctored" ramrod was used to push the wad home. But with modern sophistication, and greater skepticism, the Bullet Catch has become more difficult to achieve. Guns chosen at random, sealed boxes of ammunition, marked bullets, and subsequent microscopic examination of both the bullet and the cartridge, and watchful

A Change of Performance each Day.

RICHARDSON'S

THEATRE

Will be performed a new Eastern Melo-Drama, called The

Turkish Heroine;

Or, The FORCE OF LOVE.

Osmin (Sultan of the East) Mr. LEWIS——Nourhassan (his Son) Mr. COOPER——Alaric (Grand Vizier) Mr. PETO
Hammett (Friend to Selim) Mr. ODEY——Grand Mufti — Mr. SMITH——Selim (Prince of Palmyra) Mr. LAMORE
Guards, Attendants, &c. &c.
Almira (Queen of Palermo) — Miss DELAMORE——Abra (her Friend) — Mrs. PARKINSON
Spectre of Almira's Mother — Mrs. GREEN——Ladies of the Seraglio, &c.

AFTER WHICH,

SIGNORA JOSEPHINE

Girardelli,

The Great Phenomenon of Nature, from the Continent,

Who has had the honour of appearing before most of the Crowned Heads in Europe, and the Theatres Royal in London, with unprecedented applause, will exhibit the Power of RESISTANCE against HEAT in an uncommon manner, by

Passing RED HOT IRONS

Over her Hair, also over her Tongue, Arms, and Legs,

She will hold her ARMS over an immense BODY of FLAME,

Wash her Hands in Boiling Lead,

Pour the same into her Mouth! with many other wonderful Feats which must be seen to be credited.

To conclude with an entire New Pantomime, with splendid Scenery, Tricks, &c. called

Harlequin's RAMBLES;

Or, The WONDERS of LONDON.

Harlequin Rambler, Mr FLOWERS——Old Wise Acre (Pantaloon) Mr. FIELDING——Young Flimsey (Lover) Mr. ODEY
Dancing Bear Man, Mr LEWIS——Gardner, Mr GREEN——Dancers, Peasants, &c——Clown............Mr WALBURN
Fanny Wise Acre (Columbine).......Mrs ADAMS——Market Woman...........Mrs SMITH

A FRICASEE DANCE, by Messrs. WALBURN and HOLYOAK.

The Scenery consists of a Collection of VIEWS taken from the spot by the most celebrated Artists.

The TRICKS invented and executed by the first Mechanists in the Metropolis.

To conclude with the GRAND WATERFALL OF NIAGARA IN AMERICA.

BOXES, 2s.——PIT 1s.——STANDING PLACES, 6d.

MOTTLEY & CO. PRINTERS.

A handsheet advertising Signora Josephine Giradelli the Fire Proof Lady. A remarkable woman who could put molten lead into her mouth and spit it out marked with her teeth; pass red-hot irons over her body and limbs, her tongue and her hair; thrust her arm into a blazing fire; and thought nothing of washing her head in boiling oil.

witnesses to ensure against any "switch" these are what the modern performer has to contend with, and yet, somehow they succeed and continue to mystify.

One of the most convincing was Chung Ling Soo, whose speciality in magic was an Oriental act, although he had never been to China in his life and had been born in New York City of American parents and christened William Ellsworth Robinson. For a number of years Robinson toured by himself or as assistant to other great magicians. But a real Chinaman was proving a stunning draw at the time, so Robinson changed his name to Chung Ling Soo and challenged and beat his oriental colleague. Robinson had no patter so he devised a purely silent act and as the "Oriental Mystic" he mesmerized audiences across the world. For years he had used and perfected the bullet catch, but in London on the night of March 23, 1918, it went wrong. Or did it? The mystery of Chung Ling Soo's death transcended even

A modern Fire-Eating Act from Circus of Horrors.

EMI FILM DISTRIBUTORS LTD AND NATIONAL FILM ARCHIVE, LONDON

the excitement over his live acts and it is now generally believed that the magician tampered with his own gun in an elaborate and sensational form of suicide.

As dangerous in its way is the act of Fire Eater. The principle of a wetted mouth and tongue providing a thin insulation against fire is obvious enough, but the execution is still impressive and Human Volcanoes are certain draws in any side show or "carny." Many have suffered fearful burns, some few have "exploded" and survive only as human wrecks for they have forgotten, albeit only temporarily, or become overconfident about the four "don'ts" of fire eating: DON'T eat fire in a draught or high wind – and many a side-show tent is open to every draught that blows or can be if someone should open up the tent flap at the wrong time – ; DON'T wear whiskers – very few do, or for long; DON'T eat fire if you have a cold, are likely to sneeze or cough or suffer from indigestion; DON'T use ordinary fuel – the lead in it will ultimately turn you blue! But if you remember all these things, don't mind blisters and possess an asbestos mouth, fire eating is one of the easiest of side-show acts, and certainly one of the most impressive.

Fire eating is an age-old act and the variations these voracious people can put into their act seem endless. Chewing burning brimstone and then swallowing it was the forte of one fire eater in Italy. He also relished a diet of burning coals and supped on melted pitch which he ate with a spoon. He was quite happy licking a red-hot poker, and it was even said that he could kindle coals on his tongue and then broil

EMI FILM DISTRIBUTORS LTD AND NATIONAL FILM ARCHIVE, LONDON

Knife throwing. Another popular side-show act. From Circus of Horrors.

meat on them. He did this quite regularly and with some enjoyment five times a day at the Duke of Marlborough's Head in Fleet Street in London. Such a diet can have done him no good at all and so to assuage "the bad effect of frequent swallowing of red-hot coals, melted sealing wax, resin, brimstone and other inflammable matter," he would drink plentiful quantities of warm water and oil, and one would think he needed to.

Sword swallowing is another old side-show trick. It is said to be easy once the natural urge to vomit when any foreign body is shoved down the throat has been overcome. Even experienced sword swallowers take care not to eat for several hours before their performance. But accidents can happen. A horrifying tale is told of one Benedetti, a noted sword swallower, the climax of whose act was to swallow a bayonet still attached to a rifle and swing the weapon round his body holding the steel in his teeth. For years he had done this before enthralled audiences, then one day the bayonet snapped inside him. Fortunately he had the presence of mind to stand on his hands while attendants held his feet and shook him. Luckily the bayonet popped out, but it was many a day before he tried that trick again.

Impressive as sword swallowing undoubtedly is, it is nothing to the effect of swallowing neon lights which, when lit, produce the most ghostly of glows inside the body, and subject the performer to the most dreadful of risks either of a short circuit or, worse, of the neon tube breaking. Others seem to enjoy swallowing the most repellant of objects, Human Ostriches they are known as. Frogs, goldfish – the performer swallows copious amounts of water before he begins – live rats and such like. For the remarkable ability of the human body to regurgitate is rarely put to the test. Houdini, amongst his many other skills, was a talented regurgitator.

The world of the flea circus is another facet of the side-show scene. Perverse and temperamental little creatures, the great flea master of all time, Bertolotto, who dominated the flea stage for a remarkable portion of the nineteenth century wrote in his famous treatise on the flea:

"Fleas are of an obstinate disposition; some of them will carry their stubbornness to such a pitch when in chains that they will not move a step, nor will they take any kind of food in spite of all my endeavors to make them. They will contract their legs and remain motionless as long as they think they are observed and generally die in five or six days, victims to their obstinacy."

Possessed of tremendous strength for their size, Bertolotto reckoned that it took eighteen fully grown and plump fleas to weigh a grain, yet one flea could pull 360 times its own weight and that when harnessed by the hind leg to a golden chain which was attached to a miniature ship on a carriage. The male which was shorter and darker was less suited to his purpose than the female, who, as he put it, "for color, rotundity of form and elegance of carriage well deserves the appellation of the Fairer Sex," an aspect of fleas which is revealed to only the most enthusiastic observers.

In past days, in the heyday of the flea circuses, it was always human fleas which were used – dog fleas are less resilient and need feeding four to five times every twenty-four hours while human ones only need a meal every four to five days. In Bertolotto's day it was considered an honor to feed the fleas, and ladies of distinction, as he proudly declared, would fall over themselves to be allowed the privilege of feeding the fleas. It is less easy nowadays – perhaps ladies of distinction are fewer. Indeed to find human fleas at all is something of a problem to the "fancy" – even fifty years ago many a landlord, when asked by the ardent flea seeker whether his hostelry harbored fleas, would more likely than not fail to appreciate fully the reason for the request and also more often than not eject the seeker with some force.

Once caught, there seems no end to the ingenuity of the flea at the hands of the flea master. Bertolotto proudly proclaimed that he possessed a man o' war of 120 guns pulled by a flea, that he had trained fleas to pull up and let down a bucket from a well, others to fight a duel, and had a flea orchestra which played real music for a dance performed by eight fleas, dressed as four gentlemen and four ladies. A stag hunt, complete with flea riders and flea hounds and flea quarry, drew as large an audience as the flea attack on a fort defended by fleas. A flea Blondin and an Insect Léotard were particularly popular among the "Trained Apterous Insects, the only specimens of the Articulata in the world ever taught to perform."

Bertolotto, however, found all was not easy in the flea world, for his fleas would wear away their claws after a few days and then had to be withdrawn into reserve for a period of rest and recuperation while the claws grew again. Their miniature harnesses proved a problem and had to be secured to their bodies by even more miniature bandages because he could find no glue which would stick to their bodies. Nevertheless, once these problems are overcome, the flea must be the most resilient performer on the side-show stage, for he will perform up to fifty ten-minute shows a day for two weeks or more without wearying or going on strike or seeking a square meal more than once a week.

Of all the side shows that have captivated an audience in the history of entertainment – although it was, strictly speaking, a theater performance – that of the French gentleman known as the Petomane must claim preeminence. Born Joseph Pujol, this remarkable character did not discover his astonishing properties until he was nearly eight years old. Then one day when he was bathing he sat down in the water and held his breath – he nearly drowned, for by some remarkable quirk of nature he had been born with two mouths and breathing tubes, one at either end of his body.

As he grew older he began to discover the real fruits of his incredible physical construction. By sitting in a bucket he could "breathe" up as much as two liters of water. He could make beautiful bird noises, and others more suited to the taste of a Parisian audience. In fact, as he put it, he converted fart to art – all, as critics observed, disturbing only the sensibility of the ears. He could blow out a candle at five paces and his repertoire included a number of popular tunes. And it was all done by with or through the anus! His is an act which has never been repeated, and few have tried.

CHARIVARI

Almost before the last note of the band has died away the circus is on the move. As the crowds troop out to make their way home, the back-scene army of circus helpers go to work. First to come down are the sidewalls – the stilt men can be useful here. Then the quarter-poles are dismantled and soon the Big Top resembles a monstrous prehistoric marine skeleton. The electricians have been about their work coiling up the miles of cable which bring light, and heat and sound to the audience. The hum of the great generators come to a stop and the circus is taken down by the light of headlights. As soon as the last section of the king poles, the last piece of canvas has been loaded, the circus is ready to roll. It is only a few hours since the end of the performance and as the town sleeps the circus leaves. When dawn comes, the "tober," or lot, will be empty. The small, bustling nomadic show which had made the place its own for a few days has moved on. Only some wheelmarks on the ground, grass compressed by the weight of caravan, cage and side show betray the fact that anyone has been there – for circus folk will meticulously see that every trace of their presence has been removed, after all their reception in a year, two years' or even three years' time may depend on it. Overnight a fairyland has disappeared, a place which short hours ago had been alive with light and noise and drama and excitement has gone; a child might be forgiven if he wondered if it had all been a dream.

For there is still glamor about the circus, the "ever-changing, never-changing circus," as Earl Chapin May called it. It may not be the kind experienced by our forefathers, nevertheless it is real enough. Nor have the circus folk changed much at heart. Clannish, living a life apart, self-reliant, they intermarry and are proud of their heritage. They have their own expressions and slang, "tober," "josser," "bender" and many others. They are also superstitious –

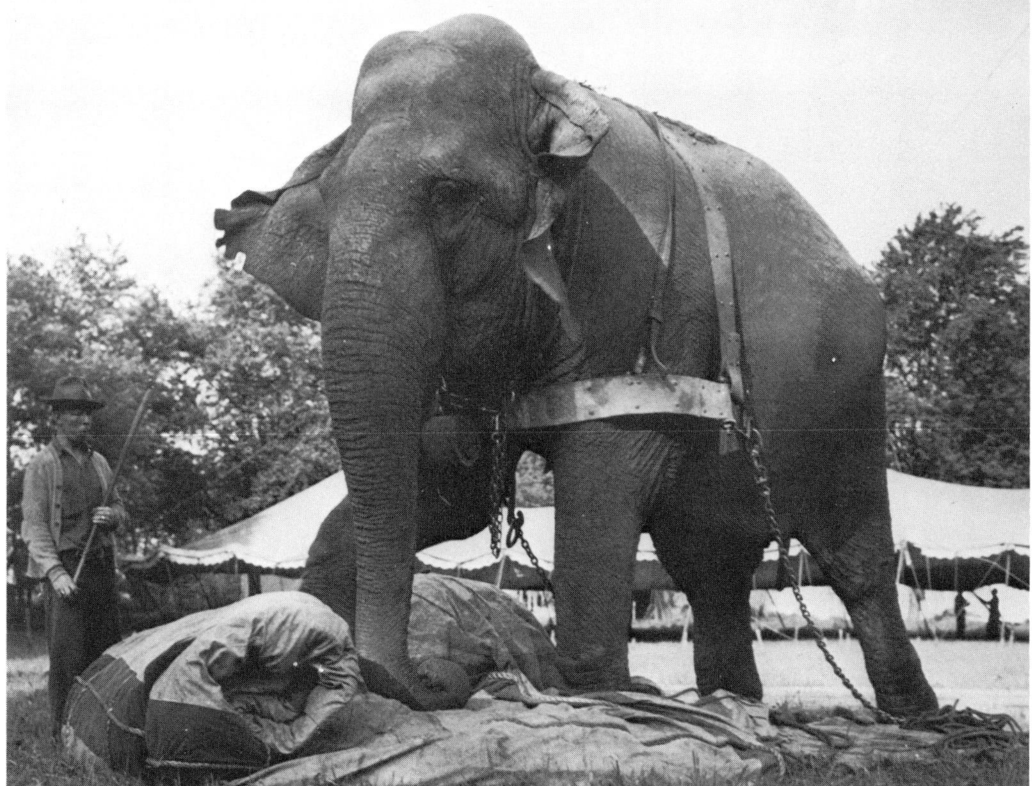

Elephant power. Helping to pack up at the Cole Brothers Circus, 1949.

particularly animal trainers who are perhaps nearer to death than the others. Some merely touch the outside of the cage before going in, others go about a complicated ritual which they religiously perform before each performance or training session.

There is a special magic about the old days of the circus; performers then lived a simple, unhurried life. An enchanting picture is conveyed of a train carrying a circus in the Czarist days of Old Russia, which would come to a halt in the middle of that huge country. The doors would open and the circus children jump out to collect flowers from field and wood, while their parents would go and bargain for eggs, chickens and vegetables from the country people. The smaller animals, released from bondage, would scamper about while the driver and his fireman would unhurriedly dismount from their wheezing engine and come to talk to their passengers and perhaps accept some tea from the ubiquitous samovar. For there was no rush in those spacious days.

Another appealing picture is created by the herd of Shetland ponies which followed on the heels of George Sanger's vast procession as it made its steady progress from one town to another. The little devils, all innocence and hair, would nose their way into any cottage door left open and pilfer any food they could find. A favorite target for their mischief were the itinerant nougat sellers who trudged their

FRED D. PFENING COLLECTION

Elephant power. The ever-willing elephants pull the Sparks Circus' bandwagon out of deep mud.

way from town to town carrying their wares on broad trays balanced on their heads. When one of these unfortunates was spotted by the ponies, like one horse they would converge on the man. In no time he had been upset and his wares, scattered on the road, devoured by the greedy Shetlands.

Getting the circus on the move must have provided different problems to those of the present day. Having dismembered the Big Top by lantern light, for this was long before the days of electricity, the wagons would be loaded and the great horse-drawn caravans set out on their way. The drivers, after a full day and an evening performance would be nearly asleep, lulled by the cool night air, the rhythmic sway of the wagons, the gentle chuckle and creak of the wheels as they crunched over the ground, and, perhaps, the contented snores of the beasts they carried. Accidents were frequent and tempers ran high when slumbering wagonmen had to be stopped to help one of their number who had driven into the ditch. For the most part the solid reliable draft horses needed no guidance. When the rains came, and the roads became a sea of mud with their deeper potholes hidden by a layer of water, then came trouble, for with wagon-drivers half-asleep, accidents were frequent. Then the circus folk must dismount and pull out the offending wagon; sometimes other horses must be hitched to the casualty. Sometimes the faithful elephants were called into use, and with a few good-natured grumbles they would soon have the wagon out of the mud with a resounding squelch and on the road again. Their only reward was pleasure at their handler's pleasure.

CIRCUS WORLD MUSEUM, BARABOO, WISCONSIN

Days of misty dawns and glorious sunrises . . . A rolling show, 1911.

In the earlier years of the circus, the elephants and their keepers would sometimes set off on their own and at their own speed and gait as soon as the day's show was over and while the rest of the circus was packing up. To hurry an elephant over rough roads was to risk getting grit and stones between the huge toes. This would soon lead to irritation and sores, and an elephant with sore feet is a very angry elephant indeed. Usually elephants trekked along in line with each one's trunk attached to the tail in front. It happened that one day the six-elephant troupe of a traveling circus was hit at a grade crossing by a train. When he discovered that only one elephant had been killed, the driver of the train who, amazingly, had survived the impact, was mightily relieved. He said so, only to be greeted with the response, "Yes, but you've torn the ass out of the other five!"

In those horse-drawn days the "boss hostler," either on horseback or in a sulky, would find the way and set the pace. "Layers out" would leave signs on the road behind him to show the following circus where to go. These might be branches stuck in the ground, a pile of sand or a cairn of rocks. Sometimes the marks would be swept away by the weather, sometimes rivals or small boys would be to blame.

So the circus would go on its way. These were days of magical sunrises and mist-shrouded mornings, of clammy reins and the feel of the countryside become alive around them. It was hard enough to stay awake on the wagons during these nights on the road, but after dawn it became well-nigh impossible, "Nobody can keep awake after the old haymaker comes up," they used to say.

It is a curious feature of those days that circus proprietors seemed to live in a constant state of surprise at the whereabouts of their competitors. On frequent occasions one reads of a circus arriving in town only to find that someone had got there first. Sanger was no exception, and it was not unusual for the "Lord" George Sanger show to be in the same town as the "Lord" John Sanger circus. And then the fur really did begin to fly. There was no love lost between the two, on the other hand both knew that a battle royal would be the best advertisement possible and people would come along just to see what happened next. From time to time their parades clashed or came within sight and sound of one another, then "Lord" George looking as fierce as he was able, would scowl at his rivals and roar "Beware the wicked uncle." But the achievement he was proudest of was the occasion when he bested The Greatest Show on Earth.

The Barnum and Bailey show was well established when Sanger's tenting show pulled into town. The Greatest Show on Earth had already given a morning performance and was scheduled for an afternoon show starting at two o'clock, so it was at that time that Sanger announced his own parade would take place. As the town flocked to see the parade, the other show played before an almost empty tent. Cheered by the success of that operation, Sanger pondered on how to thwart Bailey's evening show as well. It happened that the Boer War was at its height. Anti-Boer feeling, especially against the hated President Kruger, was rampant so it was announced that there would be a special parade after which an effigy of Kruger was to be burned. Patriotically, the town turned out to a man, woman and child, to shout and scream abuse at Kruger. Soon they started to cast more than derision. The tentman, who had stood in for the effigy as seeing an easy way of enjoying the parade, all too soon found himself the target of a hail of missiles; worse, someone managed to set fire to his false whiskers. And to enliven the scene further, a number of Bailey's tentmen now joined in enthusiastically and dumped carriage, Kruger and all in a nearby duckpond. "Kruger" departed and was never seen again. The Barnum and Bailey show crept out that night, and "Lord" George Sanger reckoned he had won a resounding victory.

This incident ended without serious casualties, but circus affrays were not always so mild. When entertainment came to town once every three or four years, the arrival of the circus was the signal for every tough in the district to start limbering up for action, for a good fight against worthy opponents was well worth a wait of a few years and the chance of "lickin' the circus" was a pleasure to be eagerly awaited.

A "clem" is the circus expression for a fight on the lot, and "Hey Rube," warning of the presence of strangers with trouble in their eyes, has been the rallying cry of the circus for more than a century. It is the signal that trouble is brewing, that the townies are massing for a fight, that every able-bodied man, and not a few women – for circus women when roused can be more wrathful than their men - should gather round, seizing any available weapon. One good thing about a circus was just how many potential weapons there were about, stakes, sledges, pickaxes and the like. To read of the famous clems of old, it is quite clear that the circus folk relished an affray with local toughs, for it was a good way for the "boys" to let off steam. The clash became almost automatic and a good fight would take place every two or three weeks. Some areas were worse than others, mining districts in particular were always notorious for generating trouble of one sort or another. The Sangers used to travel quite a lot in the mining districts of north England, and George Sanger recounted horrifying tales of steel-toe-booted miners dealing with one unfortunate showman whom they thought had cheated them.

Clems were part of the daily life of circus men of old, and the poet William Devere sums up the whole scene:

Twas just about ten years ago –
Too early yet for ice or snow –
Through bounteous Texas coming down,
A circus with a funny clown –
"Hey Rube."

The boys warn't feeling very well –
The reason why I cannot tell;
And, as they "made" each little town,
They whispered, as the gawks came round,
"Hey Rube."

They didn't say it, mind you now,
But if you scanned each frowning brow
When pestered by some "budgy" guy,
You'd almost read it in their eye –
"Hey Rube."

It's but a little phrase, 'tis true –
Its meaning well each "faker" knew;
And e'en the weakest heart was stirred
At mention of that magic word –
"Hey Rube."

They gathered round, about two score
I am not sure but there were more –
Red hot and eager for the fray;
The boys all *thought*, but didn't say –
"Hey Rube."

The ball was opened. Like a flash,
Above the battle's din and clash,
As thunderbolts hurled from the sky,
Rang, long and loud, the battle cry –
"Hey Rube."

Twas but a moment, in they went,
Each man on life and death intent;
They periled there both life and limb,
Twas wonderful to hear them sing –
"Hey Rube."

Twas finished. The smoke rolled away
As clouds before the sun's bright ray.
That Texan chivalry were gone;
They couldn't sing that circus song –
"Hey Rube."

MORAL

"Gawks," "guys," and "Rubes" another day
Whene'er a circus comes your way
And you are spi'lin' for a "clem,"
Be sure they haven't learned to sing –
"Hey Rube."

The police usually showed a marked discretion when circus trouble was brewing. In fact, were the truth known, the police were often only too delighted to see the local toughs given some well-deserved and overdue rough treatment. The larger circuses used guy ropes of chain to prevent them being cut, and sometimes had to resort to clearing the ground with the elephants – the best crowd disperser there is. The circus men were more than a match for most opposition, the advantages of discipline and the fact that they were fighting on their home ground usually proved enough. It was the smaller shows or the traveling showmen who had a hard time. George Sanger's father spent many a night wide awake with a shotgun across his knee. No one else would protect them for almost without exception magistrate and constable alike looked upon the showmen as undesirable vagrants. Nor were they immune from trouble from their own kind. In many cases fairs were held on Mondays, so as midnight struck on the Sunday before, a mad helter-skelter from the town boundary would follow as showmen rushed to get the best places. No holds were barred; showmen would block each other's wheels, sabotage the horses and do everything not necessarily short of physical violence to delay each other.

From time to time circuses would clash on the road, long before they reached their destination. One of the most famous of these affrays occurred on the road from Henley to Oxford one summer in the late 1850s. There had been a great fair in Reading for the whole of the previous week and hundreds of showmen, some with but a single stall, others with great beast wagons which housed their menageries and elaborate side shows, had gathered there. Some of the wiser ones set out for the great annual fair at Oxford almost before the last visitor had gone home and were on the road, plodding their weary way ahead of their fellows and hoping to steal a march on their less energetic competitors. The bigger shows took longer to pack up and it was not until nearing dawn that they were on the move. Soon a ragged caravan several miles long of brightly colored, gaily painted caravans and wagons was on the Oxford road. Some were slower than others and were soon passed. But the two biggest shows, deadly rivals at the best of times, were closing fast. They met, and an affray of massive proportions took place on the road. The big boys were fairly evenly matched, but soon their supporters and allies from the shows had joined in too and a free-for-all of memorable proportions took place. Why no one was killed has forever remained a mystery, but broken bones there were by the score and the police on this occasion had to be called in to prevent serious bloodshed. The young Sangers ("Lord" George, who wrote about the clash in his memoirs, was only six at the time) were in their caravan halted on the side of the road, when the whole conveyance with them still in it was bodily thrown into a ditch. Two very frightened little boys emerged to watch their elders enjoying a battle which was to go down in showman history.

Smaller skirmishes were common, especially when two circuses tried to operate on the same territory. Poster wars were commonplace, with rat bills and mud bills denouncing the opposition, and these often enough led to blood and blows. It was nothing to put up ten thousand posters in a day, a thirty-man team could plaster a medium-sized city in twenty-four hours. If there were rival posters in the way, it was easy to paste over them with your own. Fly-posting took place on any and every flat surface, barn door, fence and rail that could be found, preferably where the rain could not reach. To soothe the farmers, who naturally enough took exception to seeing their barns daubed with paper, it was explained that special glue was used which disappeared after a few weeks. The circus was long gone by the time the farmer, weary with waiting for the glue to disappear, would set about scraping the offending posters from his property. This was before the great days of the circus poster, when specimens would consist of several dozen sheets plastered on billboards and bellowing with several hundred feet of glorious color, and in words which could never be misunderstood, that Buffalo Bill was here, or that The Greatest Show on Earth was on its way. Earlier posters were more modest affairs, stuck to whatever was available with a nail and a small disc of leather, but some are gems of showman art.

A book could be written on circus advertising for the ingenuity and originality of some of those old showmen was remarkable. Astley's famous "Philosophical Fireworks" set off from a barge moored on the Thames not far from his amphitheater were certain to attract attention. In 1784 he used a balloon trailing a streamer which invited people to his circus. Balloons were used later too. In the middle of the

SAN ANTONIO PUBLIC LIBRARY

Ben Lusbie, the lightning ticket seller. A little touch of advertising magic by the Forepaugh Circus.

last century a band of Italian youths carried out a trapeze act beneath the basket of a balloon as it passed over Paris – until the police stopped the act as being too dangerous. Some years later a Madame Poitevin made an ascent mounted on a bull suspended beneath a balloon. This too was banned, by the British police, as being too cruel to the bull! Bertram Mills used to display a balloon in the shape of an elephant above his tenting circus with the single word MILLS written on it.

Barnum, of course, was the master advertiser of them all, and his inventiveness knew no bounds. In the early days of the Great American Museum, Barnum decided that he must celebrate July 4 in fitting style, so he had made a great banner announcing the delights of his museum which he strung across the street – to some trees in a churchyard across the way. It was not long before the churchmen were objecting strongly, so Barnum removed his banner, until the early hours of the awaited day. By the time the clergy had discovered how Barnum had duped them, the crowds had gathered around his museum and as the banner was now covered with the Stars and Stripes, a natural discretion told the churchmen that it would be more than their collective lives were worth to take down such a patriotic display. Barnum had won, as he usually did. On another occasion, Barnum hired a violinist to add a touch of culture to his exhibition. He was a very good violinist as it happened, but no one wanted to hear him . . . until Barnum had some posters printed showing the fiddler apparently playing upside down. The subsequent performances were packed. Joice Heth, the Feejee Mermaid, Tom Thumb, Toung Taloung – the white elephant and, of course, Jumbo, were all brought to stardom by Barnum's advertising genius.

He was rarely defeated, but one of his rivals, Titus, the man who had befriended Van Amburgh, must have thought he was once within an ace of doing so. For to Titus's amazement he discovered that Barnum was displaying an animal which was billed as "An Orang-Utan or Man of the Borneo Jungle" and worse, that everyone was going to see Barnum's monkey and shunning his own circus. He determined to see this fabulous creature and discovered to his delight that it was nothing more than a baboon. He pointed out the simple fact that orang-utans had no tail, that this creature did, and that Barnum was defrauding the public. The master showman seemed not the slightest nonplussed. Next day the Borneo Beast was advertised as being the only orang-utan with a tail! At that Titus acknowledged defeat and the two became fast friends.

Others copied the Barnum example, some even bettered it, but there was one man in Britain who was in the same league as Barnum: "Lord" George Sanger. The small twists of publicity, the use of the written and spoken word, the value of reputation and the sheer razzmatazz of splendor and glamor and spectacle were as much Sanger's trade mark as they were Barnum's. But Sanger's particular ingenuity was unique.

One of his favorite stories concerned the time when he joined Queen Victoria's procession, and for sheer gall it takes a lot of beating. After a long and dangerous illness the Prince of Wales, who had been suffering from typhoid, at last recovered. So, as a mark of celebration and a gesture of thanks for all the concern expressed by a loyal London, Queen Victoria went on a royal progress through the streets of the capital. Sanger got wind that this was to take place some weeks before it occurred and, spending over £2,000 on repainting his tableau wagons and generally refurbishing his parade, he bided his time. A few quiet words with the police and he was ready. Amid thronging crowds the Queen made her stately progress. Few people realized that at the

Sanger's Wolves.

same time, George Sanger was gradually converging on the royal route. As the Queen passed the bottom of one street, Sanger was perfectly positioned. By the time it was realized what had happened, Sanger had closed on the royal procession. A huge crowd had formed behind, so it was not possible for him to go back. After a decorous pause, the police waved him on and Sanger with his magnificent parade added a fitting rearguard to the Queen's progress while the immaculate, dignified figure of "Lord" George raised an even bigger cheer than that given the Queen herself.

Another stunt of Sanger's was less innocuous. His circus was performing in London at the time, and at his home in Margate were a number of wolves, quite tame, as playful as dogs and as mild as could be. But something sparked in Sanger's mind that here were the ingredients of a first-class publicity stunt. The wolves were brought to London and housed in a roomy stable. Sanger then had a quiet word with one of his stable lads.

The performance that night ended on time. The crowds drifted home. The circus was plunged in darkness and some of the circus artistes retired to the local pub to discuss the day's events. The scene was convivial enough until just before closing time the door opened and a harassed circus man came rushing in. "The wolves have escaped," he announced and it transpired that sure enough they had, after apparently killing an aging horse. Immediately there was uproar. Some rushed to the stable where the wolves were housed, to see the animals with blood-dripping fangs devouring the horse - which was probable as the beasts had been starved for two days - others rushed for the police who in some trepidation came to see what was about. Sanger had chosen a young man who was christened "Alpine Charlie" to be the hero in the affair. And Charlie, who knew the wolves well, with the utmost bravery, and the maximum of publicity - for by then all the press were there - drove the ravening creatures back inside an inner stable, and the emergency was over. But not for London. Questions were asked in the House of Commons about the wisdom of allowing such carnivores into London. "Man-eating wolves. Who is safe?" trumpeted the headlines, and anyone who could get away came to see the horse-devouring wolves and the hero of the hour "Alpine Charlie."

The great parades, the wonderful posters and the steam calliope were the instruments of advertising in the Golden Years of the circus. Setting up then was a simple matter for the great circuses were highly efficient organizations with a lot of man, horse and elephant power. But their circus forebears had a less easy time.

In small towns in the middle of the last century, especially in the country districts of the inland states, it was no easy matter to find a suitable site. All depended on the talent, and sometimes the pocket, of the agent who went ahead of the circus. On arrival he contacted the police, the innkeepers and anyone else who might prove useful. A plot had to be found, accommodation acquired and straw and hay made ready for the animals. A few primitive bills taken on ahead by one of their number announced the coming of the circus; on the site a clown would do handstands to attract passers-by to the excitement of the coming event. It was small-scale, it was rudimentary, but it worked. Behind the small advance guard of the bill-poster, the circus made its slow, tedious progress toward its next stand over the uneven ways which passed as roads and which became quagmires after a shower of rain. At the outskirts of the town in a handy creek, the troupe would halt to clean the dirt from their wagons, and then, with a flourish, producing whatever musical instruments they could muster, the circus came to town.

Handbell, handbill and a noisy parade heralded their arrival. They made their way to the spot chosen for the performance and there put up palings and screens – as much to keep out non-paying, prying eyes as for protection from the weather. A ring would be marked out on the turf and in this rough enclosure they would perform before the eyes of townsfolk, hungry for entertainment. On the whole, theirs were simple acts – horsemanship would be the mainstay, for horse skills in those days were universally appreciated; a comic turn or two; with perhaps a rope walker or juggler and, perhaps, a strange animal or freak of nature as an extra attraction.

OPPOSITE:
Resplendent, Redolent, Refulgent! It would seem that the Electric Light is a greater draw than the circus itself. Cooper, Bailey & Co., 1879.

Sometimes the spectators brought their own torches, otherwise lighting was from candles and "chandeliers" – poles secured to boards on which dozens of candles had been stuck. It was always drafty and candle grease went everywhere while the light was flickering and uncertain. Rags soaked in turpentine were also used, and later circuses had flare lamps which consisted of long pipes down which kerosene dripped onto a hot plate. Then it flared up making a noise unnerving for the performers and terrifying for the animals. Finally came naphtha lights and, in time, gas and electricity.

The chance to see electric light was almost as great a draw as the circus itself. Those circuses which did not have the new invention, and could not afford it anyway, were outspoken in their denunciation of the dangerous new invention, "Electric Lights are known to be extremely dangerous and blinding to the eyes," thundered one. Another went so far as to have the following leaflet printed in a vain attempt to frighten circus-goers from taking the risks of exposing themselves to the evil of the new illumination. "Electric light," the warning said, "would hurt the eyes. Also many say they have not seen a well day since the exhibition. For persons predisposed to pulmonary complaints it will shorten their days and in many cases affect the tender brains of children." This fearsome denunciation was signed: "The Public's Servant, Dan Rice."

In a vain, and one would think an uncharacteristic attempt to take the taste from the medicine, he added:

"P.S. This is not done to impair the patronage of the London Circus. Only to put the public on their guard. This much I will say, that from reports they have a very good show." The target of this abuse from Dan Rice was Cooper and Bailey's Great London Show. How effective this tirade was cannot be determined, but more than a few must have said to themselves, "Oh yeah!"

The issue of free passes, "Annie Oakleys," was another useful publicity stunt. It was prudent to give free passes to the law and to shopkeepers who helped the circus – Ringlings also gave them to traveling salesmen who, in return, were only too happy to spread news of the circus's coming. The local paper also usually received several free passes as did the great names in the town who might have helped, or who might yet help the circus in the future. But there were always others clamoring for free passes. Some proprietors were lavish in their distribution, but to Barnum it was a constant source of irritation. At length he could bear the situation no longer and had printed a small card which he gave to those who importuned him without, as he thought, proper reason. It read: "In those days there were no passes given. Search the Scriptures":

"Thou shalt not pass" – *Numbers XX, v. 18.*

Ten Times the Largest and Best Show on Earth!

St. Joseph, WEDNESDAY, | SURE One Day ONLY! | JULY 23

COOPER, BAILEY & CO.'S GREAT International Allied Shows!

Having just Returned from a Grand Three Years Triumphal Tour Around the World. Traveling 67,000 Miles by Land and Sea, have CONSOLIDATED FOR THIS SEASON ONLY, with the

GREAT LONDON CIRCUS And SANGER'S ROYAL BRITISH MENAGERIE.

FORMING A FORMIDABLE COMBINATION.

TWO SHOWS! A DOUBLE CIRCUS! TWO MENAGERIES!

IN OPERATION DAY & NIGHT At Every Performance

Resplendent Redolent Refulgent

FAINTLY DESCRIBES THE WONDERFUL

ELECTRIC LIGHT!

The Public Mind Dazed! The Great Invention!

ALL OF OUR VAST PAVILIONS

LIGHTED BY ELECTRICITY.

168,000 YARDS OF CANVAS

Are used in the manufacture of the CIRCUS, MENAGERIE AQUARIUM and MUSEUM TENTS, all of which are illuminated by the BRUSH ELECTRIC LIGHT, making night as bright as day. Giving a volume of light EQUAL TO 35,000 GAS JETS. The entire population on the *qui vive* of expectation and curiosity to behold the real wonder of the Nineteenth century. Already you hear the remark of thousands, "We are going to the Great London Show, to see

THE WONDERFUL ELECTRIC LIGHT.

The Mammoth Pavilion Illuminated at every Exhibition in the day time as well as night—The Electric Light in Constant Operation. Every visitor to the Grand Exhibition exclaiming with wonder and delight

Beautiful! Marvelous! Grand!

A circus crowd, Ringlings 1913.

"Suffer not a man to pass" – *Judges III, v. 28.*
"None shall pass" – *Mark XIII v. 30.*
"The wicked shall no more pass" – *Nathan I v. 15.*
"Beware that thou pass not" – *II Kings, VI v. 9.*
"There shall no stranger pass" – *Amos III v. 17.*
"Neither any son of man shall pass" – *Jeremiah LI v. 43.*
"No man may pass through because of the beasts" – *Ezekiel XIV v. 15.*
"Though they roar, yet they cannot pass" – *Jeremiah V v. 22.*
"So he paid the fare thereof and went" – *Jonah I v. 3.*

In the early days when the churches were on the look out for any lapse from propriety by circus folk, these and other biblical allusions were useful ammunition. And Barnum really went to town: an Indian Zebu would be referred to as a

CIRCUS WORLD MUSEUM, BARABOO, WISCONSIN

sacred cow; the first African warthog to come to the United States was called "the Prodigal's Swine"; the camel was, of course, "The Ship of the Desert"; while the hippo was "The Behemoth of Holy Writ, spoken of in the Book of Job." Flowery allusion followed flowery allusion – he even called a tent a "Superb Firmament Pavilion." While his "Grand Moral Representation of the Deluge" with appropriate sacred music packed them in at the American Museum.

Barnum, Ringling, Bailey, Mills and many others went in for what Barnum called a "Sunday School Show" – to the extent that they called Ringlings the "Ting-a-Ling" show, where there would be rigorous fines for showmen who broke the rules, missed a parade or were rude to a customer. But there was a seamier side to the old circus, and it would seem that at the hands of the immortal old rogue Pogey O'Brien, the circus found its most reprehensible proprietor.

FRED D. PFENING COLLECTION

The immortal old rogue "Pogey" O'Brien. His circus was the happiest of hunting grounds for "operators of all kinds."

A tall, fat, good-natured man, a rough diamond if ever there was one, with a native shrewdness and humor – that was O'Brien. His real name was John, but he was always known as Pogey and at one time was reputed to own more show property than anyone else in the United States. He had started his showman's career with Adam Forepaugh and was a lifelong teetotaller who never gambled. O'Brien would be called in as the only sober member of the circus to act as bookkeeper during the frequent poker sessions that punctuated the circus's progress across the states. From time to time Pogey would be given money, but more often a cigar or two in payment for his book work. These he carefully hoarded until he had enough to start his own circus. And a raging success he made of it. But whatever standard the performance may have achieved, it is with the extra attractions that were part and parcel of the circus in those days for which Pogey became most famous.

Not all circuses were as "Sunday School" as Barnums and Ringlings, the many had their short-change artists, gamblers and other "fakers" as they were called. Long before the circus reached town "fixers" would go ahead to try to buy police immunity, or at least get an agreement that the police would look the other way. With the town "fixed" or safe, the way was clear for the "boys" to clean up. A number of circuses had their concession merchants – candy butchers who sold the barber-pole rock, or those who offered the "clothes-line privilege" which gave freedom to rob the clothes-lines they passed on their way. Concessions were dear to buy, but no circus managed to reach, or fall, to the standard of diversity and numbers of these hangers-on that Pogey's show achieved. One man, who was engaged solely to sell tickets paid $1,000 a season, a sum which he handsomely covered by short-changing customers in various ways, usually with folded bills. Others paid for the exclusive pocket-picking rights. Others bought space on which they could exercise their skill with cards and other rackets – the three-card trick, or its variant the Shell Game – Hocus, Mocus and Pocus – which used shells to cover a pea. With the town "fixed," the "fixers'" next role was to pay off promptly anyone who squealed too loudly, or any suckers who complained if the popular medicines like "Wizard Oil," proved not to be as efficacious as they had thought. From time to time these merchants went too far and the local police, "fixed" or not, had perforce to step in. Then they skipped to the next town, their equipment and props were brought on for them by the circus.

They were tough days, a priceless initiation for very many of the great circus proprietors in the Golden Years, and many a circus tradition started out of necessity. Thus began that traditional circus drink, pink lemonade. George Conklin, one of the great animal trainers of those early days, and a fine circus personality for very many years, recounts the tale of how it all started. It began with his brother Pete Conklin who traveled with the Jerry Mabie circus for seven years. During the summer they would roll in the northern United States and Canada; in winter they would operate in the South – with barely any rest between. Then one day, after all these years of amicable relations, Pete Conklin had a row with the management. The circus owner was satisfied that no one in his right mind would skip the circus, they were in the middle of Texas at the time, a lawless country where single showmen were shown no respect at all. But to their astonishment Conklin packed his bags and went. He went round, in fact, to buy a couple of mules and an old covered wagon. With this to carry his goods, he then acquired a sack of peanuts to sell to customers, and with a supply of sugar, some tartaric acid and a single lemon, Conklin was ready to become a lemonade seller. He traveled in the wake of the circus. Whenever the show stopped Conklin would set up his stall and sell his brew crying:

Here's your ice cold lemonade
Made in the shade
Stick your finger in the glass
It will freeze fast.

It was turning into a nice little business until one day, a very hot day, the lemonade seller ran out of water. There was no more water on the lot and Conklin ran about looking for anything to satisfy his thirsty customers, at length he came across one of the artistes who had just finished washing a pair of brilliant red tights. Before she could object, Conklin had picked up the tub and was rushing it back with its bright red liquid to his stall. So was born the tradition of pink lemonade at the circus.

If "Hey Rube" is the rallying cry for circus folk, there is no more dreaded cry than that of fire. The early wooden amphitheaters were martyrs to fire. There can have been few circus owners who in their time did not suffer from being burned down, and more still who have not woken terrified that fire might strike their Big Tops. With the early days of inflammable canvas, not altogether reliable electricity, and an audience who smoked, the risks of fire in a circus Big Top were immense, and the shape of the tent is such that there is an ideal upward draught to fan the flames. There is the added hazard of live, and some wild animals which, if they escaped, would cause panic and could cause death. Once again, in fighting a fire circus discipline comes in handy, for circus folk are used to obeying orders, many are accustomed to heights and are very fit; all realize that it is their livelihood at stake.

As fearsome as fire is a blow-down. Tents are safer nowadays than they used to be, nevertheless there are few

OVERLEAF: *The perennial, haunting fear of circus folk. A fire in the Big Top. A graphic scene from the film* Circus World.

P. C. FILMS CORP AND NATIONAL FILM ARCHIVE, LONDON

OPPOSITE: *Everyone wants to watch the circus. Charlie Chaplin in* The Circus.

more ardent weather watchers than circus folk. That great spread of canvas, a billowing mass of unmanageable sail, is vulnerable to any strong wind. Held down by stout guys, secured at the bottom of the tent walls by stake and pin, anchored by great steel cables thrown across the roof, on the whole a Big Top is as solid a structure as any but it can still be a vulnerable object. A few snapped ropes, or a rent ripped in one of the canvas panels will throw a greater strain on the surviving supports and should those be unable to take the added pressure then the whole may go.

Snow is an even greater hazard than a blow-down, though fortunately more rare. In the days when tent heating had not reached its modern perfection, there was nothing to melt the snow as it formed. Gradually, under the weight of snow, the canvas would begin to sag. This was the signal for everyone to start scraping and poking at the snow to dislodge it; for others with hand heaters, to go as near to the canvas as they dared to try to melt the stuff off the tent. Sometimes it worked, sometimes it did not and then with an agonizing buckling noise the canvas would rent, the quarter-poles no longer able to take the weight would snap and the whole Big Top would come crashing down, carrying the King Poles with it and crushing the seats below into matchwood.

Animals usually know when a storm is brewing. One cat authority reckons that if the lions all holler together the storm will be a short one; but if only one or two roar at each other, they are in for a long spell of foul weather.

Under conditions of emergency, the discipline and the comradeship of the circus are seen at their best. There is remarkably little jealousy in the circus – everyone is out to help each other – although to occupy the coveted center-ring position is the ambition of every artiste. In many circuses before the performance you may be shown your seat by the great Filos, a dare-devil acrobat act. It may be the Martinis, a cycle troupe, who will peddle popcorn in the interval. There is a tradition, and there used to be a clause in the contract, that no matter how great a star, circus artistes were expected to "make themselves useful." It might be in putting up the Big Top, it might be in taking it down, in placing out the seats or helping the program sellers. Whatever the task may be, it is an integral part of the freemasonry of the circus.

Many have tried to define the magic of the circus. Ernest Hemingway said that "The Circus is the only ageless delight you can buy for money . . . . It is the only spectacle I know that while you watch it, gives the quality of a truly happy dream," and it was Conklin who said that there was "never but one circus – the first one – and that the circus will go on for as long as there are children, and as long as each child is accompanied by three adults."

Those great days of the old circus have a magic of

their own. "Sir" Robert Fossett, whose circus ancestry is lost in the mist of many centuries, conveyed this magic in an interview recorded in an old newspaper cutting:

> I was risin' four – in fact, I believe it was my fourth birthday, there or thereabouts, when I popped out of my carpet-bag as an extra and unexpected side-show to the Performing Birds, my father – the first Sir Robert – was running with phenomenal success at Charlton Fair

and Masquerade. That and the conjuring tricks – for my father was a wonderful hand at wizard work. There was a tremendous crowd around as Sir Robert climbed on to the little stage, staggering under the weight of his son and heir in that old green carpet bag – an' me as near suffocated as ever I have been in my life. Havin' produced a rabbit out of the ear of a lady in the front row, and one or two smallish things like that, my governor planks the bag down before him. "And now, ladies and gents all,"

There will be circuses as long as there are children. A wonderfully evocative picture of children waiting for the grand parade. From This Way to the Big Show, *copyright 1936, by Dexter Fellows and Andrew Freeman.*

he says, "now for the Grand Illusion! Hey presto!" and out I nips from the bag, all sweat and spangles and paint, and makes my Bow! You might have heard the roar at Greenwich!

"An' now," says my father, "ladies and gents all – watch the Little Nipper do the Splits and the handspring, *and* the double summersault! Hup, Nipper!" An' I hupped, though it skeered me a bit, seein' all that mighty crowd all cheering and laughing – and that's how I entered the Profession! Lord George Sanger was runnin' a rival Bird Act across the way and also conjurin' for all he was worth. He comes up to see what all the row was about, and when he sees that it was me he ups with me into his arms and says to the old man, "Lord! Bob," he says, "*what* a Treasure you've got! And him only four? Mar-vellous! We'll have him in the Peerage yet, Bob; but as he's a trifle young for a coronet, we'll christen him the Carpet Knight!" And so they christened me, in champagne and oysters; and since then I've never looked back. Poor old George! He was the first, outside the family, to dangle me on his knee, and I was the last to gaze upon his kind face and to shed a tear over the coffin as they screwed him down.

The newspaper reporter went on to describe the scene:

Sir Robert's household were gathered around him, watching his commanding eye. He signalled. One handed to him his new white gloves, another his silk handkerchief, and another his wonderful whip, which none but he may crack. He drew on his gloves with a stately air, he tried the temper of his thong, he buttoned his coat; his white hand flashed and the band in the little balcony overhead burst out in a clash of gay music. To a mighty cheer he marched proudly and splendidly into the ring, heading the gay and glittering procession. The Circus had begun.

A Brief Note on Further Reading

In the preparation of this book I have used a wealth of sources. For any circus lover who wishes to delve deeper into the fascinating world of the Big Top, I would draw attention to the masterly four-volume work by Raymond Toole-Stott entitled *Circus and Allied Art, A World Bibliography* (Harpur & Sons (Derby) Ltd).

Acknowledgments

The illustrations on pages 39 and 230, and the extract from The Journal of Queen Victoria on page 106, are reproduced by Gracious Permission of Her Majesty Queen Elizabeth II. I would also like to thank the following for their help and cooperation in providing further illustrations:

The American Antiquarian Society; The British Broadcasting Corporation; The British Library; The British Museum; The Buffalo Bill Historical Center, Cody, Wyoming; The Circus World Museum, Baraboo, Wisconsin; Susan Crawford and the Tryon Gallery Ltd; The Denver Public Library; EMI Film Distributors; The Free Library of Philadelphia; The Guildhall Library, City of London; The Historical Society of Pennsylvania; The Library of Congress; John Lukens and Hodder & Stoughton Ltd; Metro-Goldwyn-Mayer Inc; The Museum of the City of New York; The National Film Archive, London; The National Portrait Gallery, London; The New York Historical Society; The Novosti Press Agency; P.C. Films Corporation; The Fred D. Pfening Collection; Roy Export Co; The San Antonio Public Library; Sotheby Parke Bernet & Co; The State Historical Society of Colorado; The University of Oklahoma; The Victoria and Albert Museum and many circuses on both sides of the Atlantic.

Extracts in the text are from: *The Circus from Rome to Ringling* by Earl Chapin May (Duffield & Green) pages 49 and 193; *The Sanger Story* by John Lukens (Hodder & Stoughton) page 61; and *My Autobiography* by Charles Chaplin (The Bodley Head) page 178.

Index

Page numbers given in *italic* type indicate illustrations.